*The American
Immigration Collection*

Mexican Immigration
to the
United States

MANUEL GAMIO

Arno Press and *The New York Times*

NEW YORK 1969

MEXICAN IMMIGRATION
TO THE UNITED STATES

THE UNIVERSITY OF CHICAGO PRESS
CHICAGO, ILLINOIS

—

THE BAKER & TAYLOR COMPANY
NEW YORK

THE MACMILLAN COMPANY OF CANADA, LIMITED
TORONTO

THE CAMBRIDGE UNIVERSITY PRESS
LONDON

THE MARUZEN-KABUSHIKI-KAISHA
TOKYO, OSAKA, KYOTO, FUKUOKA, SENDAI

THE COMMERCIAL PRESS, LIMITED
SHANGHAI

MEXICAN IMMIGRATION TO THE UNITED STATES

A STUDY OF HUMAN MIGRATION AND ADJUSTMENT

By
MANUEL GAMIO

THE UNIVERSITY OF CHICAGO PRESS
CHICAGO · ILLINOIS

PREFACE

This study of Mexican immigration, carried on by Dr. Gamio during 1926–27, was made possible by the Social Science Research Council. The documentary materials which form the basis of the following chapters include a series of autobiographic statements made by Mexican immigrants in the United States and written down, as they were given, by Dr. Gamio and his associates. These life-histories are to appear, soon after the publication date of this book, in a companion volume issued by the same press under the title, "The Mexican Immigrant: His Life Story."

EDITOR

INTRODUCTION

The effects of migration between the United States and Mexico are scarcely known, yet the problem is important and demands the attention of both countries toward its solution.

The migratory currents flowing from Mexico to the United States and from the United States into Mexico cannot be considered from a single point of view. Mexican emigration to the United States is made up, mainly, of unskilled labor, a great population turning to the United States for wages better than it can procure in its own country. It is true that many of these immigrants are, in Mexico, skilled laborers, but in the United States of necessity they become unskilled, because of ignorance of the language, and because of their inability to operate the modern agricultural and industrial machinery they are called upon to use.

On the other hand, Americans who go to Mexico are seldom laborers, but tourists, teachers, writers, artists, and students, and a business class consisting of owners, representatives, managers, and employees in commercial and industrial enterprises.

In view of this fact, the Social Science Research Council proposed in 1926 to make an investigation of this migration, limiting it to a study of Mexican immigration into the United States, and it recommended to the author a preliminary survey which might contribute later to a more conclusive investigation. At the end of a year's work the author presented a preliminary report to the Social Science Research Council at the conferences held at Dartmouth College, Hanover, New Hampshire, during the last week of September, 1927.

These pages contain the essential points of this report in

addition to various later amplifications. In November, 1927, the Mexican government decided to collaborate with the Social Science Research Council in order that future investigations might be made on a larger scale, and charged the author with this collaboration

Scope and method of study.—When we began this study, we were disconcerted by the magnitude of the task and the difficulties which the problem of Mexican immigration into the United States presented. Because of this initial uncertainty and the fact that we could spend only a year on our work, we decided from the beginning to make it purely exploratory. We then reduced to three the numerous points of view or modes of attack which we had been following while trying to define our problem. These points of attack, or divisions of the subject, are the following: (1) Human material: This would include the data relative to the direct investigation of the Mexican immigrants, that is, the data obtained from personal contact with them in the United States as well as in the Mexican regions from which they come. (2) Geographic material: This would consist of the data obtained by direct observation of the Mexican and American regions in which the immigrants had lived. (3) Documentary material: This would consist of data already in existence relative to the individuals and regions to which the human and geographical material already cited refer. These data would be taken not only from printed publications but also from all unpublished material which it might be possible to consult.

Human material.—For the purpose of our study it was necessary to consider the immigrant before his departure to the United States, during his residence there, and also in his repatriated condition as reimmigrant to Mexico. Furthermore,

---

[1] Unfortunately, this collaboration has lasted only until June, 1927, on account of the limited finances of the Mexican government.

it was necessary in addition to take into account American citizens of Mexican origin, or Mexican-Americans in the United States. We therefore visited the American regions where live the principal groups of Mexican immigrants, as well as the Mexican-Americans, including in our itinerary Illinois, Indiana, Michigan, Ohio, New York, Texas, New Mexico, Arizona, and California. In Mexico we made surveys in the central and northern plateaus, principally in the states of Guanajuato, Jalisco, and Michoacan, from which at the present time the majority of immigrants come. Because it was absolutely impossible for us to investigate in a thorough, scientific manner the physical, mental, social, cultural, economic, and other conditions of these individuals, in order later to be able to determine the character of their contacts with the people of the United States and with the American civilization, we had to be content with mere observation, objective and subjective.

The *objective observation* consisted in considering these individuals and their conditions of life when they were not conscious of such observation. In order to accomplish this purpose without talking with them or asking questions, we went to their fields of work, their factories, railroad camps, mines, schools, churches, lodges, amusement centers, commercial centers, and so on. Furthermore, we went into their homes, tried their meals, attended their funerals, and visited their prisons and hospitals where they were interned. Lack of experience and ignorance of the social environment in which we made our investigations made our task difficult; but by frequent comparisons and repeated observations we succeeded in clarifying these observations. In order to make this work in the United States more efficient, we chose as assistants Miss Elena Landazuri, Sc.B., and Mr. Luis F. Recinos, because they spoke English, had a certain knowledge of the American environment, and, what was very important, knew how to get the sympathy and confidence of Mexicans and Mexican-Americans. Moreover, the former had important experience in social relief work, and the latter had been a newspaper man for a number of years— circumstances which in both cases were of great value in the work of investigation. Mr. Eduardo Noguera aided us effectively in the investigation of immigrants before they left Mexico. He is a member of the *Dirección* of Anthropology. Mr. Eugene Gomez also assisted us for a short time.

The *subjective observation* consisted in finding out from the individual himself what had been the character of his material and mental life. Our first experiences in this work confirmed what modern sociological methods have already indicated, that the value of autobiographies is generally slight and relative. In fact, we deduced by various means, among them the comparison of the objective and subjective observations made, that the answers frequently did not agree with the real characteristics of their lives which we had beforehand observed directly—a circumstance which indicated that the biographies were of doubtful veracity. This was perhaps due to our abrupt intrusion and interrogation, which did not awaken in him a true process of introspection nor stimulate his memory as we had hoped, but created emotional reactions to our presence, such as fear, distrust, displeasure, and so on, or else satisfaction or vanity.

In view of this fact, we gradually corrected the method of observation, as far as was possible, in the following way. The objective and subjective studies already made had enabled us to formulate a guide or classification of the most important mental and material typical characteristics of a series of individuals.[1] Provided with this guide and aided at times by information furnished us about the person to be interviewed, we talked with him when he was in the company of other persons,

[1] This guide is included in Appendix I to this volume.

taking great care not to question him or even refer to his person or his life. We chatted in simple language upon subjects suitable to his interests and interposed remarks and comments upon other persons and their lives; after this we waited patiently his response, either in the same interview or on some later occasion. Our pretense of interest in the persons and lives of other individuals as well as in affairs entirely foreign to the persons interviewed and our own silence and indifference in regard to himself generally awoke in his mind a process of introspection: His memory was stimulated; reactions relating to the present arose and reactions of the past were recalled—all of which yielded a body of statements and confidences satisfactory because of their sincerity and spontaneity. When the confidence of the individual was thus once gained and he found himself in a state of voluntary eloquence, the observation was completed by direct questioning. As soon as the interviews were at an end we wrote down the results obtained. Occasionally in the course of these interviews we took notes under suitable pretexts so that our subjects might not be conscious that we were transcribing their ideas and their words.

The objective and subjective observations mentioned furnished us with a body of data and provisional conclusions which we later proceeded to classify into four groups: (a) data relative to the physical condition of the individuals; (b) general data as to the culture or civilization, including economic situation, state of nutrition, clothing and housing, special aptitudes in trades and farming, also ethic, aesthetic, and religious ideas, folk lore, and so on; (c) data referring to languages and mixtures of languages; (d) data relative to their social mobility, horizontal as well as vertical.

Geographic material.—The new life of the immigrant, especially in its physical and biological aspects, is directly influenced by the geographical environment of the United States, and indirectly by the geographical environment of the Mexican region from which he comes, which continues to influence him in his later development. The immigrants are scattered over the whole of the United States and come from almost all parts of the Mexican Republic. For this reason it would have been logical to study the geography of both countries, but because the task is very difficult, we limited ourselves to a consideration of the Mexican regions where the greater proportion of the immigrants come from and of the American regions where their groups are most numerous.

Documentary material: number and distribution of immigrants.—How many Mexican residents did the United States have in 1926? What was their geographical distribution in that country? What were the Mexican regions from which they came? What proportion of immigrants as a rule go back to Mexico each year in order to return again to the United States? What proportion of them return to Mexico for good?

These fundamental questions arose at the beginning of this study, and as they could not be satisfactorily answered from a consideration of the human material, we turned to the documentary sources, which we assumed would be able to furnish the necessary data. These sources were the publications of the United States Department of Labor and the United States Immigration Bureau of Washington, D.C.

In Mexico we consulted the publications and archives of the Department of Immigration of the *Secretaría de Gobernación*, with the co-operation of Mr. D. German Landa y Piña, in charge of the statistics of that Department. In the *Secretaría de Relaciónes Exteriores* and in the National Department of Statistics we also secured interesting data. Thanks to the intelligent interest which His Excellency Mr. Manuel Tellez, Mexican ambassador in Washington, shared in the investigation, as well as to the help of various consuls in the sections of the United States that we covered, much useful information was received. Lastly, we tried to get data by writing to employers of Mexicans and to teachers of schools where Mexican children went, but unfortunately we obtained but few answers.

As will be seen further on, the information from which we were able to draw significant conclusions on the geographic distribution was furnished us by the lists of money orders between the United States and Mexico, embracing a period of about ten years, which exist in the general post-office of Mexico. Mr. José Almada Becerra, chief of the Department of Money Orders of that office, very kindly aided our work.

In the classification, selection, and tabulation of data referring to this and other chapters, Mr. Paul Siliceo Pauer, Rogerio Hernandez Abreu, Earl K. James, Eugenio Gomez, and Manuel de Sotres collaborated with us. The translation of the manuscript was made by Anita Brenner and Margaret Park Redfield, and by Emma Reh Stevenson, who translated three chapters.

Geographical data.—Publications of the United States Weather Bureau at Washington, D.C., and the Direction of Geographical and Climatological Studies in Mexico City were mainly consulted. In order to obtain other complementary data, various books and publications cited in the Bibliography were consulted.

Economic data.—In the United States very satisfactory general statistics exist on the daily wages and salaries of skilled and unskilled workers. Nevertheless, no special tables exist for Mexican laborers or Mexican-Americans, and as these frequently receive salaries lower than those paid to white Americans, it is impossible to calculate these from the general tables. In view of this, it was necessary to make a table from the salaries and occupations that we were able to investigate directly.

As to the wages prevailing in the regions from which

Mexican immigration comes as well as the occupations which they discharge there, the Ministry of Industry, Commerce, and Labor, and the Ministry of Agriculture of Mexico, furnished us with numerous data. The former Ministry supplied information as to minimum subsistence of workers' families necessary under the economic and biological conditions in these parts of Mexico.

Among other conclusions derived from the wage tables we obtained information as to the social mobility of the immigrant.

The most satisfactory and significant economic data which we were able to obtain, on account of their number and indisputable reliability, are those derived from the quantities of money sent back to Mexico by the immigrants, by monthly periods, from 1919 to 1926.

Anthropological data.—In order to know the racial characteristics of the Indians, *mestizos*, and whites who make up the Mexican immigration into the United States, and in order to describe their racial contacts with the people of that country, as well as the effect of the climate upon their physical development, we consulted relevant documentary sources. Unfortunately, however, satisfactory anthropometric, physiological, and pathological data on groups of whites and *mestizos* do not exist. Since the proportion of white individuals among the immigrant class is very small, our ignorance of their racial characteristics did not affect our problem; but it was necessary to know these facts in regard to the *mestizos*, who probably form the majority of the immigrants. The data compiled under our direction some time ago in the *Dirección* of Anthropology provided some general information on the natives of the regions from which the majority of immigrants come. These data were taken from scientific studies made by Mexican and foreign investigators, and although it likewise failed fully to satisfy the requirements of anthropology, it was of some use in forming certain conclusions, and as they may be of some use in future investigations, they will be referred to in the proper chapter.

No source of information was found that would give us the information sought on the physical characteristics of the Mexican immigrants living in the United States nor of Americans of Mexican origin.

Contacts of civilization or culture.—No scientific study has been made and practically nothing has been written upon the cultural characteristics of the Mexican immigrant into the United States, and even less upon the interactions of his culture and that of modern North America. The Bibliography contains references to all such material which we were able to consult. As to the culture of the present-day Mexican folk, there were only the aforementioned data compiled in the *Dirección* of Anthropology, referring only to the Indian cultures.

Newspapers and magazines edited by Mexicans and directed toward the Mexican immigrant population of the United States and to Americans of Mexican origin supplied interesting information. Other sources consulted were the regulations, constitutions, and other publications of the mutual-aid societies, masonic lodges, amusement clubs, and other Mexican groups. Lastly, the reports of the welfare and relief societies contributed to our information.

Nevertheless, the documentary source which gave us the most data as to culture contact was an extensive list of thousands of immigrants who had come back to Mexico and who had been permitted to bring their household and other objects used in the United States duty free into Mexico. This list included automobiles, tractors, stoves, washing machines, agricultural and industrial tools, and other objects—indisputable evidence as to the cultural and material influence that the American civilization exercises upon the immigrants.

The international aspect.—In this regard we consulted the laws and regulations of both countries as to immigration and emigration, as well as articles and editorials which had been published on such subjects for some time. We also read the hearings of the United States House of Representatives, reports of Mexican consuls, reports of employers and other organizations for or against Mexican immigration.

To our great advantage we were privileged to take part in the conference of the Social Science Research Council held at Hanover, New Hampshire, in 1927. The interesting exposition and discussion carried on there by distinguished authorities in the field of social science was an important help in orienting our ideas and point of view, not only with respect to this particular study, but in general. We are especially indebted to Dr. Fay-Cooper Cole and Dr. Roland B. Dixon who generously lent their aid and advice in the development of the work and in the revision of the manuscript.

Although in beginning the work we anticipated its deficiencies, we nevertheless found them, on completing the task, even greater than we had imagined. Nevertheless, we shall be gratified if in accordance with the confidence placed in us by the Social Science Research Council we have at least indicated points of attack for future scientific investigation of Mexican immigration to the United States.

TABLE OF CONTENTS

xvii

TABLE OF CONTENTS

CHAPTER I

NUMBER OF MEXICAN IMMIGRANTS IN THE UNITED STATES[1]

Official estimate.—No exact census has yet been taken of the number of Mexicans living in the United States. The latest official count was made in 1920. In December, 1926, the Mexican Embassy, on a basis of information supplied by the American Department of Labor,[2] made the estimate shown in Table I.

Mexican immigration has thus reached astonishing proportions, and has rightly become a subject of concern to both governments, arousing discussion as to how best to deal with the situation.

Validity of the official estimate.—From personal observation and interviews with thousands of immigrants, and from a study of the annual variations in the quantities of money sent to

[1] [Since the preparation of this chapter there has appeared *Mexican Labor in the United States: Migration Statistics,* by Paul S. Taylor, "University of California Publications in Economics," VI, No. 3, 237–55. Neither the Mexican nor the American statistics are satisfactory for the period under review. Dr. Gamio inclines to favor a figure for net immigration intermediate between those arrived at from the statistics of each country. Another observer (*op. cit.*) takes the view that the net immigration has been greater than that shown by the figures of either country, relying on the volume of illegal entries as the principal factor. Neither does he believe that the statistics of the two countries are gathered on a basis which makes them comparable.—EDITOR.]

[After the manuscript of this volume went to press the writer made a study of additional statistics as to source and distribution of money orders. This study, supplementing results given in this and the following chapter, is published in Mexico City (*Talleres gráficos de la Nación*) under the title "Quantitative Estimate and Sources of Mexican Immigration to the United States." Its title, and a summary of the contents, appear in Appendix IX.—AUTHOR.]

[2] "Annual Report of the Commissioner General of Immigration," *Monthly Labor Review.*

Mexico by the Mexican immigrants living in the United States, we arrive at the following conclusions:

1. The official census taken of Mexican immigrant population in the United States cannot be accepted as definite and

TABLE I

(A reproduction of the original document)

EMBAJADA DE MÉXICO OFICINA DEL AGREGADO COMERCIAL WASHINGTON, D.C.	Febrero 11 1927	Num. B 163	IMMIGRACIÓN DE MÉXICANOS EN LOS ESTADOS UNIDOS HASTA DICIEMBRE 31 DE 1926

Periodos Comprendiendo la Inmigración Neta Despues de Deducir la Emigración de la Inmigración	Numero de Hombres	Numero de Mujeres	Numero por Total
Residentes en Diciembre 31 de 1919, segun censo....	276,526	209,892	486,418
Inmigración neta, Enero 1 a Junio 30 de 1920.......	23,331	10,694	34,025
Inmigración neta, Julio 1, 1920 a Jun. 30, 1921.....	23,533	15,359	38,892
Inmigración neta, Jul. 1, 1921 a Jun. 30, 1922......	13,913	8,882	22,795
Inmigración neta, Jul. 1, 1922 a Jun. 30, 1923......	52,051	20,036	72,087
Inmigración neta, Jul. 1, 1923 a Jun. 30, 1924......	69,323	32,892	102,215
Inmigración neta, Jul. 1, 1924 a Jun. 30, 1925......	31,399	13,619	45,018
Inmigración neta, Jul. 1, 1925 a Jun. 30, 1926......	41,519	12,929	54,448
Inmigración neta, Jul. 1, a Dic. 31 de 1926........	24,255	10,593	34,848
Totales..................................	555,850	334,896	890,746

NOTA.—Este informe está basado en datos oficiales del servicio de Inmigración de los Estados Unidos, proporcionado por las oficinas principales de Washington.

This estimate, compared with those of the three preceding American censuses, shows an increase in geometrical progression of Mexican immigrant population in the United States as follows:

OFFICIAL AMERICAN CENSUS

1900...............	103,393
1910...............	221,915
1920...............	486,418
1926 (estimate).......	890,746

exact, since this population is, in part, a transient population. A relatively large part of this population enters and leaves the United States two and even three times a year. Hence this census holds good only for the short periods in the year in which it may have been taken, since the movement is continuous and occurs before and after the count has been taken.

2. The statistics compiled by the Bureau of Immigration are of little value toward correcting the earlier numerical estimates of the census, since a great number of Mexican immigrants enter into or leave the United States without the knowledge of the immigration offices.

In order to arrive at an estimate of the fluctuations in the number of immigrants, recourse was had to the post-office records showing the number of money orders sent from the United States to Mexico during July and August of 1926 and January and February of 1927. The number of these orders, classified according to state of origin, appears in Table II. This table indicated, as direct observation has suggested, that a certain proportion of Mexican immigrants return from the United States to their own country in the winter.[1]

Inasmuch as the data for one year were not sufficient for a satisfactory general conclusion, information as to money orders sent through American postal authorities to Mexico from 1919 to 1927 was also obtained, and is presented in Table III, compiled for us by the Postal Money Order Department of the national post-office in Mexico.[2] The transient character of the Mexican immigrant population in the United States is further confirmed by the employers of such labor, who discussed this aspect of the problem before the Immigration Committee in 1926.[3]

[1] [The smaller number of money orders sent in winter is also due to greater unemployment in the United States of Mexicans who do not return.—EDITOR.]

[2] [Bank drafts are also used by Mexicans to remit money to Mexico.—EDITOR.]

[3] Hearing before the Committee on Immigration and Naturalization in the House of Representatives, Sixty-ninth Congress, first session, Washington, 1926.

[The testimony at this hearing is only partly reliable. Employers distant from the border do not distinguish between an internal seasonal migration of Mexicans who spend the winter in the northern part of the United States and an international migration.—EDITOR.]

TABLE II

MONEY ORDERS SENT FROM THE UNITED STATES TO MEXICO IN
JULY–AUGUST, 1926, AND JANUARY–FEBRUARY, 1927*

State	July–August, 1926	January–February, 1927
Alabama	11	1
Alaska	1	....
Arizona	940	1,055
Arkansas	2	1
California	8,582	6,313
Colorado	586	357
Connecticut	1	4
Delaware	1	4
Columbia District	4	1
Florida	42	21
Georgia	....	3
Idaho	46	23
Illinois	2,923	2,107
Indiana	1,242	837
Iowa	157	140
Kansas	750	366
Kentucky	2	10
Louisiana	28	36
Maryland	6	4
Massachusetts	9	53
Michigan	955	450
Minnesota	103	25
Mississippi	5	5
Missouri	227	144
Montana	156	23
Nebraska	224	99
Nevada	152	68
New Hampshire	....	2
New Jersey	46	99
New Mexico	299	286
New York	424	329
North Dakota	16	....
Ohio	445	428
Oklahoma	151	214
Oregon	299	98
Pennsylvania	578	685
Rhode Island	2	....
South Dakota	33	2

* Money orders deposited in the United States and destined for Mexico are
concentrated in two series corresponding to distinct postal areas of the United
States. These series are remitted monthly to Mexico, one by way of Laredo and
the other by way of El Paso. Actually this table of money orders does not include
two full months, July and August in summer, and two full months, January and
February in winter, but approximately half of the orders corresponding to these
first two months and half of those corresponding to the last two. By way of com-
pensation, we tabulated to represent summer the orders received in July by way of
El Paso and those received in August by way of Laredo. A similar method was
used in tabulating the orders corresponding to January and February.

TABLE II—*Continued*

State	July–August, 1926	January–February, 1927
Tennessee............................	....	14
Texas..............................	3,318	3,109
Utah...............................	168	90
Virginia............................	1	4
Washington.........................	15	11
West Virginia.......................	8	16
Wisconsin...........................	310	111
Wyoming...........................	176	59
Total......................	23,446	17,709

TABLE III

-MONEY ORDERS SENT TO MEXICO BY MEXICAN IMMIGRANTS
FROM 1919 TO 1927 (IN PESOS)

Month	1919	1920	1921	1922	1923
January.....	348,659.48	673,378.48	593,151.92	304,362.30	798,414.62
February....	260,211.84	495,625.39	413,498.67	255,991.94	741,987.35
March......	238,295.18	663,689.71	394,451.37	309,440.53	911,793.66
April.......	258,111.45	724,996.62	326,476.33	309,610.82	831,025.83
May........	452,583.76	528,448.16	335,412.74	338,761.18	1,127,696.29
June........	311,962.98	669,914.98	351,594.08	480,283.60	1,600,536.71
July........	353,674.20	782,257.79	336,746.68	537,920.68	1,671,493.12
August......	451,409.94	822,863.10	330,531.05	611,085.51	1,828,035.33
September...	460,972.48	944,925.10	326,146.32	640,922.21	1,890,704.38
October.....	650,182.20	970,473.98	337,901.62	980,830.57	1,846,173.91
November...	578,246.59	774,349.55	416,231.49	844,861.17	1,575,445.60
December...	654,189.97	864,372.66	346,725.62	851,414.75	1,180,168.90
Totals...	5,020,500.07	8,915,295.52	4,508,867.89	6,465,485.26	16,013,475.70

Month	1924	1925	1926	1927
January.....	629,334.50	686,516.75	731,833.45	1,114,132.71
February....	486,525.35	629,037.05	716,924.18	1,041,677.19
March......	868,696.88	680,290.34	874,516.04	1,257,799.41
April.......	886,504.52	687,238.22	809,044.37	1,200,270.05
May........	1,023,953.50	710,948.44	925,012.51	1,334,999.59
June........	1,037,293.40	907,401.79	1,164,325.27	1,581,575.01
July........	1,104,900.78	942,365.65	1,281,028.49	1,663,350.75
August......	1,059,018.63	977,582.12	1,290,854.01	1,790,469.64
September...	1,008,064.54	901,663.54	1,305,032.26	1,573,520.47
October.....	933,940.14	953,347.76	1,409,238.12	1,502,166.62
November...	886,682.25	933,678.93	1,394,825.64	1,349,574.98
December...	815,568.11	940,060.56	1,404,411.81	1,220,653.06
Totals...	10,752,482.58	9,950,131.16	13,307,046.15	16,630,189.48

NOTE.—The value of these money orders was deposited in American gold and paid by the Mexican postal authorities in Mexican gold at the day of payment rate of exchange.

It will be observed from Table III that quantities sent in the first four or five months of the year are lower than for the other months, thus confirming the observation that a certain number of immigrants return to Mexico for the winter and spring, and re-enter the United States for the summer and fall. Although December is a winter month, figures are still high for it, because often labor is contracted to the end of the year.

The figures in Table IV represent the excess of officially admitted Mexican immigrants and non-immigrants in the United States from January 1, 1920, to December 31, 1926. The addi-

TABLE IV

According to census of 1920...............	486,418
Excess admitted in United States:	
Jan. 1, 1921—June 30, 1921.............	34,025
July 1, 1920—June 30, 1921.............	38,892
July 1, 1921—June 30, 1922.............	22,795
July 1, 1922—June 30, 1923.............	72,087
July 1, 1923—June 30, 1924.............	102,215
July 1, 1924—June 30, 1925.............	45,018
July 1, 1925—June 30, 1926.............	54,448
July 1, 1926—Dec. 31, 1926.............	34,848
Total Mexican residents in Dec., 1926..	890,746

tion of these figures to the number of Mexican immigrants and non-immigrants reported in the United States by the census of 1920 is suggested as the approximate number of Mexicans in the United States in December, 1926.

Table V represents the number of Mexican immigrants and non-immigrants departed from and returned to Mexico from January, 1921, to December, 1926, according to the Mexican migration service. The addition of these figures to the number of Mexican immigrants and non-immigrants shown by the census of 1920 approximately represents the number of Mexican residents in December, 1926.

The result of this comparison could not be more startling and paradoxical. There is a difference of 632,777 between the Mexican estimate, 257,969, and the American estimate, 890,-746. The analysis we have made of the American and Mexican data allows us to surmise the two factors that explain in part, at least, this discrepancy.

Non-registration of Mexicans who depart from the United States.—The first of these factors is the fact that it is not

TABLE V

Year	Departed from Mexico to U.S.	Returned to Mexico from U.S.
1920.	50,569	64,620
1921.	9,165	106,242
1922.	33,180	50,171
1923.	80,793	85,825
1924.	57,269	105,834
1925.	41,759	77,056
1926.	56,534	67,970
Total.	329,269	557,718
Plus census of 1920.	486,418	. . . .
Total.	815,687	
Minus returned to Mexico. . .	557,718	. . . .
Total Mexican residents in Dec., 1926.	257,969	. . . .

obligatory for Mexicans on leaving the United States to register at the American Immigration Office. On the other hand, it is compulsory for Mexicans returning from the United States to register at the Migration Offices. As evidence of this assertion, let us compare the number of Mexicans who have entered into and returned from the United States from 1920 to 1925 according to official data from Mexico (Table VI) and Washington (Table VII). Thus the number of Mexicans returned from the United States to Mexico from 1920 to 1925, according to

Mexican data, 489,748, and the number of same given by American data, 38,740, shows a difference of 451,008.

How is it to be explained that only an insignificant minority of Mexicans register at the American Immigration Offices on leaving the United States, while a very much larger number register at the Mexican Immigration Offices on entering Mexico?

We reach the conclusion that the first is due to the fact that for the American immigration service the entrance of im-

<table>
<tr><td colspan="3" align="center">TABLE VI</td><td colspan="3" align="center">TABLE VII*</td></tr>
<tr><td>Year</td><td>Departed from Mexico to U.S.</td><td>Returned to Mexico from U.S.</td><td>Year</td><td>Admitted in U.S. from Mexico</td><td>Departed from U.S. to Mexico</td></tr>
<tr><td>1920......</td><td>50,569</td><td>64,620</td><td>1920......</td><td>68,392</td><td>11,154</td></tr>
<tr><td>1921......</td><td>9,165</td><td>106,242</td><td>1921......</td><td>46,794</td><td>7,902</td></tr>
<tr><td>1922......</td><td>33,180</td><td>50,171</td><td>1922......</td><td>30,295</td><td>7,500</td></tr>
<tr><td>1923......</td><td>80,793</td><td>85,825</td><td>1923......</td><td>75,988</td><td>3,901</td></tr>
<tr><td>1924......</td><td>57,269</td><td>105,834</td><td>1924......</td><td>105,787</td><td>3,572</td></tr>
<tr><td>1925......</td><td>41,759</td><td>77,056</td><td>1925......</td><td>49,729</td><td>4,711</td></tr>
<tr><td>Total..</td><td>272,735</td><td>489,748</td><td>Total.</td><td>376,985</td><td>38,740</td></tr>
</table>

* The complete period from 1920 to 1926 is not considered because American data for 1926 are lacking at this writing.

migrants to the United States is the question of main importance, while the departure of persons is for them a question of minor consideration. We understand that the American Immigration Law does not constrain Mexicans to register on departing from the United States. Furthermore, the title of the office devoted to these affairs is "Bureau of Immigration," which clearly indicates that the departure of persons from the United States is for their purposes of secondary importance.

The Mexican Migration Law (*Ley de Migración*) regulates both ends of the problem, that is, both immigration and emigration.

Mexicans on re-entering Mexico register with the Mexican authorities for the following reasons:

1. The Mexican Law compels registration of both immigrants and emigrants.[1]

2. One illegally entering Mexico incurs the risk of being considered a revolutionist or enemy of the government.

3. To return to Mexico, no fee need be paid and no delay is involved, since it is only necessary, for legal entrance, to fill the questionnaire presented by the migration officials.

4. It would be both troublesome and costly, and unnecessary, to cross illegally at some points far from the ports of entry, especially for those coming from distant points, since there are few organized smuggling facilities from the United States to Mexico, and there are no especial interests in Mexico to support them.

These considerations permit us to conclude that the figures supplied by Mexican statistics regarding Mexicans who pass from the United States to Mexico measure the movement more nearly correctly than those of the Department of Labor at Washington. Therefore, the number of Mexicans who return to their country is by far larger than that shown in the *Annual Reports* of the Bureau of Immigration, taking into consideration that only an insignificant number of them register at the American Immigration Offices on leaving the United States.

Illegal entry of Mexicans into the United States.—[2] The second of the factors mentioned is the high number of Mexicans who enter the United States illegally every year. To justify this assertion let us deduct from the number of persons who have returned to Mexico from the United States, 557,718 (see

[1] In the Mexican Department of Migration of the *Secretaría de Gobernación*, the names of the 329,269 Mexicans who departed from Mexico to the United States from 1920 to 1926, and of the 557,718 who returned to Mexico from the United States in the same period, are available.

[2] A note on this subject is included in Appendix II.

Table V), the corresponding number of those who have gone from Mexico to the United States, 329,269. This leaves a difference of 228,449 individuals, who, apparently, have returned to Mexico, without first departing from this country. In other words, during this period of six years, 329,269 Mexicans departed for the United States, and—surprising fact—in the same period not only that number returned to Mexico, but 228,449 more! The explanation of this paradox is that those 228,449 individuals of apparent spontaneous generation, and many others as well, departed illegally from Mexico and entered the United States in the same manner. On leaving the United States those individuals naturally did not register at the American Immigration Offices, but on returning to Mexico they did register with the Mexican authorities, for the reasons mentioned before.

The main and immediate reasons for illegal entrance of Mexicans into the United States, as we could observe personally, and from interviewing a great many Mexican immigrants as well as smugglers, contractors, employers, etc., are as follows:

1. Difficulties presented by the immigration laws, of which, as a rule, the Mexican immigrants are completely ignorant, and which, among other requirements, stipulate literacy, a condition which many immigrants cannot fulfil.

2. Loss of time and expense entailed while waiting on the Mexican side during the unwinding of the long and complicated red tape.

3. The sum paid to the smuggler is generally smaller than the eighteen dollars needed to cover the consular *visé* and the head tax.

4. Individuals whose labor has been previously contracted for in Mexico cannot legally enter the United States, so they enter illegally.

It is true that illegal entrance into the United States carries the constant risk of deportation; but statistics show that the number deported is not great.[1]

In view of the poverty, timidity, and general inexperience of the immigrants, and the racial prejudice which exists against them in the American border states, illegal entrance would not be so prevalent were it not for other and more decisive factors. The real forces which move illegal immigration are, first of all, the smugglers or "coyotes" who facilitate illegal entrance to Mexican immigrants, and the contractors or *enganchistas* who provide them with jobs. The smuggler and the contractor are an intimate and powerful alliance from Calexico to Brownsville. Second, indirectly, but logically and fundamentally, the origin of illegal immigration is to be found in the farmers and ranchers, and railroad, mining, and other enterprises to which Mexican labor is indispensable.

Immigration is not only powerfully drawn from the United States but is likewise propeled by conditions in Mexico. The real impulse began just before 1900, when conditions which it is not necessary to detail here obliged Mexicans to leave their country in increasingly large numbers in search of better wages and conditions.

This immigration developed rapidly and could soon be numbered by the hundreds of thousands. As a result, a large part of the commercial and industrial activity in the frontier cities and states developed by using Mexican labor, and it would now be impossible or exceedingly difficult to continue such enterprises without it. This fact has been proclaimed constantly by employers, who bring to bear their political and

[1] [The number returned to Mexico either by deportation or by granting the privilege of voluntary return (particularly the latter) is probably more important than is here suggested. Illegal residence has become increasingly difficult. —EDITOR.]

financial influence to gain their point, and to combat the existing hostility to the immigration.

The propinquity of the two countries and the enormous extent of the boundary make it absolutely impossible to prevent immigration, unless a large army of Mexican and American police were to patrol the line.[1]

[1] [This view is open to objection. Patrol of the border has become increasingly efficient. See Paul S. Taylor, *Mexican Labor in the United States: Migration Statistics*, "University of California Publications in Economics" (Berkeley, 1929), VI, No. 3.—EDITOR.]

CHAPTER II

SOURCES OF MEXICAN IMMIGRATION AND THE DISTRIBUTION OF IMMIGRANTS IN THE UNITED STATES

Where the immigrants come from; the contrast in climates.— The money orders sent to Mexico, presumably by immigrants to their families, during July and August of 1926, were directed

TABLE VIII*

States	No. of Money Orders Received	% of Total	States	No. of Money Orders Received	% of Total
Michoacan......	4,775	20.0	Yucatán........	78	0.3
Guanajuato.....	4,659	19.6	Mexico.........	66	.3
Jalisco.........	3,507	14.7	Querétaro......	58	.2
Nuevo León.....	1,913	8.0	Guerrero.......	57	.2
Durango........	1,400	5.9	Colima.........	55	.2
Distrito Federal.	1,196	5.0	Vera Cruz......	54	.2
Zacatecas.......	1,140	4.8	Nayarit.........	51	.2
Chihuahua......	1,046	4.4	Oaxaca....·....	48	.2
Coahuila........	903	3.8	Hidalgo........	45	.2
San Luis Potosí..	869	3.7	Tlaxcala........	13	0.1
Tamaulipas.....	484	2.1	Chiapas........	2	0
Sinaloa.........	473	2.0	Tabasco........	2	0
Aguascalientes...	462	1.9	Campeche......	1	0
Sonora.........	294	1.2	Morelos........	1	0
Baja California..	115	0.5	Quintana Roo...	0	0
Puebla.........	78	0.3	Total......	23,846	100.0

* The number of persons who sent money orders from the United States during July–August, 1926, was 23,446, while 23,846 persons in Mexico received money orders. This was due to the fact that in some cases one person sent two or more money orders to two or more persons in Mexico.

in large part to the states of the central plateau (*mesa central*), and, in lesser proportion, to those of the northern plateau (*mesa del norte*). From these states, then, comes the larger part of the Mexican immigrants.

These two large zones, which are bounded on the east and west by the Sierra Madre, on the north by the American border, on the south by the southern escarpment, enjoy conditions of altitude, temperature, and rainfall which make an ideal climate for the development of human life.

The northern zone descends slowly as it reaches the border; therefore a large part of the states of Chihuahua, Coahuila, Nuevo León, and Sonora do not possess the same ideal climate but are characterized by extremes of temperature like those prevailing on the other side of the border.

The difference in altitude, latitude, and temperature between the United States and Mexico seriously hinders the adjustment of the Mexican immigrant, for with the exception of the states to the west of the Rocky Mountains—New Mexico, Arizona, and California, which in some respects have a climate similar to that of the northern regions of Mexico—the extremes of temperature elsewhere are very great and the humidity greater than that of the Mexican plateaus. This is especially true in the northern states of the East and Middle West. Complete statistics on mortality and illness of the Mexican immigrant—especially high among those who are immigrants for the first time—do not exist.[1]

[1] The Outdoor Relief Division of the County Charities, Los Angeles, Calif., during the fiscal year from July 1, 1925, to June 30, 1926, extended state aid to 6,609 American children and to 5,708 Mexican children. The next largest foreign group (British) contributed only about 500 cases. The Mexican relief cases included disproportionately numerous instances of juvenile problems, unemployment, desertion, tuberculosis, and other sickness difficulties. Venereal disease and tuberculosis predominated.

C. E. Durham, director of the Bureau of Vital Statistics, Texas State Board of Health, calculated that while for the white population in that state 1 child out of 19 did not see its second birthday, for the Mexican population 1 out of 5 did not live that long.

Of the 144 Mexican cases in the Southern California State Hospital at Patton on April 22, 1927, G. M. Webster, medical superintendent, stated that "of the cause of insanity in this class of patients among men 55% appear to be de-

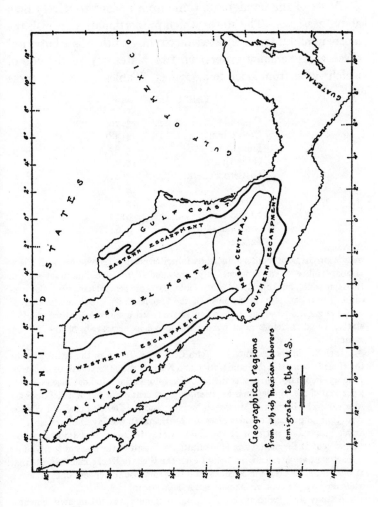

Geographical regions
from which Mexican laborers
emigrate to the U.S.

Most of the immigrants come from regions relatively high above sea-level. The states which proportionately furnish the most immigrants are located (according to the distribution of these 23,446 money orders) on two plateaus² the altitude of which varies from 4,000 to 8,000 feet. Tables IX–XI list these

TABLE IX

	Per Cent
Coahuila.............	3.78
Chihuahua...........	4.38
Durango.............	5.87
Guanajuato..........	19.54
Distrito Federal......	5.01
Jalisco..............	14.70
Michoacan...........	20.27
Nuevo León..........	8.02
San Luis Potosí.......	3.64
Zacatecas...........	4.78

mentia precox, a psychosis induced by inherited tendencies together with a lack of adaptability to environment. 30% are manic depressive, due practically to the same cause, but considered recoverable. 15% are general paralysis: this condition has its etiology in syphilis. Of the females, 75% are dementia precox; 25% are general paralysis. These figures are based upon comparatively limited statistics and therefore must not be considered as necessarily of absolute accuracy."

Included in the testimony of John C. Box, of Texas, in the hearing before the House Committee on Immigration and Naturalization, Sixty-ninth Congress, January–February, 1926, was the following information: In Los Angeles, where 7 per cent of the population is Mexican, 27.4 per cent of the public-relief cases are Mexican. The Bureau of Municipal Nursing and the Division of Child Welfare state that 40 per cent of their cases are Mexican. In the Jay Home of the children's hospital 25 per cent of the children are Mexicans. At Pasadena, where 2.8 per cent of the population is Mexican, 6 per cent of the cases of the Welfare Department are Mexican. In Long Beach the Welfare Department reports that 21 per cent of its cases are Mexican, and that they use 16 per cent of the budget, while only 11 per cent of the population is Mexican.

A study of ill health among Mexican immigrants in an urban environment is to be found in "Analysis of Mexican Patients at Chicago Dispensary," by Britton and Constable, *Nation's Health*, VII (July, 1926), No. 7.

² The states of Jalisco and Michoacan include also two escarpments on the coasts, but it should be stated that the emigration comes almost exclusively from the regions of those states situated in the central plateau.

sections with the percentage of money orders which they respectively contribute.

TABLE X*

PERCENTAGE CONTRIBUTED BY EACH STATE OF MEXICO TO IMMIGRATION IN
ARIZONA, CALIFORNIA, AND NEW MEXICO, ACCORDING TO POSTAL MONEY
ORDERS FROM THESE LAST STATES ADDRESSED TO MEXICO DURING JANU-
ARY, 1927

Arizona	California	New Mexico	Total	Percentage	Where Collected
42........	172	6	220	2.76	Aguascalientes
8........	66	0	74	0.93	Baja California
0........	0	0	0	0.00	Campeche
26........	102	8	136	1.71	Coahuila
4........	68	0	72	0.90	Colima
0........	4	0	4	0.05	Chiapas
136........	304	48	488	6.12	Chihuahua
36........	326	18	380	4.77	Distrito Federal
74........	472	16	562	7.05	Durango
142........	1,482	74	1,698	21.31	Guanajuato
2........	22	0	24	0.30	Guerrero
4........	12	0	16	0.20	Hidalgo
368........	1,362	48	1,778	22.31	Jalisco
0........	6	2	8	0.10	Mexico
92........	1,038	22	1,152	14.46	Michoacan
2........	2	0	4	0.05	Morelos
4........	58	0	62	.78	Nayarit
6........	16	2	24	.30	Nuevo León
0........	8	0	8	.10	Oaxaca
4........	12	4	20	.25	Puebla
2........	10	0	12	.15	Queretaro
6........	34	10	50	.63	San Luis Potosí
0........	0	0	0	0.00	Quintana Roo
28........	170	0	198	2.48	Sinaloa
94........	108	0	202	2.53	Sonora
0........	0	0	0	0.00	Tabasco
0........	42	6	48	.60	Tamaulipas
2........	0	0	2	.03	Tlaxcala
0........	22	0	22	.25	Veracruz
0........	0	0	0	0.00	Yucatán
138........	552	18	708	8.88	Zacatecas
1,220........	6,470	282	7,972	100.00	....

* A winter month was selected to emphasize the great climatic difference between American and Mexican regions.

Guanajuato, Jalisco, and Michoacan, places of mild climate, are the principal contributors, though it would seem that

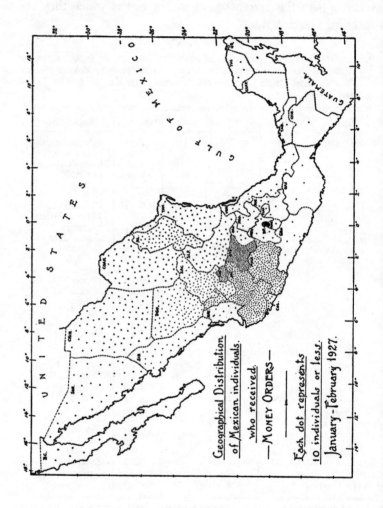

Geographical Distribution
of Mexican individuals
who received
—Money Orders—

Each dot represents
10 individuals or less.
January-February 1927.

the states of Sonora, Chihuahua, Coahuila, and Nuevo León, which, because they are near the border, are advantageously

TABLE XI

PERCENTAGE CONTRIBUTED BY EACH STATE OF MEXICO TO IMMIGRATION IN ILLINOIS, INDIANA, AND MICHIGAN, ACCORDING TO POSTAL MONEY ORDERS FROM THESE LAST STATES ADDRESSED TO MEXICO DURING FEBRUARY, 1927

Illinois	Indiana	Michigan	Total	Percentage	Where Collected
39	7	7	53	1.57	Aguascalientes
1	0	0	1	0.03	Baja California
0	0	0	0	0.00	Campeche
38	9	18	65	1.93	Coahuila
1	1	1	3	0.09	Colima
2	0	0	2	0.06	Chiapas
27	7	3	37	1.10	Chihuahua
151	34	26	211	6.27	Distrito Federal
39	16	13	68	2.02	Durango
768	275	97	1,140	33.86	Guanajuato
1	0	0	1	0.03	Guerrero
7	0	0	7	0.21	Hidalgo
386	137	68	591	17.55	Jalisco
8	3	2	13	0.39	Mexico
521	250	97	868	25.78	Michoacan
1	0	1	2	0.06	Morelos
0	0	0	0	0.00	Nayarit
47	24	15	86	2.56	Nuevo León
7	0	0	7	0.21	Oaxaca
10	1	1	12	.36	Puebla
12	1	0	13	0.39	Querétaro
55	11	17	83	2.47	San Luis Potosí
0	0	0	0	0.00	Quintana Roo
1	0	0	1	.03	Sinaloa
0	0	0	0	.00	Sonora
1	0	0	1	.03	Tabasco
20	2	5	27	.80	Tamaulipas
0	0	0	0	0.00	Tlaxcala
7	0	1	8	0.24	Veracruz
3	0	0	3	0.09	Yucatán
49	6	8	63	1.87	Zacatecas
2,202	784	380	3,366	100.00	....

situated for emigration to the United States and where climate conditions are more nearly like those in the United States, are also principal contributors.

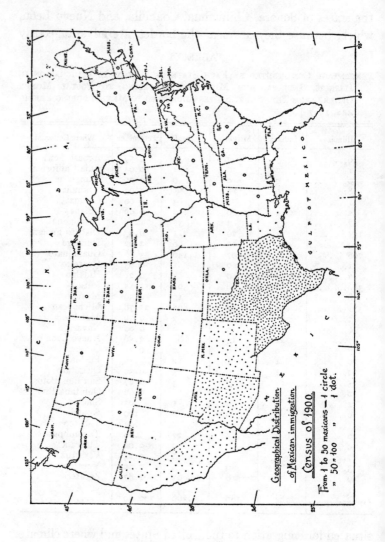

Geographical Distribution
of Mexican immigration.
Census of 1900.
From 1 to 50 mexicans — 1 circle
    "   50 " 100 "   — 1 dot.

One might suppose that the immigrants coming from the central tablelands would choose to go to California, Arizona, and New Mexico, where the climate is relatively the same, and that the immigrants from Chihuahua, Coahuila, Nuevo León, and Sonora would go to the states of the east and midwest where a more rigorous climate prevails. Nevertheless this is not the case. An examination of the data on distribution by states and cities shows that in California, for example, there is a relatively high proportion of immigrants from Sonora, Chihuahua, Coahuila, and Nuevo León; while in the northern east and midwest states, especially Illinois, Indiana, and Michigan, the largest proportion of immigrants comes from the states of Michoacan and Guanajuato, which are in the mild central plateau.

The official weather reports compiled by the Mexican and United States governments show that in states from which come most of the immigrants the mean annual variation in temperature is not 20° F., while in some parts of the United States to which the Mexicans go it is almost 100°. The great difference in humidity is likewise to be considered. The scant economic means and the ignorance and inexperience of the Mexican immigrants hamper them in their struggle with the hostile climate, and they frequently succumb to disease.

One might conclude that the simple fact is that the immigrants come from those Mexican states having the largest populations. But this is not true. Of the three states in the republic which have more than a million inhabitants, Jalisco is the only one which provides a high proportion of emigrants, while Puebla, on the central plateau, and Veracruz, on the east coast, contribute very small percentages, 0.32 and 0.22, respectively. Probably the reason for the high percentage of emigration from Jalisco, Guanajuato, and Michoacan lies in the fact that conditions there for agriculture are difficult, the land having

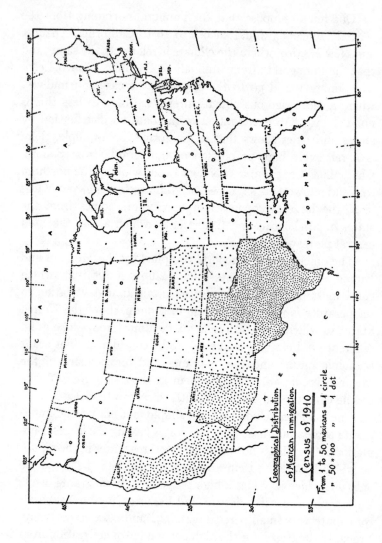

Geographical Distribution
of Mexican immigration.
Census of 1910

From 1 to 50 mexicans = 1 circle
  „   50 „ 100   „   1 dot

always been in the hands of a small number of big proprietors. For this reason, the excess population of the prolific *peón* class has been obliged to emigrate periodically. This region, because of its fertility and great production of cereals, and its excess population, has rightly been called the granary and *"peón purveyor"* of Mexico. The same circumstance, in smaller degree, can be said of Aguascalientes, Durango, Zacatecas, and San Luis Potosí.

From the escarpments and the coasts come the lowest percentage of immigrants, except in those states near the border, Lower California, Sonora, and Tamaulipas, which furnish 0.48, 1.23, and 2.01 per cent, respectively, and Sinaloa, from which the United States is easily accessible so that the percentage there rises to 1.98. The small amount of emigration from the coasts is probably due to the fact that the agrarian problem, so acute in the central plateau and in lesser degree on the northern plains, is much less important in the tropics; therefore there is not an excess population which must emigrate.

Distribution of the immigrants in the United States.—We have already noted that for obvious reasons Mexican migration to the United States developed in the border states first. An examination of the geographic distribution of immigrants will show (Table XII) that in 1900 Texas had a population of 71,062 Mexican settlers; Arizona, 14,172; California, 8,096; and New Mexico, 6,649; while in no other state did their number reach 500. Possibly the greater total in Texas was due to the fact that this state had the largest population technically American, but really Mexican racially and Spanish linguistically. Naturally this attracted more Mexican settlers.

The development of natural resources and the increase of prosperity in California assumed great proportions in a short space of time—1900–1910. This caused a great demand for labor, and therefore the number of Mexican immigrants grew

TABLE XII*
GEOGRAPHIC DISTRIBUTION OF MEXICANS IN UNITED STATES

States	ACCORDING TO AMERICAN CENSUSES			ACCORDING TO DESTINATIONS OF MONEY ORDERS IN JULY AND AUGUST, 1926
	Number of Mexicans			Number of Money Orders
	1900	1910	1920	
Alabama...............	43	81	146	11
Arizona...............	14,172	20,987	61,580	940
Arkansas..............	68	132	280	2
California.............	8,086	33,694	88,771	8,582
Colorado..............	274	2,502	11,037	586
Connecticut...........	22	19	44	....
Delaware..............	2	2	52	1
District of Columbia....	38	26	73	4
Florida................	84	145	167	42
Georgia...............	14	25	55	....
Idaho.................	28	133	1,215	46
Illinois...............	156	672	4,032	2,923
Indiana...............	43	47	686	1,242
Iowa.................	29	620	2,650	157
Kansas...............	71	8,429	13,770	750
Kentucky.............	19	28	138	2
Louisiana.............	488	1,025	2,487	28
Maryland.............	26	10	87	6
Massachusetts.........	41	71	148	9
Michigan.............	56	86	1,333	955
Minnesota............	24	52	248	103
Mississippi...........	48	72	110	5
Missouri..............	162	1,413	3,411	227
Montana..............	47	67	236	166
Nebraska.............	27	290	3,611	224
Nevada...............	98	752	1,177	152
New Hampshire........	3	6	10	....
New Jersey............	55	97	420	424
New Mexico...........	6,649	11,918	20,272	299
New York.............	353	555	2,999	424
North Carolina........	4	10	30	....
North Dakota..........	1	8	29	16
Ohio.................	53	85	952	445
Oklahoma.............	134	2,744	1,818	151
Oregon...............	53	85	8	445
Pennsylvania..........	110	135	17	578
Rhode Island..........	5	8	68	....
South Carolina........	2	2	176	....

* The number of money orders directed to a given state cannot conclusively be regarded as an index of the number of Mexicans in that state. It is probable, for example, that more recently arrived Mexicans in California have more family connections in Mexico, and therefore send back money more frequently, than do older Mexicans resident in Texas.—EDITOR.]

TABLE XII—*Continued*

States	ACCORDING TO AMERICAN CENSUSES			ACCORDING TO DESTINATIONS OF MONEY ORDERS IN JULY AND AUGUST, 1926
	Number of Mexicans			Number of Money Orders
	1900	1910	1920	
South Dakota..........	13	15	251,827	33
Tennessee..............	29	45	1,166	....
Texas.................	71,062	125,016	7	3,318
Utah..................	41	166	....	168
Vermont...............	3	6	....	....
Virginia...............	18	12	80	1
Washington............	73	145	450	15
West Virginia..........	7	10	80	8
Wisconsin.............	499	399	178	310
Wyoming..............	58	188*	1,801	176

in this period to 33,694, approximately quadrupling the number in 1900. Texas, Arizona, and New Mexico developed more slowly, and the increase of Mexican immigration was in proportion. In Arizona, through this period, it was doubled, reaching 29,987 in 1910. In Texas it was almost doubled, being 125,744 in 1910, and in New Mexico the increase raised the total number to 11,918. Immigration began to spread from these first states to those adjoining, increasing in 1910 in Louisiana to 1,025, in Oklahoma to 2,744, in Colorado to 2,502, and in Nevada to 732. Mexican labor throughout this period was employed chiefly in the cultivation and harvest of cotton, corn, sugar-cane, and fruits, but also on the railroads, in stock ranches, and in mines. The immigrant population increased enormously in Kansas, from 71 in 1900 to 9,429 in 1910. This was probably due to the fact that Kansas City became a temporary stopover and important distributing center of immigrants going to the eastern and midwestern states, where the demand for Mexican labor increased more perceptibly than in others. In Missouri the increase in immigrant population

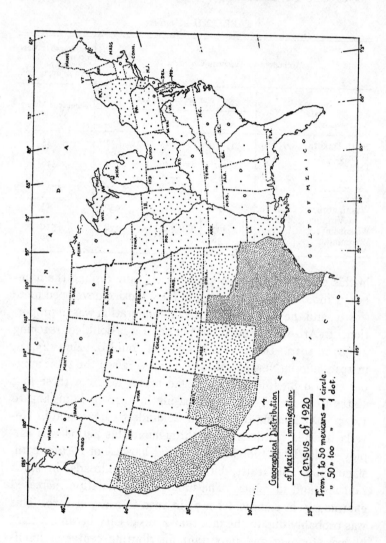

Geographical Distribution
of Mexican immigration
Census of 1920
From 1 to 50 mexicans = 1 circle.
  "   50 " 100   "   = 1 dot.

was also considerable, in 1910 reaching a total of 1,413, as a result of which St. Louis, Missouri, became also a distributing center of Mexican labor, though of secondary importance. The number of immigrants to other states also increased, but the population of few went over 500.

From 1910 to 1920 California continued to develop economically, but the increase in Mexican immigration was not proportionately great, the number, 33,694 in 1910, was little more than doubled in 1920, reaching 88,771. This relatively small increase might be accounted for by the fact that the anti-Asiatic campaign vigorously carried on in this period also retarded Mexican immigration. In Texas, New Mexico, and Arizona the demand for Mexican labor increased proportionately to the development of these states, and the numbers rose to 251,827, 61,580, and 20,272, respectively; that is, the 1910 figures approximately doubled. In Oklahoma and Louisiana about the same relative increase occurred, but in Colorado the 1910 figures were quadrupled, probably because of the great development of mining. In Utah the immigration reached a figure approximately seven times that of 1910, and in Nevada it was almost doubled, as also in the states containing distributing centers, that is, Missouri and Kansas. The demand for Mexican labor was intensified in this period, chiefly for the cultivation of beets, and for industries such as iron, cement, automobiles, and packing-houses, in the East and Midwest. In 1920 Mexican immigration was twenty times greater in Michigan than in 1910; ten times greater in Wyoming and nine in Nebraska and Idaho; five times greater in New York, Pennsylvania, and Illinois; and four times in Iowa.

Considering the post-office money-order records for July and August, 1926, the season when the immigration reaches its highest amount, we find that the states from which the greatest number of drafts were sent are as follows: California, 8,582;

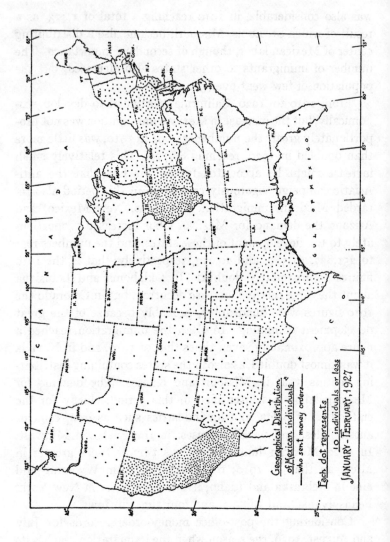

Texas, 3,318; Illinois, 2,923; and Indiana, 1,242. This seems to indicate an increase in California, a reaction from the slowing-down of the preceding period; in Texas, normal increase and great increase in Illinois and Indiana. Michigan sent 955 money orders; Arizona, 940; Kansas, 750; Colorado, 586; Pennsylvania, 578; Ohio, 445; New York, 424; and Wisconsin, 310. These figures show that, in general, immigration during the last period did not continue its geographical distribution with relatively regular progression of the three preceding periods, but increased proportionately more in the northern states of the East and Midwest than in the southern states, except California and Texas.

Distribution of immigrants in American cities.—With the exception of Maine, Vermont, and North and South Carolina, Mexican immigrants sent money to Mexico during these months from all the states in the American union. These money orders came from 94 American cities of more than 25,-000 inhabitants and from 1,417 cities of less than 25,000. This is a total of 1,511 post-offices, and represents approximately 4 per cent of the total of 36,970 populated centers in the United States.[1] This distribution seems to indicate that a high proportion of the immigrants are engaged in rural labor, in smaller towns and cities, and that a smaller proportion employed in industrial enterprises. Though it is true that a large number are doing agricultural work, in cities like Chicago, Los Angeles, San Antonio, and in the vicinity of Pittsburgh and of others of similar importance, large numbers of Mexican immigrants are employed in industry. On the other hand, these immigrants come from approximately 552 Mexican cities.

[1] *New Reference Atlas of the World* (New York, 1926).

CHAPTER III

THE MEXICAN IMMIGRANT WAGE-EARNER

Mexican immigration into the United States is, fundamentally, an economic phenomenon, the automatic result of increasing demand for labor in the one country and available supply of laborers in the other. Let us see what the results have been so far.

That it has been beneficial to American employers appears from the testimony of representatives of large industrial and agricultural enterprises involving probably five billion dollars, who declared to the Immigration Committee of the House of Representatives[1] that they owed their development partly to Mexican immigration, and who even went so far as to say that they were so much dependent on it that were immigration to cease, or be cut much below the present average by a quota, they would be left on the verge of bankruptcy.

As to the Mexican immigrants themselves, a measure of the extent to which they generally better their own living conditions and standards is found in the fact that from 1919 to 1927 they sent money to their families in Mexico on a yearly average of $10,173,719.31, Mexican money, or approximately one-half of this amount in American money. A total of $91,563,473.81 *pesos* was thus remitted during the nine years (see chap. i, Table III).

Of course not all Mexican immigrants remit money. A tabulation of 12,321 money orders (Table XIII) sent from various parts of the United States during July, 1926, shows a total of $592,061.35 *pesos*, or an average value of each draft of

[1] Hearing before the Committee on Immigration and Naturalization, Sixty-ninth Congress, first session, Washington, 1926.

30

$48.05. This, of course, was not the value of each money order, for there were 154 variations in the amounts sent, from a minimum of 0.52 *pesos* to a maximum of $207.25 *pesos*, the limit allowed by the post-office. The relative frequency of amounts remitted appears in Table XIII.

Those hostile to Mexican immigration argue that these remittances represent economic loss to the United States, and add that further loss is occasioned by the large sums spent in relief work among the immigrants, larger for Mexicans, proportionately, than for other immigrants or for Americans in need.

The argument set forth in reply is that the amount sent by immigrants to their relatives in Mexico is very small considering the benefit rendered by Mexican labor to American industry and agriculture, and that the sums spent to help the immigrants are furnished, partly, directly or indirectly, by those enterprises which profit by their labor, which contribute to federal, municipal, or private sources from which the relief comes. Furthermore, it is argued, a relatively high proportion of the Mexicans included in the statistics of relief work are American citizens of Mexican origin.

The American Federation of Labor is hostile to Mexican immigration, for several reasons. The Mexican laborer generally works for a wage much lower than the American. Without the competition of the Mexican immigrant, says the American Federation of Labor, the American worker would receive higher wages than he does. The immigrant's answer to this is that he is obliged to work for a lower wage because, since the unions generally refuse admission to him, he cannot demand union rates. This membership is refused as a rule when the immigrant is not an American citizen, and the Mexican is usually unwilling to become one. The Federation insists that he be naturalized, and adds that even when he is admitted to union membership without this prerequisite he is not a satisfac-

TABLE XIII*

RELATIVE FREQUENCY OF AMOUNTS REMITTED BY POSTAL MONEY ORDERS

Number of Drafts	Amount in Mexican Currency†	Percentage
41	2.07	0.33
96	4.15	.78
77	5.18	0.63
143	6.22	1.16
87	8.29	0.71
1,737	10.36	14.10
167	12.44	1.36
101	14.51	0.82
115	16.58	.93
44	18.65	0.36
2,056	20.73	16.69
70	22.80	0.57
124	24.87	1.01
75	25.91	0.61
58	26.94	0.47
1,140	31.09	9.26
52	33.16	0.42
45	35.23	.37
55	37.31	0.45
945	41.45	7.67
1,208	51.81	9.81
542	62.18	4.40
219	72.54	1.78
327	82.90	2.66
117	93.26	0.95
855	103.63	6.94
100	113.99	0.81
115	124.35	.90
90	124.55	.73
66	155.44	.54
54	165.80	0.44
352	207.25	2.86
1,043	Other denominations	8.48
12.321		100.00

* The money orders here tabulated proceeded from Arizona, California, Colorado, Idaho, Iowa, Kansas, Louisiana, Minnesota, Missouri, Montana, Nebraska, Nevada, New Mexico, North Dakota, South Dakota, Oklahoma, Oregon, Texas, Utah, Washington, and Wyoming, and were remitted through the El Paso, Texas, post-office during July, 1926. These money orders were deposited in United States currency and paid in Mexico at the rate varying from $2.07 to $2.08 Mexican currency to the American dollar.

† Most of the money orders are for $10, $20, $30, etc., rather than for even amounts in between.

tory member. Another reason for the hostility of the American Federation of Labor to Mexican immigration lies in the fact that some Mexican workers become members of the I.W.W., sometimes believing that this will better their wages and position and sometimes from sympathy with the principles and policy of this organization.

The question, economically, is therefore only the eternal war between capital and labor. It is true that were Mexican immigration to be cut below its present numerical average, there would be both a decrease in the volume of agriculture and industrial production dependent on Mexican labor and an increase in the wages of American labor, which could substitute for it only in part, since for these enterprises American labor is scarce. If the present conditions prevail, and no limit is placed on Mexican immigration, the labor situation will continue just as long as the economic factors which cause it and upon which it depends remain constant.

Labor groups.—Mexican immigrants in the United States fall into three labor groups: (1) unskilled laborers, (2) skilled laborers, and (3) tenant farmers or farmers on shares. Besides these there are clerks, small merchants, artists, students, professional exiled politicians, and others, but their scant number eliminates them from the immigrant mass we consider our problem.

Unskilled or common laborers in Mexico.—The economic condition of this group, which forms by far the majority in Mexico, has been very bad in the past and continues to be so to the present day, especially in the small towns and in the country. This perpetual economic evil is at the root of the alarming and abnormal trends, slow growth or even decrease, which has characterized the numerical development of Mexico's population for more than a century. This slow growth appears from Mexican census figures, and population estimates, from

1793 to 1921, furnished by the Departamento de la Estadística Nacional (see Table XIV). Because the Mexican population is

TABLE XIV

CENSUS OF THE MEXICAN POPULATION FROM 1793 TO 1921

Year	Authority	Population
1793–94......	Revillagigedo	4,483,569
1793–94......	Revillagigedo	4,483,680
1793–94......	Revillagigedo	5,200,000
1804.........	Humboldt	5,837,100
1808.........	Humboldt	6,500,000
1810.........	Semanario Económico	5,910,005
1810.........	Navarro y Noriega	5,122,354
1810.........	Navarro y Noriega	5,128,000
1810.........	Primer Congreso	6,204,000
1824.........	Poinsett	6,500,000
1830.........	Burkardt	7,996,000
1831.........	A. J. Valdés	6,382,284
1834.........	Calendario de Galvan	7,734,292
1836.........	Noticia de los estados y territorios	7,843,132
1838.........	Cámara de Diputados	7,009,120
1838.........	Juan N. Almonte, compendio de geografía	7,500,000
1839.........	Instituto de Geografía y Estadística	7,044,140
1852.........	Almonte, "Guia de Forasteros"	7,661,919
1854.........	Anales de Fomento	7,853,395
1855.........	Miguel Lerdo de Tejada	7,661,520
1856.........	Miguel Lerdo de Tejada	7,859,564
1857.........	Antonio Garcia Cubas	8,283,088
1857.........	Manuel Orozco y Berra	8,287,413
1862.........	J. M. Pérez Hernández	8,396,524
1869.........	García Cubas	8,743,614
1872.........	Secretaría de Gobernación	9,097,056
1873.........	A. Balcárcel	8,994,724
1874.........	García Cubas	9,343,470
1878.........	Secretaría de Gobernación	9,384,193
1880.........	Emiliano Busto	9,384,193
1882.........	Bodo Von Glumer	10,001,884
1886.........	García Cubas	10,791,685
1888.........	Direc. Gral. de Estadística	11,490,830
1895.........	Direc. Gral. de Estadística	12,632,427
1900.........	Direc. Gral. de Estadística	13,545,462
1910.........	Direc. Gral. de Estadística	15,160,369
1921.........	Depto. de la Estadística Nacional	14,234,799
1921.........	(Correction to date)	14,334,780

very prolific, the slow increase and fluctuations of these figures can only be accounted for by the abnormal disappearance of inhabitants, probably occasioned by three factors: first, abnormal mortality produced by disease and privations which imply a miserable economic existence; second, abnormal mortality as a result of frequent wars and revolutions; third, emigration to foreign countries.

From 1793 to 1810 only the first of these factors exerted its unfavorable influence on the growth of the Mexican population, but from 1810 to the beginning of the last quarter of the nineteenth century, during which time there was no easy communication with the United States, the first and second factors were in operation. Lastly, in the period between the end of the second period and 1921 when convenient railway communication with the United States was established, all three factors exerted their unfavorable influence.

The only constant factor has been the first, the result of the chronic economic misery of the lower classes that make up the bulk of the population. The difference of historical background, the ethnic heterogeneity of the elements that form the social structure, bad government, low industrial development, low wages, and lack of work, and many other conditions contribute to the explanation of these bad conditions; but we shall limit ourselves solely to the discussion of the insufficient wages which the common laborers received in Mexico in 1927 and which they are probably receiving today.

A wage table compiled for us from official sources, showing the prevailing wage scale in over four hundred towns and cities in the northern and central Mexican plateaus, a table too long to include here in full, shows that the average daily wage for agricultural workers in Mexico is 0.91 *pesos*, and that of an industrial worker 1.40 *pesos*, an average of 1.15 *pesos*, or $0.57 a day in American money. But in the regions from which the greatest part of the Mexican immigrants come the average daily wage is still lower.

The insufficiency of this "minimum living wage," or "misery wage," may be demonstrated in various ways, but we have preferred to do it by means of the annexed Table XV, likewise

TABLE XV

Cost of Living of a Workman's Family of Five Persons during January, 1926 (in Pesos)

	Ags.	Coah.	Chih.	Gto.	Jal.	Mich.	N.L.	Tams.	Zac.	D.F.
Food:										
Maize.............	10.00	10.00	11.00	10.00	10.00	9.00	11.00	12.00	8.00	11.00
White bread......	18.00	16.80	18.30	14.40	16.20	16.50	18.90	17.10	17.70	17.10
Beans...........	9.00	14.00	8.00	8.00	10.50	11.00	13.00	16.00	8.60	5.00
Rice.............	7.60	8.40	8.40	6.20	6.40	5.80	7.40	8.00	8.60	5.00
Meat.............	36.00	45.70	43.50	48.75	43.50	49.50	39.75	50.25	36.00	62.25
Milk.............	19.00	20.00	24.00	21.00	20.00	22.00	22.00	27.00	18.00	24.00
Sugar...........	6.00	6.66	7.35	5.40	6.00	5.85	5.85	6.30	6.90	4.65
Coffee...........	4.59	3.99	4.05	4.83	3.84	3.63	3.21	3.51	3.69	3.60
Lard.............	12.59	12.40	12.10	12.70	11.90	13.40	11.30	11.20	11.40	12.00
Chili.............	4.05	6.30	5.40	4.50	4.50	5.30	5.85	7.40	5.20	3.15
Vegetables........	6.00	6.00	6.00	6.00	6.00	6.00	6.00	6.00	6.00	6.00
Salt.............	0.40	0.50	0.55	0.45	0.55	0.60	0.45	0.55	0.55	0.45
Fuel:										
Coal.............	20.00	12.00	24.00	16.00	14.00	12.00	12.00	22.00	12.00	16.00
Oil..............	2.80	2.50	3.50	2.80	3.30	3.50	2.70	3.20	3.40	2.40
Workman's clothing:										
Shirt.............	2.58	2.66	3.34	3.16	4.16	3.84	2.50	3.00	3.00	3.34
Drawers..........	3.10	3.20	4.00	3.80	5.00	4.60	3.00	3.60	3.60	4.00
Cotton blouse.....	5.06	6.12	5.88	6.34	5.44	5.84	6.22	5.06	5.72	4.16
Cotton trousers....	6.06	7.34	7.06	7.60	6.54	7.00	7.46	6.06	6.85	5.00
Suit of clothes.....	11.12	13.46	12.94	13.94	11.98	12.84	13.68	11.02	12.58	9.16
Shoes...........	8.34	13.34	19.16	3.34	10.84	12.50	14.16	19.16	15.84	20.84
Sarape..........	4.16	8.06	8.34	6.66	8.34	7.22	5.00	7.22	8.06	10.28
Hat.............	4.44	4.44	3.88	1.94	2.50	3.06	2.50	5.84	4.72	1.12
Woman's clothing:										
Chemise..........	1.55	1.60	2.00	1.90	2.50	2.30	1.50	2.30	1.80	2.00
Underskirt........	1.50	1.85	2.20	1.60	1.60	1.90	1.85	1.95	1.55	1.35
Skirts...........	1.50	1.85	2.20	1.60	1.60	1.90	1.85	1.95	1.55	1.46
Blouse..........	1.25	1.54	1.83	1.33	1.33	1.58	1.54	1.63	1.29	1.13
Shawl...........	1.67	1.67	1.67	1.67	1.67	1.67	1.67	1.67	1.67	1.67
Shoes...........	2.50	4.44	6.11	1.11	3.61	4.17	4.72	6.39	5.28	6.94
Dress of baby in lactation:										
Shirt.............	0.34	0.36	0.44	0.42	0.56	0.51	0.33	0.40	0.40	0.34
Cap.............	0.25	0.25	0.25	0.25	0.25	0.25	0.25	0.25	0.25	0.25
Swaddling-cloth...	2.07	2.13	2.67	2.63	3.33	3.07	2.00	2.40	2.40	2.67
Nine-year-old boy's dress:										
Shirt.............	1.03	1.06	1.33	1.26	1.66	1.53	1.00	1.20	1.20	1.33
Drawers..........	1.29	1.33	1.67	1.58	2.08	1.92	1.25	1.50	1.50	1.67
Cotton trousers....	2.53	3.06	2.94	3.17	2.72	2.92	3.11	2.53	2.86	2.08
Cotton blouse.....	2.02	2.44	2.36	2.53	2.18	2.33	2.49	2.02	2.29	1.67
Shoes...........	2.09	3.34	4.79	0.84	2.71	3.13	3.54	4.79	3.96	5.21
Hat.............	1.11	1.11	0.97	0.49	0.63	0.70	0.63	1.46	1.18	0.28
Lodging:										
Rent.............	8.22	11.50	16.44	8.22	11.50	11.50	15.61	25.44	8.22	13.97
Cleanness:										
Soap............	5.90	7.80	5.90	5.70	6.30	6.40	6.50	7.10	7.70	5.50
Bath............	9.86	11.83	19.23	6.41	4.93	4.93	6.90	11.83	5.92	8.38
Total.........	247.48	283.02	315.75	250.42	262.65	273.69	270.67	328.28	256.34	298.89

derived from official sources. In it is calculated the "minimum wage of comfort" by which a worker's family consisting of five members might defray the costs of normal life in various states from which immigrants to the United States come. In this cost-of-living scale no expenditures for education or recreation are included—in fact, nothing except what is of urgent necessity to life. According to this table, in order that a Mexican laborer might be able to live normally he would have to receive a wage of 247.48 *pesos* a month, or $123.74 in American money, in some states such as Aguascalientes; or 328.28 *pesos*, or $164.14, in other states such as Tamaulipas. The average of the two figures is 287.88 *pesos*, or $143.94 in American money. The true wage scale cited above shows that the actual mean daily salary for the Mexican worker is 1.15 *pesos*, or 0.57 cents in American money. This, in a month of thirty-one days, is equal to 35.65 *pesos*, or $17.67 in American money. That is to say, the mean wage of a Mexican worker would have to increase approximately eight times in order that he might meet the cost of the normal necessities of life.

Before 1910 the working day was generally twelve hours, "from sun to sun." Later, governments established the eight-hour day in the principal cities and industrial regions; but in many rural sections it is still customary to work ten or twelve hours a day.

Since the miserable pay of the workman insures him only insufficient food, inadequate clothing, unhealthful homes, and deficient medical attention, the work he does during such a long working day is not and cannot be truly productive. The worker, a victim of chronic fatigue, manages by all means possible to save his energies, working effectively for only a few hours and slacking up and killing time the rest of the day. On the other hand, when the pay is higher and the working day eight hours, the work is more productive, as foreign employers established in Mexico are able to confirm. It is inevitable, therefore, that the Mexican worker should emigrate to the United States, to avoid all these difficulties, especially in those times when unemployment is unusually general.

Unskilled or common laborers in the United States.—To compute a table of wages received by Mexican workers in the United States is a very difficult task because the level of these wages fluctuates as the demand changes for the seasonal labor that the majority of the immigrants perform. On the other hand, the accurate wage tables that already exist in regard to Americans workers are of little use to us, for frequently the Mexicans earn less salaries than do Americans. In view of this fact it will be understood why the Table XVI is so meager. The data for this table were collected for the most part through direct investigations in the regions which we covered, while others were furnished by Mexican consuls and by some of the employers of Mexican laborers. In this table are shown, in addition to the wages paid by the day or hour, those which are paid according to the quantity of work performed, that is to say, per job, as, for example, according to the quantity of fruit picked or the acreage of beets sown. The minimum pay is $1.50 a day, and at times a little lower still, as in Texas, whereas in other regions the laborers get as high as $6.00 a day. Nevertheless it is necessary to strike an average of all the wages in the table, and this gives $3.38 a day, or $104.78 in a month of thirty-one days. This pay is six times as great as the $17.67 a month which the worker gets in Mexico.

We lack sufficient data to compile a table on the cost of living of Mexican laborers in the United States, and therefore cannot compute the relation between this cost of living and the prevailing wage. Nevertheless, the question may be attacked indirectly. The monthly wage of the worker in Mexico is, as has been noted, the eighth part of the cost of living of that

TABLE XVI*

AVERAGE DAILY WAGE OF MEXICAN COMMON LABORERS IN VARIOUS
PARTS OF THE UNITED STATES

OCCUPATION	STATE	WAGE (IN DOLLARS)		
		Min.	Max.	Aver.
Agriculture:				
Unskilled labor (cotton)........	Alabama	$2.00	$6.00	$4.00
Unskilled labor (cotton)........	Arizona	2.50	3.00	2.75
Unskilled labor (cotton)........	Arkansas	2.00	6.00	4.00
Unskilled labor (cotton)........	California	2.50	4.00	3.25
Unskilled labor (cotton)........	Louisiana	2.00	6.00	4.00
Unskilled labor (cotton)........	Mississippi	2.00	6.00	4.00
Unskilled labor (cotton)........	Texas	1.50	2.00	1.75
Unskilled labor (melon).........	Arizona	2.50	3.00	2.75
Unskilled labor (watermelon)....	Arizona	2.50	3.00	2.75
Unskilled labor (orange)........	California	2.75	....	2.75
Unskilled labor (grape).........	California	4.00	6.00	6.00
Unskilled labor (raisin)...	California	2.50	4.00	3.25
Unskilled labor (beets).........	Michigan	3.00	....	3.00
Unskilled labor (beets).........	Minnesota	4.00	4.50	4.25
Industry:				
Mining:†				
Peónes (underground)........	Arizona	4.40	....	4.40
Barreteros..................	Arizona	4.95	....	4.95
Peónes (exterior).............	Arizona	2.75	....	2.75
Carretilleros.............	Arizona	2.75	....	2.75
Brick-kiln:				
Cortadores..............	California	4.00	....	4.00
Dampeadores...............	California	3.50	....	3.50
Metedores de moldes.........	California	2.50	3.00	2.75
Areneros....................	California	3.50	....	3.50
Paleteros...................	California	3.00	....	3.00
Templadores................	California	4.00	....	4.00
Arriadores.................	California	3.50	....	3.50
Cargadores.................	California	4.00	....	4.00
Asentadores................	California	3.75	....	3.75
Pichadores.................	California	3.75	....	3.75
Arregladores...............	California	3.75	....	3.75
Apiladores.................	California	3.75	....	3.75
Railroad:				
Railroad...................	Kansas	2.00	2.40	2.20
Iron, cement...............	Chicago	3.50	....	3.50
Other Industries.............	Chicago	4.50	5.00	4.75
Other Industries.............	Chicago	4.00	....	4.00
Traqueros o vigilantes........	California	2.80	3.80	3.30
Peónes....................	California	0.31‡	(8 hours)	2.48
Peónes....................	Texas	.30‡	(8 hours)	2.60
Camellos o excavadores.......	California	0.31‡	(8 hours)	2.48

TABLE XVI*—*Continued*

OCCUPATION	STATE	WAGE (IN DOLLARS)		
		Min.	Max.	Aver.
Packing:				
Amarradores...............	California	$0.35‡	(8 hours)	$2.80
Cosedores..................	California	.50‡	(8 hours)	4.00
Peladores..................	California	.40‡	(8 hours)	3.20
Sacadores de pezunas.........	California	.35‡	(8 hours)	•2.80
Lavadores.................	California	.35‡	(8 hours)	2.80
Cargadores.................	California	0.35‡	(8 hours)	2.80

* [Of course, steady employment may not be assured. These occupations are highly seasonal. —EDITOR.]
† No English translation was given by Mexican laborers for their occupations.
‡ Per hour.

country. If in the United States the cost of living kept the same relation with the pay he receives, it would be necessary for this cost of living to rise to $1,295.46 a month. Such an assumption is absurd, for in reality there is no proportion between the relation of the cost of living of the two countries and the respective wages. In Mexico the cost of living is very high and the pay very low, while in the United States in comparison the pay is very much higher and the cost of living lower. The great difference as to the wages paid in the two countries is an indisputable fact, so that it is only necessary to show that the cost of living is relatively much lower for the Mexican worker in the United States than in Mexico. Agricultural production in the United States is more efficient and more diversified than in Mexico for many reasons, among them the use of modern farm machinery, the application of scientific methods of cultivation, the efficient organization of labor, and the abundant means of communication. The best proof of this is that it is continually necessary to import agricultural produce into Mexico, including corn, which is the basis of the Mexican diet, for which reason it results that these products cost more in Mexico than in the American market. The industrial production of Mexico is quantitatively so low that it is necessary to import the greater part of the articles of industrial character which Mexico consumes, with the natural result that such objects purchased by the laborer in the Mexican market are usually much dearer than when bought in the United States, their home market.

In the United States the Mexican laborer not only earns enough to satisfy the elemental requirements for minimum comfort, a condition not yet attained in Mexico, but he also spends money for education, recreation, and so on. It is sufficiently convincing to note that the Mexican laborers in the United States often own property they never succeed in acquiring in Mexico, such as automobiles, phonographs, and refrigerators. In the chapter on the characteristics of the cultural contacts, we refer more fully to this subject and include a table enumerating the objects introduced into Mexico in 1927 by 2,104 repatriated immigrants who were exempted from the payment of import duties. Lastly, it is a well-known fact that the workers in Mexico cannot save, and that it would be impossible to do so because of the small wage, whereas in the United States they do save, as is shown by the quantities of money, relatively considerable, which are mentioned at the beginning of this chapter.

Although there are not a few occasions where unscrupulous employers impose working days of ten or more hours upon Mexican laborers, as a general rule the normal industrial working day in the United States is limited to eight hours. Efficient organization and strict discipline bring it about that labor is really effective during the working day and that there is little chance to waste time, with the consequences that the Mexican laborer, recently arrived and lacking great vitality because of earlier privations, at once finds all his energies consumed and sometimes becomes sick or goes back to Mexico. Some employers who do not understand the background of the Mexican worker and assume that they are capable of the same resistance as the American worker accuse them of laziness and disinclination to work. Others who have had long experience with Mexican labor attempt to rebuild their physical vigor and make their work more efficient. Nevertheless, the effects of the long working days and the small wages to which they are subject in Mexico leave such deep marks that even after they have lived for several years in the United States and have come to discharge their duties efficiently, they complain continually of physical exhaustion.

These unskilled laborers constitute the great majority of the immigrants. Even for them the change from Mexico to the United States is great, since the environment is totally different. First of all, there is the close co-operation, the specialization, and the distribution of individual activity, in contrast to the generalized individual activity and loose co-operation characteristic of Mexican labor, especially in the small towns and rural districts from which the immigrants come. For example: An American woodcutter does nothing but cut wood, and society is so organized that by doing the one thing only he can supply all his needs and at the same time increase his efficiency as woodcutter. A Mexican woodcutter, on the other hand, cuts wood and also does other things, not only because he does not earn enough by cutting wood to pay the baker and the blacksmith, but because he is accustomed to perform the actual work of his everyday needs. He sows, cultivates, and prepares at home the food he eats; he makes his own primitive furniture, his sandals, and frequently his blankets; he digs clay, cuts lumber, and builds his own house; he harnesses his own mules, makes his burro pack, or rides horseback. As a rule he walks from three to five miles a day to and from his work. He performs his work generally on his own account and with primitive tools. In the United States such a Mexican woodcutter is less efficient than his American competitor, especially throughout the period of adjustment to totally different conditions and customs.

The great part of unskilled labor in the fields is transient. During the summer and fall such men follow the crops across various states of the American union; many of them return to Mexico for the winter; a few go instead to the American southern states. It is almost impossible to determine in which parts of the year the demand for Mexican unskilled labor is greatest, or least, but in order to give a general idea of this matter, we shall set out what limited conclusions we were able to reach.

The demand for Mexican labor in industry is comparatively small but constant, and the worker in general keeps his position the year around, and if because of the rigors of the season he migrates south during the winter, it is probable that on his return he goes again to the same work. These conditions of course change when the economic trends of such industries fluctuate.

Agriculture's demand for such labor is very great but also very variable, and is limited to certain seasons of the year and to certain parts of the country. Early in spring arises the demand for labor to work the land and to do other tasks in the regions where the climate is mild. During the summer, and principally in July and August, the demand is at its peak, for then the crops need the greatest number of hands. In Texas, California, and some other states of the Southwest the demand for labor continues to the beginning or middle of autumn, as some crops last to the end of this season. In December the demand for such labor entirely stops and large groups of workers find themselves obliged to return to Mexico, while others remain in the United States, especially in parts of Texas and the Southwest where the winters are less severe.

As a rule, the harvesters and transient laborers are single men or men who have left their families in Mexico or in American cities. But American employers generally prefer men with wives and families, for two reasons: they stay with their work, and their families generally help, thus providing the employer with more working hands.

Skilled laborers in Mexico.—The condition of the skilled workers is much better than that of the common or unskilled laborers, but it is not good or even satisfactory. The intrinsic superiority of the work they do naturally yields them a better wage than that received by unskilled labor, and more favorable living conditions. In addition to this there are other factors which have contributed to the economic and social betterment of this class of workers. The majority of this class work in industries, and it is well known that these pay better than agriculture, which engages the majority of the unskilled laborers.

Moreover, the skilled laborers are organized into unions, such as the Confederación Regional Obrera Mexicana. The organization of labor in Mexico since 1910 has been influenced by the action of the revolutionary government, by the efforts of returned Mexican immigrants who have observed the ways of organized labor in the United States, and by the contact of the American Federation of Labor with labor elements in Mexico. Labor is now organized in the important cities of the Mexican Republic and in some rural districts.

It would be hard to compute the average wage of the Mexican skilled worker, taking into consideration all parts of the country, but as an example we include Table XVII, compiled from official data representing the average wages paid in various industries in the federal district—wages which are only rarely greater than those paid in other parts of the country.

This table also includes the wages received in certain industries, such as metallurgy, mining, and oil, which do not exist in the federal district. It should be noted that the wage designated at

TABLE XVII

AVERAGE DAILY WAGE PAID TO SKILLED LABORERS IN SOME INDUSTRIES OF MEXICO (IN PESOS)

Brewery	4.16
Manufacture of mattresses	2.04
Manufacture of curtains and steel doors	3.98
Pastry and biscuits	3.02
Tobacco manufacture	4.62
Manufacture of gaseous water	5.51
Shoe manufacture	4.09
Manufacture of pasteboard and carton boxes	2.11
Foodstuff and preserves	2.49
Candy manufacture	2.27
Manufacture of cloth	4.05
Manufacture of sewing thread	2.34
Soap manufacture	3.13
Ceramics and porcelain	3.56
Furniture manufacture	4.43
Metal works	3.43
Coal mines	2.97
Mining	2.11
Flour mills	4.95
House moving	3.05
Stationery and printing	4.63
Oil	7.25
Clothing stores and workshops	2.19
Shirt workshop	2.96
Carpenter's shop	3.61
Lithography workshops	4.33
Tailor's workshop	3.82
Average wage	3.59

the right of each industry mentioned in the table is the average of the various wages received by the different occupations in each industry.

We have previously stated that the salary of the skilled worker is not normal, that is to say, not sufficient to supply his necessities. In the industries considered in Table XVII the average daily wage is $3.59 *pesos*, or $121.29 *pesos* a month, while the salary of minimum comfort should be, as explained before, $287.88 *pesos* a month in order to be enough to pay for the normal necessities of life.

Skilled laborers in the United States.—Our investigation refers principally to unskilled labor because the majority of the immigrants fall into that class. Very few of the skilled laborers find work of the same sort which they have done before, and most of them have to begin all over again as unskilled workers. Some of these may become skilled laborers in the course of time. It should be remarked that even then, because they are not union members or for other reasons, they receive wages much lower than American workmen of the same class. Of these laborers, the great majority is not transient, and after some time they may acquire a little land and a home, especially if they live in a small town or a rural district.

The adjustment is especially difficult when, as in a great number of cases, the laborers change occupations and adopt whatever opportunity is available in the United States. Smiths, carpenters, and masons arrive without knowing where to turn for work best suited to their ability and experience, since there are great differences in the needs to be supplied and the manner of supplying them between the new environment and the old. As a rule, employment agencies and contractors take on these men as unskilled labor, and they go to work in the cotton, sugar-cane, or beet fields, or in fruit orchards, or they are sent to do common labor in railroad camps. On the other hand, common laborers who in México worked as farm hands go to iron, cement, and furniture factories, packing-houses, etc., and although in these places they do unskilled labor nevertheless it is for them a great change. The employers of such men state that their work is satisfactory, but the men themselves, as well as those in the factories as in the fields, state that they would do better were they given work for which they had more training, and they are probably right.

Tenant and share farmers in Mexico.—We cannot here go into the history of the Mexican agrarian question, and we therefore merely state that one of the principal causes, and perhaps the most important, of the revolutions that have agitated Mexico for more than a century lies in the urgent and never satisfied need for land on the part of the masses of the people, as well as for agricultural education and implements·for tilting the soil efficiently. Since the easy ways of communication with the United States opened the escape valve of immigration, hundreds of thousands of men who had no lands of of their own and whose small wages were not enough for them to live on, or else who could not even count on these small wages because there was no demand for work, turned to the United States.

The millions who did not migrate, although they were in the same miserable condition as those who did, expressed their agrarian aspirations in the successive revolutionary movements beginning in 1910. The governments resulting from these revolutions have managed to satisfy these demands to some extent.[1] Unfortunately, these measures have not yet attained the results that are hoped for, namely, increased national agricultural production and consequent decrease in the importation of foreign agricultural products, increase of the low wages which the workers receive, especially the unskilled, and lastly the decrease or even cessation of the great emigration directed toward the United States. The government of Gen-

[1] Land distributed in the period from 1915 to 1926 embraced 3,588,875 *hectares*, or 1.82 per cent of the total area of Mexico.

eral Calles sought to remedy the situation by various means, such as distributing land by the colonization system, giving practical agricultural instruction to the rural population and economic aid to small landholders, and interesting the returned immigrants in colonization and agricultural exploitation.

The tenant farmers, who are relatively few, and the share farmers, who are very numerous, might be able to keep on cultivating their land, although inefficiently. The conditions according to which the farmers and share farmers in Mexico divide the crops are more or less like those observed between Americans and Mexicans in some parts of the United States.

TABLE XVIII

Mexican Farm	Total	Owners	Managers	Tenants
Operators........	12,142	1,625	117	10,400
Value of land and buildings......	$71,207,258	$12,036,003	$5,598,026	$53,573,229
Farm acreage....	1,576,722	444,435	351,310	780,977
Improved land...	700,116	83,645	15,301	601,170

Tenant and share farmers in the United States.—These are farmers on a small scale who own, manage, or rent the land, or work it for a share of the crops. They are men who have been in the United States for a number of years, working as skilled or unskilled laborers, and who are therefore comparatively familiar with the environment. This class of people is as a whole permanent and settled, going back to Mexico only from time to time to return again to the United States. We do not know what is actually the number of such Mexican inhabitants, but it is probably so small that it cannot yet be cause for alarm. The United States census of 1920 gave the figures shown in Table XVIII.[1] The insignificance of these figures may be ap-

[1] [The number of Mexican tenant and share farmers has probably increased since 1920.—EDITOR.]

preciated by comparing them with the values of the corresponding possessions of Americans during the same period:

Number of acres of land in farms.................... 910,939,194
Acres of land improved............................ 473,774,566
Value.. $63,786,058,855

The number of Mexican farm operators, 12,142, corresponded, according to the same census figures of 1920, to 486,418 Mexican immigrants who then resided in the United States.

Conclusion.—Both skilled and unskilled Mexican laborers are praised by American employers and landowners who favor immigration and benefit by it. It is even said that they could not get American workmen for the low wages and long hours that Mexicans accept. The contracts give the advantage to the employer, and, furthermore, if an employer breaks a contract the workman cannot well defend himself, partly because he rarely has the money to do so, and partly because he does not know the law or the language. To this employers answer that no matter how bad the conditions or even the abuses, the Mexican workmen as a whole are better off than in Mexico, else why do Mexican workmen return again and again? Although the immigrant often undergoes suffering and injustice and meets many difficulties, he undoubtedly benefits economically by the change. He learns the discipline of modern labor. He specializes. He becomes familiar with industrial and agricultural machinery. He learns about scientific intensive agriculture. He observes and learns about the transformation of raw material into industrial products. He becomes a laborer of the modern type, much more efficient than before. Could all the immigrants return to Mexico, they would do much to make of it a great industrial and agricultural country.

Unfortunately, when immigrants return, as a rule, they go back singly or in very small groups, and are therefore soon absorbed back into the old conditions, becoming identified with the small town or rural backward culture which they left. Usually they leave again, and sometimes return and leave still again; but each time they return the same thing occurs. To take lasting advantage of whatever these men have learned in the United States, large organized centers, some distance away from centers of the old type, would be necessary.

In conclusion, from the economic point of view, Mexican transient immigration is beneficial to both countries, inasmuch as the United States cannot supply the need of labor which exists in certain regions for certain types of work, at a time when Mexico cannot offer better living conditions to its own workers. On the other hand, permanent immigration is harmful to both countries, especially if it takes place on a large scale; and even if it does carry with it temporary economic benefits, in the long run it can cause great harm. For the United States this might be expected to make itself felt in labor struggles and perhaps in racial conflicts, whereas for Mexico it would mean the loss of its best working population, for it is exactly these that emigrate.

CHAPTER IV

INTERRACIAL RELATIONS

If we had satisfactory anthropological data on both white Americans and Mexican immigrants, we might describe the real physical differences between the two groups. We might then consider not only the sociological and psychological aspects of the interracial contacts, but also the biological aspects. In the absence of such data, conclusions as to the biological results of race contact are largely conjectural. Most of the current discussions have really to do with social, cultural, or economic facts and not with the actual racial problem.

Let us consider the relationship between social groups prevailing in Mexico. There are three groups: Indians, *mestizos*, and whites. Between them there is no real race repulsion or prejudice. That which exists is economic and cultural, since the whites generally belong to higher strata in these two respects and the Indians to the lowest. Contact between these groups is the direct result of economic and cultural factors. Thus, the whites who are on a low cultural and economic level mix their blood with the Indians as naturally as with the whites. Similarly, the pure-blooded Indian who reaches a high economic and cultural level finds no barrier to intermarriage with the elements classed as "pure white,"-the most interesting example of this being Benito Juarez, the most illustrious president Mexico has ever had. The cross between *mestizo* and white or *mestizo* and Indian is much more frequent, however, than that between racial extremes, since the *mestizos* are intermediate between the high and low social strata, and therefore there is less difference between them and the highest and lowest, economically and culturally, than between the two extremes.

51

This Indo-Spanish cross which has been going on since the conquest is not, however, the only example of intermarriage with the Indian, for the Indo-Germanic mixture has reached fair proportions in Mexico, in Guatemala, and in other Latin-American countries. If, then, both white Spaniards and white Germans mix freely with the Mexican, in Mexico, it is not surprising that the Mexican immigrant is deeply offended at discovering a racial prejudice against him in the United States.

The origin of this prejudice is not to be sought in known physical inferiority, since the medical examinations to which immigrants submit show that, as a whole, their characteristics are normal. It may be added that individuals deficient or diseased are not admitted. Furthermore, the proportion of those barred for this reason is much the same as in the case of other nationalities. These examinations are, of course, superficial and do not reveal the fundamental anthropological traits of the Mexican immigrants.

What little anthropological data exist on contemporary Mexican peoples[1] refer to only a few of the emigrating groups, and in the main describe only the pure-blooded native Indian. Furthermore, these data are anthropometric rather than physiological. In any case they do not indicate the racial inferiority of the groups measured.

If, then, there are no anthropological data which demonstrate the physical inferiority of the Mexican immigrant, and if physiologically he is similar to any other immigrant, according to the data of the Bureau of Immigration, why do racial repulsion and prejudice exist against him? If in Texas the pigmentation of the Mexican individuals in a group including indigenes, *mestizos*, and whites were arranged in a series according to the

---

[1] A compilation of available anthropometric data is to be found in "Conocimiento antropologico de las agrupaciónes indigenas de México," by Paul Siliceo Pauer, in *Ethnos* (2a época), Tomo I, No. 1, Nov., 1922—Jan., 1923.

Broca tables, the result would be a theoretical scale of prejudices which would conform fairly to the actual situation. The darkest-skinned Mexican experiences almost the same restrictions as the Negro, while a person of medium-dark skin can enter a second-class lunchroom frequented also by Americans of the poorer class, but will not be admitted to a high-class restaurant. A Mexican of light-brown skin as a rule will not be admitted to a high-class hotel, while a white cultured Mexican will be freely admitted to the same hotel, especially if he speaks English fluently. Mexican children suffer similar discrimination in schools where there are American children, and for this reason it has in places been found preferable to establish separate schools.

The racial prejudice of which we speak has not arisen recently, from the presence of Mexican immigrants, but dates back to the time when white Americans first came into contact with Indians, Spaniards, and Indo-Spaniards in the frontier regions immediately after these states were annexed to the American union. It is natural that they should have called them Mexicans and made social discriminations with regard to them at first, as was done with German or Italian immigrants. But the second or third generation of Germans or Italians became Americans in appearance and customs, and the social discrimination disappeared; whereas the Mexicans, though they might be American citizens of the second or third generations, nevertheless remained or were kept apart socially, and were almost always called "Mexicans."

Practically all Germans or Italians of the second or third generation are completely American, while only a minority, and possibly a very small minority, of Mexicans are. They continued living, after the annexation, in the same traditions and social environments, which was their own and which, indeed, has to some extent influenced the American local element. The minority which adopted the English language and American habits, customs, and education even then did not become thoroughly fused with the American element, as did the other foreigners. The present generation of those Mexicans, which is the third, is American, from the material viewpoint; domestic life, work, clothes, education, are modeled on the American. Nevertheless, racially they are not wholly or partially American; and notwithstanding that they are American citizens, they remain on economic, political, and social levels always inferior to those occupied by Americans of like condition and capacity.

As an extension or reflection of this racial prejudice, individuals of Mexican origin but of white skin are also socially discriminated against. The stigma of indigenous blood is so deep that the word "Mexican," which implies a little or a great deal of Indian blood and the corresponding pigmentation, has acquired in the South a derogatory character. In general, to distinguish between white and brown Mexicans, the whites are euphemistically called "Spanish," and they themselves adhere to this distinction. The head of one large family, established in the United States for more than two hundred years, but whose color and features show marked indigenous blood, answered to discreet questioning about his family antecedents: "I am Spanish; my ancestors were Spaniards who were in Mexico and later came to New Mexico. They were relatives of Cabeza de Vaca."[1]

American citizens of Mexican origin are, as a rule, called "Mexicans" in courts, hospitals, and theaters. The American

[1] I had amusing experiences in this respect. Once in New Mexico, having been invited to a Rotarian banquet, the host in his introduction explained that I came from Mexico and spoke of scientific work in that country which I had done, so that my nationality was clearly established. Yet the reporter who described the banquet began his article with: "The well-known Latin, Señor M. Gamio." I asked for an explanation of this, and was told by a courteous American that

of Mexican origin does not hold the same prejudice against the Mexican immigrant. There are prejudices, differences, sometimes even hostility, but this is not racial and we shall speak more fully of it elsewhere.

Racial prejudice, though existing throughout the United States, is not expressed with the same intensity and bitterness in every part of the American union. In Texas it is very marked, in the other southern states less so, and in the northern states of the East and Midwest even less. But everywhere the prejudice exists strongly enough for the fusion between white Americans and Mexicans, be these latter American citizens or merely immigrants, to occur in such small proportion that it need hardly be taken into account.

The two factors which seem clearly established, and which are corroborated again and again in the individual cases which we observed,[1] are these: (1) White Americans do not intermarry with Mexican immigrants nor with Americans of Mexican origin. (2) Americans of Mexican origin intermarry with Mexican immigrants frequently, and social discrimination is not a factor in these unions.

These factors lead to an important conclusion, making clear the defense of Indo-Spaniards against the racial repulsion and prejudice directed toward them. The only enduring conquest is racial conquest, since any other after a time is not conquest but exclusion. If racial prejudice had not existed in the United States, there would be at present no citizens nominally American but really Mexican, for they would long ago have become part of the nation racially. Moreover, the Mexican border

---

"the reporter knows you come from Mexico, since he was at the luncheon, but, in order not to wound your feelings or slight a guest as distinguished as yourself, he must establish the difference in this manner between you and the Mexicans in this state."

[1] This matter is more fully discussed in Appendix III.

states would have at present a population predominantly American, whereas, as a matter of fact, not only is this population Mexican but within the United States there exists a vast zone parallel to the boundary line, inhabited by people nominally American but really Indo-Spanish or Mexican, who, although they have adopted American customs and American material civilization, remain racially, sentimentally, and traditionally one with the Mexicans on the other side of the Rio Grande and a part of the whole body of the Indo-Spanish people.

The generic denomination of "La Raza" in which all of these social elements include themselves is a proof of the actuality of these facts. Indeed, in other chapters we shall see that there are several appellations with which the Mexican immigrants name the Americans of Mexican origin in Texas, Arizona, and other border states. At the same time Americans of Mexican origin designate with different terms the Mexican immigrants. However, one and all unanimously declare that they belong to "La Raza," although they have not an exact idea of the meaning of that expression. They cannot, therefore, give more detailed explanations, and when they are questioned upon the matter they insist that they belong to that indefinable group composed of Mexican immigrants and Americans of Mexican origin that they call the race, "La Raza."

CHAPTER V

CULTURE BACKGROUNDS AND CULTURE CONTACTS

In studying contact between American civilization and that of the Mexican immigrants, we must first consider the separate character of each. The first is a modern, integrated, and homogeneous civilization, with material and intellectual characteristics shared by all the people living within the borders of the country with some variations between social levels, but always preserving its typical characteristics.

The Mexican immigrants, on the other hand, arrive in the United States with widely diverse cultural baggage, differing completely from that of the United States and also exhibiting marked differences within itself. Roughly divided, three cultural groups corresponding to racial elements can be described among the Mexican immigrants as follows:

1. Modern civilization derived from Europe or the United States, but developed within and modeled to Mexican environment. To this belong the social minorities of white Mexicans and *mestizos*. The proportion of immigrants of this type is very small, and therefore it is not necessary to consider them as a part of the general problem.

2. Ancient aboriginal civilization, different in type from the modern, and much simpler, that is, with fewer material and intellectual culture elements. It represents the type of social groups still in relatively inferior stages of development. In Mexico the majority of Indians and a minority of *mestizos* are included in this cultural group. From this group comes a fairly large proportion of the immigrants, the number of which can-

not be calculated but which direct observation indicates to be considerable.

3. *Mixed civilization.*—This is between the two former groups. It characterizes a great proportion of *mestizos*, Indians, and fewer whites. Probably the majority of immigrants belongs to this mixed cultural type.

Let us consider, therefore, in detail, the indigenous and the mixed cultures, since they contribute practically all the Mexican immigration.

The indigenous civilization.—This is an indigenous development undisturbed until the Spanish Conquest. It was made up of various cultural subtypes differing among themselves, the differences due chiefly to the geographic and climatic variations of the country and the cultural influences of new migratory groups. In some places, such as Tenochtitlan (now Mexico City), this culture has disappeared completely, in others it has disappeared partly; but in general it has carried over to the present, though degenerated. This degeneration is due to the fact that the Indian has been losing ground continually, or has been forced to abandon his traditional expressions and at the same time has assimilated very slowly and most incompletely the habits and culture of the upper strata.

This is in turn due not so much to unwillingness and apathy of the Indian as to the fact that the ruling classes have not wished or have not known how to substitute their culture for the aboriginal culture. Of these aboriginal groups not all provide immigrants; therefore we shall examine more fully only those to which immigrants belong.

Prehispanic antecedents of the indigenous groups.—One of the principal characteristics of the prehispanic Indians of Mexico was their migratory tendency. We may cite as an example the Aztecs, who from unknown regions of the North or Northeast moved southward until they reached what is today

Mexico City. The episodes of this famous peregrination are known through hieroglyphic characters in a codex, or native book, now in the National Museum of Mexico and well known to archaeologists; the Aztec emigrants even reached Central America and the Gulf and Pacific coasts.

The extent or intensity of the migrations would appear to be in a direct ratio to the grade of cultural evolution which characterized the various Indian groups. Indeed, the nature, the abundance, and the geographic distribution of archaeological remains prove that the most civilized groups, such as the Mayas, Aztecs, and Toltecs, covered in their migrations extensive areas, while the more primitive groups, such as the Tepehuanes, Yaquis, and Tarahumares, confined themselves to very limited areas. States of the *mesa central*—Michoacan, Guanajuato, Jalisco—those which in fact contribute the largest number of emigrants to the United States, were inhabited by Tarascans and Otomies, descendants of the archaic or subpedregalian peoples, who were apparently the earliest comers to Mexico.

The many and repeated migrations as well as the geographical differences in the zones in which successively the emigrants became established helped to produce two results: (1) the development of culture areas, (2) culture diffusion. As a specific example of this may be mentioned the important difference between cultures characterized architecturally by pyramidal structures and, on the other hand, cultures which lack this architectural feature. It is generally agreed that the prehispanic migration crossed the northern plateau to the south-central plateau; certainly in the architectural remains on the northern pleateau, such as Chalchihuites and Casas Grandes, the pyramidal structure is lacking, while in the archaeological remains on the southern plateau this feature is the most characteristic trait and is profusely represented by the pyramid with inclined wall, features of the Aztec culture as well as of the Toltec or Teotihuacan culture. It appears that for reasons which we still do not know, but which probably had to do with the development of religious ideas and the influence of a new geographic environment, there arose in the valley of Mexico (*mesa central*) the prototype of the pyramid (typified by Cuicuilco) constructed by the subpedregalian or archaic peoples, and which constituted its most important and distinctive culture trait. This early type of structure developed in this valley until it had become the pyramid of Aztec or Toltec type, which in turn came to be the most distinctive architectural element of these cultures.

When representatives of these groups, archaic, Toltec, and Aztec, moved out of the valley of Mexico, they carried with them to the regions into which they emigrated the elements of their culture. In this way originated the pyramidal structures of the Tarascan, Mayan, Zapotec, and Totonac cultures.[1]

Not all the culture traits characterizing the original area were carried to other regions where the immigration moved, but some of them persisted solely in the original area. An example of the sort is furnished by the *candeleros*, or small incense-burners, of Teotihuacan, small vases of oval or rectangular shape with very thick walls and with two cylindrical cavities communicating with the exterior through two perforations. These "candlesticks" are very numerous in the valley of Mexico in a narrow zone which has Teotihuacan for its center; but they are not found in other regions to which the Toltec or Teotihuacan culture penetrated.

We have already shown that the geographic source of the greatest part of the Mexican immigration to the United States

----

[1] [This view of the priority of the Toltec culture to that of the Maya is not shared by many other archaeologists. See, e.g., H. J. Spinden's *Ancient Civilizations of Mexico and the United States*.—EDITOR.]

is the central plateau, in which are situated the states of
Jalisco, Guanajuato, and Michoacan, and the northern mesa
and northwestern coast, where are Lower California, Sonora,
Coahuila, Sinaloa, Tamaulipas, Chihuahua, Durango, Zacatecas, and Nuevo León. Archaeological investigations established that, prior to the conquest, the regions now Jalisco,
Michoacan, and Guanajuato were largely inhabited by groups
of the Tarascan of Otomi or archaic type, a culture incompa-
rably the inferior of the Toltec, Aztec, and Maya who inhabited
the southern parts of the central plateau and the escarpments,
and coast and peninsular regions in the south which do not
contribute immigrants. In Guanajuato the archaic aboriginal
culture remained always in a very primitive state. In Jalisco
and Michoacan it developed farther, and the decoration and
design of pottery and clay sculpture became highly convention-
alized and stylized, indicating evolution beyond the primitive
archaic type found in Mexico and Guatemala. This region also
furnishes architectural structures called *yácatas*. Social institutions and intellectual forms were inferior to those of the culture
of the more southern groups already mentioned. As to the prehispanic antecedents of the aboriginal type of immigrants from
the northern plateau, except for some cultural groups (*pueblos*
in Chihuahua, the transition type like Chalchihuites in Zacatecas, and groups of Huastecan culture in Tamaulipas, cultures
in stages of evolution analogous to that of the Tarascan or
archaic of Michoacan and Jalisco), the rest were very primitive,
in both material and non-material features. These groups were
the Yaquis, Seris, Mayos, Papagos, Tepehuanes, and other related tribes.

Colonial antecedents of indigenous groups.—The almost exclusively utilitarian character of the Spanish Conquest and
domination kept a part of the primitive group of the northern
mesa, as well as tribes in Sonora and California, in a state of

almost animal slavery.   Of Spanish civilization, these Indians adopted only scant rudiments in some instances, and continued their savage existence of prehispanic times.   In Jalisco and Michoacan the conquest and colonization assumed an interesting and humanitarian aspect, in one sense, for here men of real genius like Archbishop Vasco de Quiroga observed and utilized the practical and beautiful elements of the native culture, fusing them harmoniously with analogous elements of the Spanish civilization, and developing new and important crafts and industries, often of an artistic character, such as lacquer, beautifully decorated pottery, leather tanning and carving, woodcarving, and metal work.   Yet the development of modern civilization along educational and scientific lines has not advanced in these regions, since illiteracy and fanaticism were important limiting factors during the colonial régime.

Present characteristics of indigenous groups.—Little is known accurately about the present indigenous groups as a whole from the ethnographic viewpoint, as even less is known from the physical. Nevertheless, some investigation has been made, by both Mexican and foreign students, and this information has been compiled by the Department of Anthropology of Mexico. Of it we give a condensed account in the Appendixes. This brief summary may at least give an approximate idea of the cultural level of the Indian immigrants. The sudden contact of this simplest culture and of the mixed cultural type with modern civilization produces interesting results, commented on more fully in the section on mixed culture.

The mixed civilization.—This is a heterogeneous culture which began to form at the conquest, but which as yet is not fully integrated. So far the development has been very slow and gradual, a fusion of some elements of Spanish civilization and of the modern European-American culture with elements of the Mexican indigenous civilization, which is in turn made up of contributions from different cultural groups.

Colonial antecedents of mixed culture.—Fusion between Spanish civilization and native occurred chiefly with respect to economic, religious, legal, and administrative features. The system of taxation which the Spanish authorities first established was a combination of the fiscal administration of Spain and the old native system of tributes. The religion of the colonial period, as a result of the efforts of the missionaries, was a peculiar polytheism in which native gods disappeared but their personalities and attributes became attracted to saints. As to the legal fusion, the laws of Indies can well be considered a union of Spanish codes with laws directly derived from the need of the natives and the prehispanic laws which had existed to meet them. In the cities the municipal governments were also a product of Indo-Hispanic interadjustment. The most important or most productive union occurred principally in art, architecture, and fine arts, producing works which breathed of both native and Spanish tradition, and were truly original, interesting, and unique.

Present characteristics of mixed culture.—The development of the mixed civilization was more rapid and intense during the eighteenth century because after Mexico declared her independence from Spain, she threw wide her doors to the European cultural current. During the last thirty or forty years factors have appeared which have confused the grouping into the culture types and have modified the mixed and even the Indian culture types. Railways and other means of communication which facilitated contact within the Mexican Republic and with the United States; the spread of popular education; the rapid industrial or agricultural development of some regions and the decadence of others; the social, economic, and cultural transformations and reversals produced by revolution; the return of hundreds of thousands of immigrants from the United States who brought new ideas and tendencies—these are some of the profoundly influential factors which, thrust suddenly into the slow evolution of the masses, have produced such strange and fantastic cultural fusions, substitutions, and juxtapositions that it is difficult to identify and classify without falling into serious error the characteristics of the immigrants belonging to the cultural groups in question.

For instance: Some groups characterized by the essentials of the civilization we classify as "mixed" have recently received sporadic injections of modern culture, the outgrowths of which are more visible than the original groundwork, and for this reason such groups are often classified as belonging to modern civilization when in reality they do not. The reverse also occurs. Civilization fundamentally modern, outgrowing certain characteristics of the mixed culture, since these are on the surface and therefore visible, often cause such groups to be classified erroneously as of mixed civilization. Then sometimes it happens that only the material civilization evolves to the level of the modern type, while the ideas and attitudes prevailing are still in those of the mixed group. Moreover, sometimes a single group exhibits material and non-material characteristics of both modern and mixed type, and finally, though more rarely, there are groups whose intellectual development is modern and whose material condition is properly of the "mixed" cultural type.

Contacts of preceding types of civilization in the United States.—The change from the aboriginal and mixed cultures to the highly modern civilization of the United States is therefore exceedingly abrupt. The contact therefore results in substitutions and artificial integrations, even more intense and contradictory than in present-day Mexico. The abnormality of the situation is heightened by the geographic and climatic change.

The cultural contacts of the Mexican immigrants in the United States are complicated by the fact that besides the modern American civilization there is another and different Mexican-American culture, that of the Americans of Mexican origin. This civilization is American nominally, and exhibits the principal material aspects of modern American civilization, but intellectually and emotionally it lives in local Mexican traditions. This element can be said to constitute a peculiar nationality, within the United States. To the immigrant it is a sort of go-between, since these Mexican-Americans do not feel racial prejudice against him. Though a struggle occurs between the purely Mexican culture and this semi-Mexican, in the end it often absorbs the Mexican immigrant. With it there can occur a closer fusion than with the purely American culture, for with the latter it already shares many traits, while the great difference between the purely American and the purely Mexican, together with the factor of race prejudice, makes an intellectual, emotional, and traditional disparity too great to be bridged rapidly and perhaps never completely.

In later chapters the various cultural aspects of the Mexican immigrants and the nature of their contacts with the social elements of the American civilization will be treated in more detail, but it is thought proper at this point to give some general conclusions.

1. *Intellectual culture.*—Among the Mexican immigrants in the United States may be noted a great persistency of cultural characteristics of Mexican origin, and as a result few such American features are acquired.

2. *Material culture.*—Among the Mexican immigrants in the United States few features of Mexican material culture persist; as a result many American characteristics are taken over.

3. Among the Mexican-American elements, or Americans of Mexican origin, the Mexican type of intellectual culture exerts a great influence, while the Mexican type of material culture exerts much less.

4. Among the white American elements in contact with the large groups of Mexican immigrants in states such as California, Texas, and Arizona certain intellectual and material influence of Mexican cultural type may be noted; for example, in music, decorative arts, architectural style, and cookery.

We are aware that the value of these conclusions might be questioned, for although they are based on careful observation made by us and our assistants, and on information furnished us by other investigators, after all they can only be considered as personal opinions and interpretations. Furthermore, the American cultural influences exerted on the immigrant during his stay in the United States may be only temporary, because of restrictions imposed by the American environment. A group of Mexicans living, for example, in Minnesota, where they are unable to get foodstuffs, newspapers, and other articles from Mexico or from Mexican centers in the United States, might very naturally appear to have absorbed the American culture very thoroughly, especially in its material aspects. But if this group is transient, as is often the case, and goes back to Mexico, or to American localities where there are large numbers of Mexicans, it will probably lose many, or at least some, of the American influences, and Mexican characteristics will again reappear.

With these thoughts in mind, we attempted to study the cultural condition of Mexicans returned to their original homes after having lived for some time in the United States. This plan was not successful because at the time of this investigation (in 1927 and part of 1928) the return of immigrants had decreased greatly in the regions visited, namely, Guanajuato, Jalisco, and Michoacan; because of the religious conflicts in these regions nearly all the repatriates, instead of returning to their states, went to less disordered sections of the country. As far as we could ascertain, these people hid their cultural characteristics of American origin in order not to appear to their neighbors to have affected foreign customs.

The material obtained on cultural influence of an intellectual nature was not very abundant and did not permit us to reach really satisfactory conclusions. We therefore began an investigation of the influence of American material culture suggested to us by the observation of immigrants returning from the United States through the various frontier points.

These repatriates carried with them objects they had acquired and used in the United States. We noted that some groups crossing the frontier carried large numbers of objects, while others had but few. This was due, according to the custom officials, to the fact that the *Secretaría de Relaciónes* issued *Circular 202* of December 14, 1926, exempting from duty objects brought in by repatriates who intended to colonize lands. Each of these persons had to submit a list of the objects belonging to him so that custom inspectors could examine them and prevent contraband. In the controller's office we were able to examine and tabulate the list of objects belonging to 2,104 immigrants returning to Mexico from the United States during 1927 by way of Ciudad Juarez, Laredo, Agua Prieta, Piedras Negras, Matamoros, Reynosa, Naco, Ojinaga, Sasabe, and Ciudad Guerrero.[1]

We believe that these quite objective data permit of more satisfactory conclusions than the purely personal interpretations and opinions previously referred to. An examination of the table summarizing these data enables us to reach the following conclusions:

Taking into consideration the generally miserable conditions of the great mass of immigrants that enter the United States, it is obvious that in the case of 2,104 individuals considered, new needs have been created during their stay in the

[1] The full list is contained in the Appendixes.

United States. Most notable is the tendency to raise the standard of domestic comfort, as is indicated by the number of objects brought in which these immigrants either did not use in Mexico or which were there very rare among them (see Table XIX). Clothing of American origin is represented by a high ratio in this table, notwithstanding that simple clothing used by the common people is manufactured and sold at low prices

TABLE XIX

Articles	Ratio of Number of Objects of Class Indicated to Every 100 Immigrants Listed
Bathtubs......................	38.19
Wood or metal toilets.........	12.73
Refrigerators.................	3.80
Metal kitchen utensils........	77.99
Washing machines............	0.38
Stoves......................	27.58
Beds.......................	82.88
Mattresses..................	70.53
Chairs.....................	134.58
Sewing machines.............	16.57
Typewriters................	1.42

in Mexico. In fact, the trunks, valises, and bundles which contained clothing alone numbered 3,653, a ratio of 173.51, so that the number of separate articles of clothing must have reached tens of thousands. The fact that part of this clothing was for sale does not prevent this from being a case of cultural influence, for they represent the collective taste as to clothing acquired by the Mexican immigrants in the American environment.

The possession of automobiles is absolutely unheard of in the humble social class to which the immigrants generally belong. Nevertheless, 37.69 per cent of the persons in question, or more than one out of every three, owned an automobile on his return to Mexico. Of these, 27.81 per cent represented passenger cars and 9.88 trucks. According to information received, nearly all cheap cars had been acquired new, while the expensive ones were bought second hand. The fact that the immigrant takes back to Mexico such a relatively large number of automobiles is partly an advantage and partly a waste. Many sections of rural Mexico where the repatriated immigrant goes to colonize have no suitable automobile roads, and either there is no gasoline or else it is expensive or hard to get, with the result that automobiles are often useless. The good that results is that the possession of automobiles stimulates the owners to build roads, however poor these might be due to the humble circumstances of the owners. It would have been better had they brought in more buggies and carriages, actually represented only by the figures 1.14 and 6.41, respectively.

As for cattle, which would have been so useful for improving the native breeds, relatively few were brought in, horses, burros, cows, goats, etc., being 25, of which 15.81 represented goats. The ratio of chickens reached 122.35 and of incubators 2.61. The number of agricultural and industrial tools was moderate, for the boxes containing these represented a ratio of 13.72, in addition to the tools that were separated. The proportion of plows was 8.64, cultivators 0.95, and planters 1.04.

Considering that the large majority of immigrants do not know how to read or write when they go to the United States, the intellectual progress made there might be expressed to a certain extent by the quantity of books brought back; the boxes in which these came numbered 65, and represented a ratio of 3.08. Assuming that each box contained an average of 40 books, or a total of 2,600, there was at least 1 book for each individual of the groups considered.

The musical and artistic tendencies of the immigrants are indicated by the figure as to phonographs, which is 21.82, and as to records, which is 118.00. The ratio of other musical instruments is 4.44, which is small. Perhaps the price of stringed instruments is generally high for the immigrants, and those manufactured in Mexico are much cheaper than the American ones. Nevertheless it is remarkable that player-pianos, which are probably the most expensive of musical instruments, have the highest number, namely, 1.04.

CHAPTER VI

THE MENTALITY OF THE IMMIGRANT

Perhaps two-thirds of Mexicans of school age are illiterate. The rate is higher among those economically and culturally inferior classes from which the immigrants come. The United States immigration laws require literacy as a prerequisite to entry, but because so many immigrants evade the immigration authorities and cross the border at unguarded points, there are many illiterates among Mexicans found in the United States. The Mexican immigrant as a rule has little money and must work hard; there is no time left to him for school. His formal education for this reason makes little or no progress. Some, in order to be admitted to the United States, learn to read and write Spanish imperfectly. Less often an arrived immigrant learns to speak a little poor English; even a little is of help in securing better work and better wages. The children of immigrants, on the other hand, may receive a fair amount of schooling, although their opportunities in this respect are not infrequently inferior to those of native American children.[1] The education which his parent receives, however, is not obtained in any classroom, but is the education of practical experience in the new environment, a training in the elements of agriculture, industry, and hygiene all the more significant in view of his relatively primitive antecedents.

The illiteracy rate does not, of course, measure the inherent mental competence of the Mexican; no more do intelligence

[1] Material on Mexican education in the United States may be found in the *Report of the Commission on Education of the El Paso Congress* held under the auspices of the Home Missions Council, and in the *Texas Educational Survey General Report*, Vol. VIII.

tests devised and applied by Americans, often in the English language. The mental capacity of the Mexican child is probably normal, although some investigators conclude that he is mentally inferior to an American child of the same age—a conclusion probably affected by racial attitudes and by a translation into terms of mental competence of differences in economic and cultural position.

Some educators and psychologists have realized the inapplicability to Mexicans of intelligence tests devised for American children. We quote from a dissertation on this subject by Mary Wright Coan, working under Dr. Helene Evers at the University of New Mexico:

1. Spanish-speaking children do much better on intelligence tests when directed in Spanish.

2. Spanish-speaking children show only a slight improvement when tested twice in English.

3. There are too many retarded and over-age pupils in the lower grades with the younger children. Best work cannot be secured from such heterogeneous grouping.

4. Just how well a Spanish-speaking student comprehends English should be discovered before any intelligence test is given.

5. Different methods of giving tests should be employed when giving tests to Spanish-speaking children who have a poor comprehension of the meaning of English words.

To this we must add another reason perhaps more important than the difference in language which might serve to explain the difference in the performance of mental tests. An American child as a rule develops in a relatively scientific atmosphere. This child interprets the phenomena around him according to tendencies already fixed for him in the standard American home. His mind works on lines more or less scientific or pragmatic, rarely supernatural or magical. In school, he enters a world of ideas with which he is already familiar. He responds normally to mental tests, not only because he is used to rational thinking, but also because these tests are similar to elements in his experience previous to entering school.

The son of the Mexican immigrant of mixed or indigenous culture, however, develops in an environment of personal attitude based on tradition, convention, and supernatural belief. He sees problems met sometimes by will and effort, and sometimes by the intervention of mysterious, vague, unexplicable, and unexplained beings, without whose aid personal effort may not alone be sufficient for success. This child, taking the mental test in an American school, suffers real mental conflict. If the tests are in English, failure is almost certain since the child cannot think in English as rapidly or effectively as he would in Spanish, as the experiments of Miss Coan have shown. If the tests are given in Spanish, the child can think well enough, but the answer to the problem presented is complicated by inexpressible and vague tendencies. There arises in him the impulse to get help from outside mysterious agency, and therefore he pursues confused digressions, so that the result does not represent all the working of his brain nor the total effort put forth. As a rule the teacher ignores this and attributes to the child a mental capacity less than he really has. Furthermore, the tests should take into consideration the marked artistic tendency of Mexicans, children and adults alike, and the real difference this makes in ways of conceiving ideas and of expressing them.

It could be said with reasonable assurance that were mental tests to be given in schools in Mexico to American and Mexican children, the American children might seem to show deficiency. The real explanation would be, of course, the reverse application of the reasons just given for the relatively poor showing of the Mexican child in the American environment.

The performance of the Mexican immigrant to intelligence testing is thus to be understood not merely as the response of an inherent intelligence, but also as a response determined by the cultural experiences of his more primitive environment. His mentality is therefore not merely native ability; it is acquired; it is an aspect of his culture. This culture is a folk culture, plainly distinguishable in type from modern civilization. The difference in mentality between an individual with folk backgrounds and one brought up in a modern, urbanized environment is reflected in the behavior of each.

A person truly identified with modern civilization interprets his individual experiences and the phenomena around him scientifically, whether the basis for this science be his own or derived from the knowledge of others. If he becomes ill, he goes to a doctor and is cured scientifically. If he must defend himself or his family from social attack, he goes to the law to remedy his situation, either himself applying to the organization of society or procuring a lawyer to do so. The farmer who fears loss of crops because of floods, frost, or hail consults the meteorologist in order to protect his crops from any such impending evil.

On the other hand, the person identified with indigenous or mixed culture interprets his own activities and those outside of him by a peculiar criterion all his own, or goes to people he considers authorities, but who know as little of modern scientific interpretations as himself. His concepts, like those of such authorities, are generally based on unquestioned convention and on the intervention of the supernatural, an attitude traditional from remote times and little changed by contact with modern civilization.

Such an individual treats his sicknesses with herbs or some other folk remedy, accompanied by magic ritual. If his own efforts are not enough to cure him, he goes to a medicine man or a witch, and only in a rare and extreme case does he consult a doctor. To settle troubles with his neighbors; to fight drought, fire, or flood, loss of crops, and catastrophes of all kinds; or to prosper materially or succeed in love affairs he turns also to magic, pagan religion, and supernatural help.

This "folk-lorism" goes back to prehispanic times, when although the natives had no science such as that to which we are accustomed, they did have professionals officially recognized in the practice of religion, simple astronomy, or rudimentary medicine, and these specialties were probably so specialized and esoteric as not to be part of the lore of the folk. However, folklorism was practiced clandestinely and popularly. The wealthy, and, we might say, the upper classes culturally, went to the "official" sources for cure and help, while the masses went to witches, medicine men, and people of that sort. Father Sahagun gives us interesting information on this point.

In the colonial period this folk-lorism was similarly practiced, and indeed the body of folk lore became larger and more complex. At the beginning, there was on one side Spanish professionalism and also Spanish superstition and folk lore, and, on the other, Indian professionalism and also popular superstition and folk lore. With the military and economic fall of the Indian nations came the fall of the official Indian religions, and the esoteric wisdom of the cultured and wealthy classes, so far as it survived, became identified with the lore of the folk, the two becoming one body of tradition which retained only vestiges of prehispanic professionalism. With this surviving Indian tradition the popular thought and practices of the Spanish masses likewise fused, and there resulted a Spanish-Indian folk lore derived from widely diverse sources. It is this that is characteristic of the typical Mexican immigrant. The upper minority in Mexico retained European culture and developed along European lines, but the enormous lower majority thus created a culture absolutely different and markedly personal and national.

The immigrant in the United States.—Although, as will be seen, in religion the Mexican immigrant undergoes a great change in the United States, this is not the case in so far as his folk-lorism goes. Materially, he becomes identified with modern American civilization—housing, clothing, domestic utensils, use of machinery, etc.—all these he makes his own. But his folk-lorism is not only retained; it continues developing and spreads to Americans of Mexican origin and even to native Americans.

In most of the life-stories which we collected the folk factor plainly appears. Some of the ballads, poems, stories, and songs which we collected were composed in Mexico and retained in the United States, usually with slight change, while others were made in the United States by Mexicans or Americans of Mexican origin. In these latter is found the reflection of the new environment upon the Mexican spirit. The influence of the Mexican folk in the United States is to be seen, lastly, in the picturesque and vivid names of Mexican restaurants, stores, drug stores, and pool halls which he frequents.

Birthdays, or rather "saint's days," are celebrated with music and dancing, as are also baptisms and weddings. There is usually a small hired orchestra, or perhaps a piano may be rented or hauled to the scene of the *fiesta*. Suppers of Mexican food, *enchiladas*, *tamales*, are served. The music is a combination of American fox-trot alternating with the singing of Mexican ballads to the accompaniment of guitars. Many of the immigrants own phonographs.

A funeral is an extremely important occasion, and every effort is made to make it as elaborate as possible. Mass is said and there is always a wake, at which there is less drinking than on such occasions in Mexico. On such occasions the church receives financial tribute; funeral mass costs ten dollars, a baptism five, a marriage twenty, and burial privileges in Catholic cemeteries come high but they are always paid for.

The evil eye, a superstition widespread in Mexico, known in Europe and much less known in the United States, is a common belief among the Mexican immigrants. There are witchwomen and herb doctors who cure this and other ills, by means of their own preparations and magical spells. Typically Mexican are the "chills of fear," counteracted with a specially prepared and blessed brew which is accompanied with a ceremony in which Catholicism, European magic, and Indian magic combine curiously. This brew is called "water of fright." Herbs are widely sold and used, though sometimes "the business is spoiled," as one herb-vendor explained, by doctors paid and kept by the companies that employ the immigrants.

Superstitions peculiar to the American-Mexican population in the United States are also numerous: Sweethearts may not give each other handkerchiefs, for this means forgetfulness and desertion; the guests at a wedding do not dance in the room where the bride sits, as this is a bad omen; girls "wish" on a star or on the moon, with their arms out and body forming a cross, and also believe that a wish made at 9:15 at night invariably comes true. Meeting a group of nuns in the street means bad luck, and also two yellow taxis seen together are a bad omen, to counteract the effects of which the person seeing them pats or strikes his companion twice on the back. These few examples suffice to give an idea of how the folk mind of the Mexican immigrant finds food everywhere, as well in old tradition as in new.

The form and content of the Mexican immigrant mind is made known in the songs and other documentary materials to which we have already made reference, and to these we now turn for closer consideration.

Our materials are of four sorts: first, *corridos* (ballads), *canciónes* (songs), and music; second, herbal medicine; third, the names of Mexican stores and other places of business; fourth, superstitions and magical beliefs.

Corridos and other folk and popular songs.[1]—Some of these are transmitted only orally, while others are printed and are indeed often illustrated. They circulate in almost all parts of the country in which there are Mexicans or Mexican-Americans. In accordance with their geographical origin they can be classified in two groups:

1. Compositions which originated in Mexico and which may be more or less changed by the immigrants who carry them to the United States. In these songs the influence of the American environment cannot be seen. They are accordingly less expressive of immigrant life than are verses of the second class. The majority of these compositions are transmitted orally from one country to another by the immigrants, a fact which explains the alteration they have undergone. In some cases printed copies are brought from Mexico; in San Antonio we made a collection of *corridos* printed in Mexico by Vanegas Arroyo.

[1] The songs mentioned here and illustrated in the next chapter, written by the immigrants themselves or by others of the same cultural level in Mexico, are not, of course, the only songs sung among the Mexicans. Space does not permit the inclusion in this report of a collection of more sophisticated and commercial songs sung by Mexicans. Lists of such songs were secured through music-stores selling sheet music and phonograph records to Mexican clientèles.

Mexican immigrants preserve music genuinely Mexican, while their children, growing up in the United States, as well as many Mexican-Americans, more frequently enjoy the more American type of song. In a music-store in San Antonio we overheard the following dialogue between a Mexican father and his son: The father wished to buy some Mexican songs, but the son objected, saying, "No, father; these songs are silly and mournful; don't buy them; they are old-fashioned. I like things that are up to date." "What do you want?" asked the father. "I like songs like 'I Love My Baby,' " replied the boy. He was asked to sing this song, but he could remember only a small part of the beginning. At this the father said, "Son, I am no musician, but nevertheless when I was courting your mother I could sing many songs from beginning to end." "But, father," said the boy, "we only want music to dance by." And the clerk later commented on this conversation, saying regretfully, "The only kind of music they ask for here is superficial, of no account."

2. Verses made in the United States by Mexicans, and, more rarely, by Mexican-Americans. These often reflect the influence of the American environment, are therefore of special interest for this study, and will be specially considered in the next chapter.

Medicinal herbs.—In Mexico a large part of the Indians and *mestizos* are wont to be treated for illness by the use of medicinal plants with properties, real or imaginary, that have been passed on from prehispanic times.

This is especially common in the country where there are few doctors; in contrast the number of herb doctors of various sorts is considerable. In almost all parts of America where there are Mexicans and Mexican-Americans there are Mexican drug stores in which there is a great sale of every sort of medicinal plant. As the clerks are forbidden to say what sicknesses these plants are good for and are simply allowed to sell them, they could not give us information upon their uses. The patients themselves usually surround themselves with a mysterious silence when they are interrogated upon this subject.[1]

[1] The Mexican drug stores found in every large Mexican immigrant community are fertile fields for collecting folk lore of this type. In one such in Chicago, where Mexican *metates* and Mexican groceries were sold as well as drugs, we obtained a list of Mexican medicines. These included laurel and walnut leaves, squash and flaxseed, snake and toad oil, and the following medicinal plants imported from Mexico: Yerba-mora (*Solanum nigrum*); Yerba-gato (*Valeriana tolucana*); Yerba-mula; Yerba-del-Cancer (*Cuphea* sp.); Yerba-buena (*Mentha viridis*); Yerba de San Nicolas (*Tecoma mollis*); Amole; Contrayerba (*Psoralea pentaphylla*); Copal (*Bursera* sp.); Cabellitos de maiz (*Maydis stigmata*); Culantrillo (*Adianthum tenerum*); Canahuala (*Polypodium* sp.); Gordolobo (*Gnaphalium* sp.); Gobernadora (*Covillea tridentata*); Huachichile (*Locselia coccinea*); Epazote (*Chenopodium foetidum*); Estafiate (*artemisia mexicana*); Itamo Real (*Passiflora* sp.); Muicle (*Jacobinia mohintle*); Ojasén (*Cassia* sp.); Oreja de ratón (*Dichondra argentea*); Pirul (*Schinus molle*); Parraleña; Romero (*Rosmarinus officialis*); Raiz costomate (*Physalis costomatl*); Simonillo (*Conysa filaginoides*); Zacate Limón (*Andropogon citratum*); Semilla de acocote; Torongil (*Cedronella mexicana*); Tabardillo; Yerba de vibora; Yerba de venado.

Names of Mexican business houses in the United States.—
Following the popular usage in Mexico, the names of bakeries,
barber shops, restaurants, and grocery stores do not usually
refer to the function of the establishments; they are florid or
sentimental terms often of patriotic reference. In many cases
they employ the names of Mexican states, cities, or heroes, or
suggest the picturesque antiquities of Mexico. Occasionally
Americans of German, Jewish, or Syrian ancestry employ such
names in order to attract Mexican trade. The term *La Raza*
("The Race") is a common title of this sort. Others are:
"Azteca," "The Future," "The Maid of Puebla," "Moctezuma," "The Man of Xochimilco," "Michoacan," "The
Flower of Mexico."

Superstitions and magical beliefs.—Of documents of this
class relative to the folk mentality of the immigrant a vast
number could be collected. Our own collection of life-history
documents, which are not incorporated in the present volume
for lack of space, contain many examples. A few samples of
this sort of material may be included here.

The following document was obtained in the course of an
interview with a Mexican woman in San Antonio.

She says with regard to the evil eye that her daughter as a child was
very attractive and she took great care of her and never wanted any one
to touch her. Every day there was a beggar woman who came to ask alms
and she asked her to let her take the child. The mother always refused
and one day in vexation said that she was too dirty to touch her daughter.
The beggar woman became angry and told her that she was going to put
the evil eye upon the little one and so went off. The child immediately
fell sick and began to cry as if she had a pain somewhere and grew worse
and worse until finally she doubled up as if in a spasm. Then the mother
of Señora X understood that what was the matter with the child was that
she had had the evil eye caused by the beggar woman and she persuaded
Señora X to go off and find the old woman and bring her back. They were
obliged to question the old woman a long time but finally she scrubbed
the body of the child all over with the wrong side of her white petticoat
and then spat out a mouthful of water on her petticoat stretched out over

the child in such a way that the water was strained through the petticoat before touching her. At once the child began to get better and was cured. But when two people are the cause of the evil eye at the same time the matter is more complicated; then both have to let fall a mouthful of water at the same time taken from the same glass and transfer this water to the mouth of the bewitched person. Another time two "bad" women at the door of a house of prostitution brought the evil eye upon the little girl by noticing her legs. The child became paralyzed and had to be carried to the house of prostitution where the two women were asked to drink water at the same time from the same glass and to spit this upon the legs of the child and to put it in her mouth. Thus she was cured. Señora X knows that there is a way of making one person fall in love with another but she does not know how to do this and has never attempted it.

The folk lore of the immigrant involves a great deal of detailed magical ritual in connection with the treatment of disease. The following is a recipe, taken down verbatim, for "water of fear," used to cure people afflicted with *El Espanto* ("The Fright").

A copper kettle, like those from Mexico, which are very good, is placed on the fire to heat and then there is put in a liquid which has already been prepared. This is made of holy water with three little red crosses of red ribbon, a handful of earth which is collected at the first cross road and a gold ring. All this must be put in the kettle and the sick person must look at it very hard. If he is surprised by a sudden hiss from the kettle, he will get well. Then the mixture is chilled and the sick person takes it to drink and then lies down to sleep. This has to be done at eleven in the morning for several days. I cured my daughter so.

The following report of an interview with a Mexican immigrant is a fair sample, representing the part which magic plays in the life of the group.

We used to live next door to a *guera*[1] married to a Negro. Then we were getting on very well; I had my five-room house, with good furniture, beds in every room, chairs, in short we were very well fixed. I am not afraid of work, and a large house is very little for me to clean and put in order. I earn, sometimes by washing, sometimes by cleaning, five dollars a day. People are envious of me on account of the work I have. That

[1] A blonde, i.e., a native white American woman.

guera was bad and she was envious of me and then she put a charm on us, Miguel and I. (I mean by putting a charm on [*congestionar*] making bad blood between people.) One night the *guera* said to Miguel that he should come to take supper with them, and what he had never done before, he left my supper and went. There they gave him what do I know what sort of potion or wine all dark and strange. Day after day he went there and he never talked to me, a very frightful thing. Finally he left the house; three words we exchanged but they were very harsh, and I knew no more of him. I remained secure in the house without letting anyone know anything. "Where is Don Miguel?" people said to me. "He went to the cotton fields," I answered, feeling horribly inside. This was not hatred, but such sorrow I cannot describe it. I could not work, I did not leave my house because I said, "Here I am secure; I will stay where he left me until I see what happens to me." So the days passed and I had to begin to sell my furniture and my fruit business and my clothes and at last there wasn't a thing worth twenty-five cents left. One day Mr. P., who had been a very good friend and kind person to us, asked me why I didn't go to see a spiritualist who he said could tell me what was happening to Miguel. I pretended that I knew where Miguel was, since I did not wish to say that he had gone off, and besides the spiritualist cost a *peso*. But two days afterwards Mr. P. returned and said to me: "Go along now, take this *peso* and go to see this man and tell me what he does." I went, and first of all the man put some stamps on his eyes, then some pieces of cotton and then he wrapped himself up in a cloth.

"You were not married," he said to me.

"Yes, I am married," I said.

"You were married according to the civil ceremony, but according to the law of God you were not married."

"That is true," I said.

"Well, your husband is fond of you, but they have put a charm on him. But take a needleful of thread in your right hand, make three knots, and put it on the palm of the left hand." I took hold of that bunch of thread; as if blown away it flew out of my hand into an ash tray which the man was holding. "Your husband is bewitched," he said to me. "How could I understand how the bunch of thread went into the tray? I do not know." "Take this thread," he said to me, "and make three knots again and put it on the palm of your left hand and then put your other hand on that palm. Hold the thread in your hands a while and if the knots loosen up your husband will come soon." With difficulty I made the knots because it seemed as if my fingers had grown bigger and I put the thread in the palm of my hand with a kind of paste which he gave me so that it would not fly away. I covered it over with the other hand and after a while when I uncovered it I had no knots. He said to me, "Tomorrow at the latest your husband will return."

On the following day Miguel returned. He brought with him ten *pesos*, and on the next day, Sunday, because he came on a Saturday, he went away again but he told me where and at what he was working. He never was a bad one for work but after this he scarcely ever returned with ten *pesos* and from that time on he hasn't had good luck in work. It's gone badly with him and at small jobs he earns almost nothing. I have had bad luck since that time, too, and we have not been able to get on.

Then I lived, as I told you, in a large house. But it was a house where a Negress had been hanged and who knows what horrible things had happened and they said that it was haunted. I am not afraid of anyone and I have never seen a ghost. But it was as if this house was stained and very sad and I felt oppressed in it. One day Miguel told me that the night before when he was sitting down suddenly the whole house shook from its foundations. No wagon was passing, nothing was on the other side, we were in the middle of a lot of land. Miguel saw nothing but felt himself somewhat shaken up. I said that I was going to fumigate this house to see if I could not get the sadness out, so I went and asked a lady how to do this. She told me that every day for fifteen minutes I should take my prayer-book and pray while I burned incense. I did this for several days and one day there was an explosion in the house as if an automobile tire had burst. Then I washed it all with lye; I fixed it all up and I felt that the bad influences had gone.

E.L.: Was it evil spirits that were there?

F.C.: No, child, it was bad thoughts, those passions, black and strong, the crimes, everything bad like that which stays in a house and falls upon one.

E.L.: And then did the ghost stop appearing or was it still haunted?

F.C.: The ghost? Do you know what that was? I don't want to talk evil of anyone, but I had a neighbor who had a love affair with a man and in the night she used to go out all wrapped up so that people would not know her, because she was married, to see the man. I did see her. But I did not see a ghost and I have never seen one. When Maria was a little girl alone with her I used to cross the *avisperito* [this is a terrible slum district] and I never saw anything except people.

CHAPTER VII

THE SONGS OF THE IMMIGRANT[1]

Many of the songs composed by the Mexican immigrant express his experiences in the new country and his reactions to the new experiences with a fidelity and a naïveté which make them a valuable source of information on his likes and his dislikes, his hopes and his disappointments. They constitute, taken together, a sort of collective autobiography. In this report space will permit the quotation of no more than a few of the songs of this class.

Some recount the misfortunes of the immigrant, his disappointment and disillusion. Many such deal with the unpleasant results of labor contracts entered into through the too unscrupulous labor agent.

LOS INMIGRANTES
(Los Enganchados)

THE IMMIGRANTS
(Los Enganchados—"The Hooked Ones")

El 28 de Febrero,
　Aquel día tan señalado,
Cuando salimos de El Paso
　Nos sacaron reenganchados.

On the 28th day of February,
That important day
When we left El Paso,
They took us out as contract labor.

Cuando salimos de El Paso
　A las dos de la mañana,
Le preguntó al reenganchista,
　Si vamos para Louisiana.

When we left El Paso
At two in the morning,
I asked the boss contractor
If we were going to Louisiana.

Llegamos a la Laguna
　Sin esperanza ninguna

We arrived at Laguna
Without any hope.

[1] [This chapter was prepared by Margaret Park Redfield from materials collected by Dr. Gamio.—EDITOR.]

Le pregunté al renganchista Si vamos para "Oclajuma."	I asked the boss If we were going to Oklahoma.

Por esas líneas del Kiri[1]
    Pasa un tren muy volador
Corre cien millas por hora
    Y no le dan todo el vapor.
	Along the line of the Katy
	There goes a very fast train.
	It runs a hundred miles an hour
	And then they don't give it all
	    the steam.

Y el que no lo quiera creer	And he who doesn't want to believe it,
No más que venga a montar No más que monte de noche	Just let him get on board. Just let him get on board at night;
Lo verá donde va a dar.	He will see where he gets to.

Llegamos el día primero
    Y al segundo a trabajar
	We arrived on the first day
	And on the second began to
	    work.

Con los picos en las manos Nos pusimus a trampar.[2]	With our picks in our hands We set out tramping.

Unos descargaban rieles
    Otros descargaban "tallas"
Y otros de los compañeros
    Echaban de mil malallas.
	Some unloaded rails
	And others unloaded ties,
	And others of my companions
	Threw out thousands of curses.

Los que sabían el trabajo
    Iban recorriendo el "llaqui"
Martilleros y paleros
	Those who knew the work
	Went repairing the jack
	With sledge hammers and shov-
	    els,

Echándole tierra al traque.	Throwing earth up the track.

Ocho "varas" alineadas
    Nos seguíamos disgustados
A los gritos y las señas
    Nos quedábamos paraos.
	Eight crowbars lined up,
	We followed disgusted;
	To shouts and signs
	We remained indifferent.

[1] Katy, or Missouri, Kansas, and Texas Railroad.
[2] The English word "tramp."

Decía D. José Maria
  Con su boquita de infierno
Mas valiera estar en Kansas

  Que nos mantenga el gobierno.

Decía Jesus el Coyote
  Como queriendo llorar
Valía más estar en Juarez

  Aunque sea sin trabajar.

Estos versos son compuestos
  Por un pobre mexicano
Pa ponerlos al corriente
  Del sistema americano.

      CHICAGO, ILL.

Said Don José Maria
With his hell's mouth,[1]
"It would be better to be in Kansas
Where the government would maintain us."

Said Jesus, "El Coyote,"
As if he wanted to weep,
"It would be better to be in Juarez
Even if we were without work."

These verses were composed
By a poor Mexican
To spread the word about
The American system.

      CHICAGO, ILL.

LOS BETABELEROS

Año de mil nuevecientos
Veinte y tres en el actual
Fueron los betabeleros
A ese "michiga" a llorar.

Por que todos los señores
Empezaban a regañar
Y don Santiago les responde:

Yo me quiero regresar
Por que no nos han cumplido

Lo que fueron a contar.
Aquí vienen y les cuentan

THE BEET-FIELD WORKERS

In the year 1923
Of the present era
The beet-field workers went
To that Michigan, to their grief,
Because all the bosses
Began to scold,
And Don Santiago says to them:
"I want to return
Because they haven't done for us
What they said they would;
Here they come and they tell you

---

[1] I. e., "cursing."

Que se vayan para allá,	That you ought to go up there
Por que allá les tiene todo	Because there you will have everything
Que no van a batallar,	Without having to fight for it.
Pero son puras mentiras	But these are nothing but lies,
Los que vienen y les dicen.	And those who come and say those things are liars.
Cuando ya estamos allá	When we get there
Empiezan a regañarnos	They begin to scold us,
Y luego les respondemos:	And then we say to them:
"Nosotros nos regresamos	'We are going back
Porque allá en San Antonio	Because there in San Antonio
Nosotros sólo gozamos.	We just enjoyed ourselves.
El 18 de febrero,	The 18th of February,
Ah que día tan señalado!"	Oh, what a day to remember!'
Cuando llegamos a Houston	When we arrived at Houston
No hallábamos ni que hacer	We didn't find anything to do.
El tiempo estaba muy duro	The times were very hard,
No se quería componer.	And didn't seem to want to get better.
Cuando llegamos a Houston	When we arrived at Houston,
Trabajando noche y día	Working night and day,
No nos daban de comer	They didn't give us anything to eat,
No más que pura sandía.	Nothing more than just watermelon.
Al pasar del estado de Texas	On leaving the state of Texas
A las dos de la mañana	At two in the morning
Le pregunté al enganchista	I asked the boss contractor
Que si íbamos a Louisiana	If we were going to Louisiana.
Llegamos a Kansas City,	We arrived at Kansas City.
Gritaba Juan "El Coyote"	Juan, 'El Coyote,' yelled out,
Con su sombrero de lado,	With his hat on one side,
Yo no volveré a Kansas	'I will not go back to Kansas
A trabajarle al condado	To work for the county.'
Gritaba Juan "El Coyote"	Juan, 'El Coyote,' yelled out

Con esa boca de infierno:
Yo no volveré a Kansas
A trabajarle al gobierno.
Despedida no la doy
Porque no la traigo aquí

La dejé en el estado de Texas
Para que se acuerden de mí.

HOUSTON, TEX.

With that mouth of hell,
'I will not go back to Kansas
To work for the government.
I shall not sing my farewell
Because I do not have it with
    me;
I left it in the state of Texas
To make them remember me.' "

HOUSTON, TEX.

Sometimes the mood is one of homesickness. The higher standard of living is not the only consideration to motivate the immigrant.

EL RANCHO DONDE YO NACI

No me gusta bailar en salones
    Como al estilo de por aquí
a mi me gusta piso de tierra
    como en el rancho donde yo
    nací.

No me gusta la pistola escuadra

    como al estilo de por aquí
a mi me gusta carabina negra
    como en el rancho donde yo
    nací.

No me gusta camisa de seda
    como al estilo de por aquí
a mi me gustan las "yompas"
    azules
    como en el rancho donde yo
    nací.

THE FARM WHERE I WAS BORN

I don't care to dance in the halls
That you have here;
What I want is an earth floor
Like on the farm where I was
    born.

I don't care for your automatic
    pistols
That you have here;
What I want is a black rifle
Like on the farm where I was
    born.

I don't care for your silk shirts
That you have here;
What I want is a suit of blue
    jumpers
Like on the farm where I was
    born.

No me gusta coche ni automóvil | I don't care for your carriages or automobiles

como al estilo de por aquí | That you have here;
a mi me gusta carreta debueyes | What I want is a cart with oxen
como en el rancho donde yo nací. | Like on the farm where I was born.

No me gustan los calzones anchos | I don't like your wide trousers

como al estilo de por aquí | That you have here;
a mi me gustan pegados al cuero | I like them close to the skin
como en el rancho donde yo nací. | Like on the farm where I was born.

SAN ANTONIO, TEX. | SAN ANTONIO, TEX.

Perhaps no subject arouses the distaste and even disgust of the immigrant as the free-and-easy conduct of the Americanized Mexican girl, contrasting as it does with the traditional restraint upon the Spanish-American woman. The "flappers" are the theme of many Texas *corridos* and *canciones*. One such bears the title and employs the refrain, *¡Ay, Mama! ¡Que Pantorillas!* ("Oh, Mamma! What Legs!"). Another, entitled "Las Pelonas" ("The Bobbed Heads; the Flappers"), is too long to quote in full. One stanza follows:

Los paños colorados | Red bandannas
Los tengo aborrecidos | I detest,
Ya hora las pelonas | And now the flappers
Los usan de vestidos. | Use them for their dress.
Las muchachas de S. Antonio | The girls of San Antonio
Son flojas pa'l metate | Are lazy at the *metate*.
Quieren andar pelonas | They want to walk out bobbed-haired,

Con sombreros de petate. | With straw hats on.
Se acabaron las pizcas, | The harvesting is finished,
Se acabó el algodón | So is the cotton;
Ya andan las pelonas | The flappers stroll out now
De puro vacilón. | For a good time.

Some Mexicans, however, take these problems of culture conflict more easily. Perhaps the writer of the following verses has made more than one trip to the United States—he knows what to expect.

LA DE LA 'NAGUA AZUL

De las dos que vienan "ay"
  Cual te gusta, valedor,
Esa de la 'nagua azul
  Me parece la mejor.

Que dices, chata, nos vamos

  Pa' los Estados Unidos
Donde gozan las mujeres
  Al lado de sus maridos?

Si me quieren sé querer,

  Si me olvidan sé olvidar,

Como lo quieran hacer,
  Para mi todo es igual.

Que dice, mi reenganchista,

  No le dije que volvía,
Mándeme par "onde quiera"
  Que ya traigo compañía.

REFRÁN

Si me quieren, etc.

Pues, muchacho mexicano
  Yo si te sabré decir
De los dos reenganches que hay,
  ¿Para donde quieres ir.?

SHE OF THE BLUE SKIRT

Of the two who are coming there
Which one do you like, friend?
She of the blue skirt
Seems the best to me.

What do you say, snub-nosed;
    shall we go
To the United States
Where women have a good time
Living with their husbands?

If you love me, I know how to
    love;
If you forget me, I know how to
    forget.
Whatever you want to do,
It's all the same to me.

What do you say, my contrac-
    tor;
Didn't I tell you I'd be back?
Send me wherever you will,
Because now I bring someone
    with me.

REFRAIN

If you love me, I know how to
    love, etc.

Well, then, Mexican fellow,
I'll say yes to you.
Of the two jobs that there are
Where do you want to go?

No me manden para Kansas,	Don't send me to Kansas
Ni tampoco pa' Oclajuma	Nor to Oklahoma either,
Son estados degraciados	They are terrible states
Que aborrecen al que fuma.	Which hate the man who smokes.
[*Refrán*]	[*Refrain*]
Si fueres pa' California	If you go to California
No lleves mujer bonita	Don't bring along a good-looking woman,
Porque allí hay muchas panteras	Because there are many panthers
Y cualquiera te la quita.	Who may get her away from you.
[*Refrán*]	[*Refrain*]

Some Mexicans are, apparently, more at home in the new environment. The following was composed as a parody on the song "Las cuatro Milpas," then very popular in Mexico.

EL FOTINGO	THE FORD
[Con música de "Las cuatro Milpas"]	[To the music of "Las cuatro Milpas")
POR T. FLORES	BY T. FLORES
Cuatro ruedas tan sólo han quedado,	Only four wheels remain
del "Fotingo" que era mío[1]	Of the Ford which was mine;
del pobre carrito	Of the poor buggy
que compré en abonos	That I bought in instalments,
todo se acabó. ...	It's all gone. . . . .
Las linternas están apagadas,	The lights are out,
el motor tiene "parado"	The motor is cold,
llantas ya no tiene	It has no tires
ni asientos ni puertas	Nor seats, nor doors—
todo se acabó. ...	All are gone. . . . .
Y recuerdo las noches aquellas	And I remember these nights

[1] "Fotingo" is the name given the Ford car.

en que con las "guisas"[1]
y con el moonshine
vacilaba y me las tronaba.[2]

On which, with the girls
And with some moonshine,
It staggered around and I smoked *marihuana*.

que noches aquellas ya no vol-
verán.
Nunca olvido cuando era "bu-
lega"[3]
Las veces que me siguieron
el Ford corría tanto
que me parecía
se iba a desarmar
Era bueno y jamás se rajaba

What nights those were which will never return!
I'll never forget when I was a bootlegger
The times that they followed me.
The Ford ran so much
That it seemed to me
It was going to fall apart.
It was a good one and never broke down

ya fuera en subida
o cuando iba a bajar
Los amigos siempre dijeron
que más que "fotingo"

Whether it was going up
Or whether it was going down.
My friends always said
That it looked more like an Overland

parecía "Overland."

Than a Ford.

PHOENIX, ARIZ.

PHOENIX, ARIZ.

The lines which follow suggest that the Mexican's migratory habits are not a product of his native temperament. A Mexican in Texas "views with alarm" the coming of the railroad to his town. The song was composed in Victoria, Texas, upon the occasion of the completion of a railroad line to that place.

EL FERROCARRIL

La máquina pasajera
no puede hacer cosa buena
porque "oscurece" en su casa

THE RAILROAD

The fleeting engine
Can't do anything good
Because at dusk it is at home

---

[1] "Guisas" is a term applied to girls.
[2] I. e., to smoke *marihuana*.   [3] Bootlegger.

y amanece en tierra ajena.	And at dawn in a strange country.
¡Ay! ¡que dolor!	Oh! What sadness!
Tendrían los mexicanos	The Mexicans will have to see
al ver el ferrocarril	The railroad train
que traen los americanos.	That the Americans bring.
La máquina chiquitita	The very littlest engine
es la que ha quedado aquí	Is the one that has been left here,
y la quieren llegar	And they expect it to go
hasta San Luis Potosí	As far as San Luis Potosi.
Oigan y oigan	Listen, listen,
el ferrocarril bramar.	To the train puffing;
el que lleva a los hombres	The train which carries men away
y nunca los vuelve a traer.	And never brings them back again.

But assimilation of the Mexican is often confined to adoption of new techniques. No Mexican is so despised as he who "denies his race."

EL RENEGADO	THE RENEGADE.
[Se canta con música mexicana "Dame un beso"]	[This is sung with the Mexican music "Dame un beso"]
Andas por hay luciendo	You go along showing off
gran automóvil	In a big automobile.
me llamas desgraciado,	You call me a pauper
y muerto de hambre	And dead with hunger,
y es que ya no te acuerdas	And what you don't remember is
cuando en mi rancho	That on my farm
andabas casi en cueros	You went around almost naked
y sin huaraches.	And without sandals.
Así pasa a muchos	This happens to many
que aquí conozco	That I know here

cuando aprenden un poco	When they learn a little
de americano	American
y se visten catrines	And dress up like dudes,
y van al baile.	And go to the dance.
Y el que niega su raza	But he who denies his race
ni madre tiene,	Is the most miserable creature.
pues no hay nada en el mundo	There is nothing in the world
tan asqueroso	So vile as he,
como la ruin figura del renegado	The mean figure of the renegade.
y aunque lejos de tí,	And although far from you,
Patria querida,	Dear Fatherland,
me han echado	Continual revolutions
continuas revoluciones,	Have cast me out—
no reniega jamás	A good Mexican
un buen mexicano	Never disowns
de la Patria querida	The dear fatherland
de sus amores.	Of his affections.

LOS ANGELES, CALIF.   LOS ANGELES, CALIF.

The second generation, born in this country, is not yet a numerous group. But that there are already some problems of culture conflict between the generations is suggested by the following song, here quoted only in part:

EL PADRE DEL CHARRO VARGAS	THE FATHER OF CHARRO VARGAS
Ya está en San Antonio	There is here in San Antonio
el padre del Charro Vargas,	The father of Charro Vargas.
éste si que es un demonio	He is a regular devil
con uñas y barbas largas.	With long nails and a beard.
Esto nunca lo tolero	"This I will never tolerate,"
dice el padre de Varguitas,	Says the father of Varguitas,
que en lugar de ser bolero	"That instead of being a cowboy
ande con los periodistas.	He goes out with writers.

Pues en su tierra señores

  sólo cuidaba marranos,
era el peor de los pastores

  entre todos sus hermanos.

Y mugroso como él solo
  con su tazota de atole,
siempre estaba sobre el lodo

  masticando su pinole.

De charro no tiene tal,

  en cambio en las fiestas patrias
se vistió con un costal
  muy ajustado en las patas.

De todos era la risión
  con su endiablado caballo,
y dijo allí un guasón
  que era el charro más payo.

Por esa muy justa razón
  yo tu padre, 'hora quiero
de tu vida explicación;
  aquí en el extranjero.

Más te digo por trasmanos
  que sé que vendías terrenos,
y también moles poblanos
  y algunos zapatos buenos.

Supe que fuiste inventor

"Because in his own country,
  sirs,
He just looked after the pigs,
He was the worst of all the
  herders
Among all his brothers.

"Dirty and all alone
With his big bowl of *atole*,
He was always on top of the
  mud
Eating up his *pinole*.

"There is nothing of the *charro*
  in him,
But on national holidays
He dressed up in a sack
Very tight around the legs.

"He was the laughingstock of all
With his runt of a horse,
And a joker there said
That he was the most comical
  charro of them all.

"For this very good reason
I, your father, now wish
An explanation of your life
Here in a strange land.

"I will tell you, by secret ways
I know that you sold land
And also *mole Poblano*
And good shoes besides.

"I knew that you were the inventor

de un Cemaforo muy bueno,	Of a very good Semaphore,
pero eso de escritor ...	But this thing of being a scribbler
eso sí que es retebueno.	Is quite a good thing,
Pero para otras gentes	"All right for other people
que tengan tantito seso,	Who have at least some brains,
pues tu sólo tienes dientes	But you have only teeth
pa masticar con exceso.	To eat too much with."
—T. A. Soto	—T. A. Soto

Different from the song so far quoted, which are autobiographical in character and express the attitude of the writer with the directness of the lyric, is that type of Mexican song commonly known as the *corrido*. It may be well to confine the term *corrido*, or "ballad," to the songs which tell a story. The *corridos* are, of all the songs collected, nearest to the human-interest story of the popular newspaper. Like the human-interest story, they express the interests and attitudes of the people. The heroes of the *corridos* are types that catch the popular imagination—swaggering bandits who boldly defy all the rest of the world, brave men foully assassinated, or men who "kill for love." Examples of the first sort are "The Tragedy of Gregorio Cortez" and "Jesus Cadena," a very elliptical account of a fight in a dance hall.

LA TRAGEDIA DE GREGORIO CORTEZ	THE TRAGEDY OF GREGORIO CORTEZ
En el condado del Carmen	In the county of Carmen,
miren lo que ha sucedido	Let them see what has happened.
murió el "chirife mayor"[1]	The sheriff died,
quedando Ramón herido.	Leaving Ramón wounded.
"Insortaron" a Cortez	They went on the pursuit of Cortez

[1] Sheriff.

por toditito el estado:

Over the whole state.

"Vivo o muerto que la apre-
hendan

"Let him be caught dead or alive

porque a varios ha matado."

Because he has killed several
people."

Iban los americanos

The Americans started after
him.

que por el viento volaban

Like the wind they flew

porque se iban a ganar

Because they were going to get

tres mil pesos que les daban.

Three thousand *pesos* reward.

Decían los americanos:

The Americans said:

¿Si lo vemos que le hacemos?

"If we see him, what shall we do?

¿Si le entramos por derechos

If we go right at him

muy poquitos volveremos?

Very few of us will go in the
front way."

Se anduvieron informando,

They went around getting information

como tres horas después

And about three hours afterward

supieron que el malhechor
era Gregorio Cortés.

They knew that the evildoer
Was Gregorio Cortez.

Tiró con rumbo a González,

He went in the direction of
Gonzalez.

varios *sheriffs* lo vieron,

Several sheriffs saw it

no lo quisieron seguir

But they did not want to follow him

porque le tuvieron miedo.

Because they were afraid of
him.

Allá en el "brosville"

There in the *brosville*

del rancho

Of the ranch

lo alcanzaron a rodear

Some men, more than three
hundred,

poquitos, más de trescientos

Succeeded in surrounding him.

allí les brincó el corral.

There he jumped the corral
fence.

Decía Gregorio Cortés,

Said Gregorio Cortez,

con su pistola en la mano:	With his pistol in his hand,
"No siento el 'berlo' matado	"I'm not sorry he was killed,
lo que siento es a mi herma-	What I am sorry for is my
no."	brother."
Decía Gregorio Cortés	Said Gregorio Cortez,
con su alma muy encendida,	With his soul very hot,
"Maté al 'chiffe'·mayor,	"I killed the head sheriff,
la defensa es 'permetida'	It was in self-defense.
Todo el mundo tengo andado,	I have gone over the whole world.
ya me canso de andar,	Now I am tired of going;
al llegar a San Antonio	When I get to San Antonio
yo me voy a presentar."	I am going to give myself up."
Se "incontró" a un mexicano,	He met a Mexican.
"platícame que hay de nuevo	"Tell me the news.
yo soy Gregorio Cortés."	I am Gregorio Cortez."
Y iban los perros "jaunes"[1]	And the hound dogs went out;
Y iban sobre la huella	They followed his tracks,
pero alcanzar a Cortés	But to catch Cortez
era alcanzar una estrella.	Was like catching a star.
Decía Gregorio Cortés	Said Gregorio Cortez,
"paí'qué se valen de planes	"What good are their plans
si no pueden agarrarme	If they cannot catch me,
ni con esos perros 'jaunes.' "	Not even with these hound dogs?"
Gregorio le dice a Juan:	Gregorio says to Juan:
"Muy pronto lo vas a ver,	"You'll see something very soon.
anda háblale a los 'chiriffes'	Go tell the sheriffs
que me vengan a aprehender."	To come and take me!"
Luego llegan "chiriffes"	Then the sheriffs arrived.
Gregorio se presentó,	Gregorio stepped forth,
"Por la buena sí me llevan	"I will give myself up
pero de otro modo no."	But I won't be taken any other way."
Agarraron a Cortés	They seized hold of Cortez.

[1]Hounds.

ya terminó la cuestión,
la pobre de su familia
la lleva en el corazón.
Aquí va la despedida
por la voluntad de Dios
estos sucesos pasaron
en mil "nuevecientos" dos.
Ya con ésta me despido
por las hojas de un ciprés,
aquí se acaba cantando
la tragedia de Cortés.

SAN ANTONIO, TEX.

Now the matter is ended.
His poor family
Carry the pain in their hearts;
Here comes the goodbye.
Through the will of God
These events took place
In nineteen hundred and two.
And now I say goodbye,
By the leaves of a cypress.
Here finishes the singing
Of the tragedy of Cortez.

SAN ANTONIO, TEX.

JESUS CADENA

El 16 de Septiembre
  De mil novecientos ocho
Jesús traiba su pistola
  Calibre de treinta y ocho.
Los amigos de Jesús
  Eran como una docena
Toditos a una voz:
  ¡Viva Jesús Cadena!

JESUS CADENA

The 16th of September
Of nineteen hundred and eight
Jesus was carrying his gun,
A thirty-eight caliber.
The friends of Jesus
Were about a dozen;
All cried with one voice,
"Long live Jesus Cadena!"

Jesus and his friends go to a dance and there pick up a fight. He faces his adversary:

Decía este Jesús Cadena:
  "Mi pistola no la enfundo
'Ora los hago a mi ley

  O los separo del mundo."

Said that Jesus Cadena,
"I will not put away my pistol,
Now I shall make you do as I
  please,
Or I shall send you away from
  this world."

Decía este Jesús Cadena:
  "Voy a ver a mi querida,

Al cabo que me han de hacer,

Said that Jesus Cadena,
"I am going to see my sweetheart.
After all, what can they do to
  me?

No me han de quitar la vida."

They are not going to take my life."

Las dagas y las pistolas
   Par dondequiera se vieron,
Pero no se hicieron nada
   Porque se reconocieron.

Daggers and pistols
Could be seen everywhere,
But they did nothing
Because they recognized one another.

Corridos usually deal with names, dates, and places. If the ballad is a popular one, however, it will be preserved in the memories of men for a long period, new versions will arise, and the heroes will tend to become legendary rather than real. The ballad of José Lozano, who was assassinated while performing his duty on the side of law and order—a position which always commands less sympathetic interest than that of the outlaw—will, one would venture, be shorter lived than that of Gregorio Cortez. In fact, the general tone here is rather that of a more or less compulsory obituary notice than of an exciting tale. It may be noted, however, that Lozano is accorded the highest possible honor by being classed with Villa and Zapata.

JOSE LOZANO

En la pasada semana,
   Una tragedia ocurrió
que a todos los mexicanos
   grandemente impresionó.

De une manera alevosa
   se dió muerte a un mexicano,
a un hombre de corazón:
   al bravo José Lozano.

Era este compatriota
   un hombre muy decidido
que por su arrojo y valor

   de todos era temido.

JOSE LOZANO

In the past week
A tragedy took place
Which made a great impression
Upon all the Mexicans.

Through treachery
A Mexican was killed,
A noble-hearted man,
Brave José Lozano.

This compatriot of ours
Was a very daring man
Who for his boldness and courage
Was feared by all.

De Monterrey, Nuevo León,	Of Monterrey, Nuevo León,
fué nativo este valiente	This brave man was a native,
y como buen fronterizo	And as a good frontiersman
combatía frente a frente.	He fought face to face.

Por su estatura gigante
  y por ser buen tirador,
nada mas con sólo verlo
  José infundía temor.

Through his gigantic stature
And through being a good shot,
Just through being seen,
José inspired fear.

Como todos los valientes,
  combatiendo era un león;
pero como hombre pacifico
  tenía buen corazón.

Like all brave men
In fighting he was a lion;
But as a man of peace
He had a good heart.

Dicen que tenía enemigos
  pues a la ley ayudó,
cuando el cuerpo de los Rangers

En San Antonio operó.

They say that he had enemies
Because he helped the law
When the company of the rang-
  ers
Was active in San Antonio.

Desde hace tiempo, José
  era policía especial
del ferrocarril I.G.N.
  en esta misma ciudad.

For a long time José
Was a special policeman
Of the I.G.N. railway
Of this same city.

Los mexicanos más bravos
  han tenido mala suerte,
pues a Villa y a Zapata
  a traición les dieron muerte.

The bravest of Mexicans
Have had an evil fate,
For both Villa and Zapata
Died from treason.

SAN ANTONIO, TEX.

SAN ANTONIO, TEX.

Frank Cadena, on the other hand, who murdered his sister-in-law in "a fatal moment" because he couldn't have her himself, will perhaps make a more permanent appeal to the human sympathies.

FRANK CADENA

A mis queridos lectores
  Narrar les debo por tanto,
Esta historia dolorosa
  Acaecida en Viernes Santo.

Sobre el dolor de este día
  Para católicos fieles,
Una muerta más había
  La de Paulita Jimenez.

Fué de Frank Cadena

  La cuñada distinguida
Pero en fatales momentos
  La privó éste de la vida.

Al regresar Cadena a su casa,

  Un cigarrillo venía fumando:
En su mente traía ilusiones

  Que con ello venía disipando.

Cadena ya en su morada
  Miró que Paula feliz dormía,

Pensó de nuevo cuánto la amaba

  Y que tal vez de él nunca
  sería.

Su mente ciega por el cariño,
  Siniestra impuso su desición;
Sacó el revolver de su bolsillo

  Matando luego a su adora-
  ción.

FRANK CADENA

To my dear readers
I must relate therefore
This sad story
Which happened on Good Fri-
day.

Besides the sorrow of this day
For faithful Catholics
There was added a death—
That of Paulita Jimenez.

She was the charming sister-in-
law
Of Frank Cadena,
But in a fatal moment
He deprived her of her life.

When Cadena returned to the
house
He was smoking a cigarette
With which he was scattering
away
The dreams he had in his mind.

Cadena inside the house
Saw that Paula was sleeping
peacefully.
He thought again of how much
he loved her
And that yet she would never
be his.

His mind, blinded by passion,
Impelled his actions to evil.
He took out his revolver from
his holster
And immediately killed his
adored one.

En la corte treinta y siete	In the Thirty-sixth Court
Del Distrito criminal,	Of the Criminal District
Sentenciaron a Cadena	They sentenced Cadena
A LA PENA CAPITAL.	TO CAPITAL PUNISHMENT.
Mas se espera la clemencia	But clemency is hoped for
Del señor Gobernador	From the Governor
Que conmute la sentencia	That he will commute the sentence
A la perpetua prisión.	To life-imprisonment.
Para hermanos y parientes de Cadena	For the relatives of Cadena,
Y aun para el público en general	And even for the public in general
Perenne quedará el recuerdo de la condena	Forever will remain the sentence
A quien por amor fué criminal.	Of one who was a criminal for love.
SAN ANTONIO, TEX.	SAN ANTONIO, TEX.

On the other hand, the ballad of "Paulita Rodriguez," "a sweet and beautiful young girl," who,

> Through her lack of experience
> And perhaps because she had been deceived,
> Took her own life,

is tragic enough but somewhat lacking in dramatic quality and primitive blood and terror. It, one may predict, will be preserved very largely by her own circle of friends and acquaintances.

"The Life, Trial, and Death of Aurelio Pompa," a young man who was executed in Los Angeles, expresses so well, however, the early background and ambitions of the Mexican immigrant, and also the attitudes that are developed in the American environment, that it is bought on phonograph records by Mexican laborers in many cities of the United States.

VIDA, PROCESO, Y MUERTE DE AURELIO POMPA

Voy a contarles la triste historia
de un mexicano que allá emigró
Aurelio Pompa, así se llamaba,

el compatriota que allí murió
allá en Caborca, que es de Sonora,
el pueblo humilde donde nació,

"Vámonos, madre," le dijo un día
que allá no existe revolución.

Adios, amigos, adios, María,"

dijo a la novia con gran dolor,

yo te prometo que pronto vuelvo,
para casarnos, mediante Dios.

Adios Aurelio, dijo la novia,

que sollozando se fué a rezar,
cúidalo mucho, Virgen María,
que yo presiento no volverá.

El señor cura y sus amigos,
junto a la novia fueron a hablar,

LIFE, TRIAL, AND DEATH OF AURELIO POMPA

I am going to tell you the sad story
Of a Mexican who emigrated out here—
Aurelio Pompa, so he was called.

Our compatriot who died there,
Out there in Caborca, which is in Sonora,
The humble village where he was born,

"Come on, mother," he said one day,
"Over there there are no revolutions.

Goodbye, friends; goodbye, María,"
He said to his betrothed very sadly.
"I promise you that I will return soon,
So we can get married, God willing."

"Goodbye, Aurelio," said the girl,
And she went sobbing to pray.
"Look after him, Virgin Mary,
I have a foreboding he will not come back."

The priest and his friends
Along with his sweetheart went to talk

a suplicarle al pobre Aurelio	And to beg poor Aurelio
que no dejara el pueblo natal.	Not to leave his native village.
Fueron inútiles tantos consejos	Such advice was useless
también los ruegos de su mamá	And so were the entreaties of his mother.
vámonos, madre, que allá está el *dollar*	"Let's go, mother, over there is the dollar,
y mucho, juro, que he de ganar.	And I swear I am going to earn a lot of them."
El mes de mayo de hace cuatro años	Four years ago in the month of May
a California fueron los dos	The two of them went to California
y por desgracia en la misma fecha	And through misfortune on the very same date
en una cárcel allá murió	Died there in prison.
Un carpintero que era muy fuerte,	A carpenter who was very strong
al pobre joven muy cruel golpeó,	Struck the poor young fellow cruelly,
y Aurelio Pompa juró vengarse	And Aurelio Pompa swore to be revenged
de aquellos golpes que recibió.	For those blows he had received.
Lleno de rabia contó a la madre	Filled with rage he told his mother about it
y la pobre anciana le aconsejó	And the poor old woman advised him,
"por Dios, olvida, hijo querido,"	"*Por Dios*, forget it, dear son."
y el buen Aurelio le perdonó;	And good Aurelio forgave him;
pero una tarde, que trabajaba,	But one afternoon, when he was working
con tres amigos en la estación	With three friends at the railroad station
el carpintero pasó burlando	The carpenter came by mocking at him

y al pobre Pompa le provocó,
los tres amigos le aconsejaban
que lo dejara y fuera con Dios

y el carpintero, con un martillo

muy injurioso lo amenazó,

entonces Pompa, viendo el peligro,
en su defensa le disparó
con un revólver y cara a cara,

como los hombres él lo mató.
Vino la causa, llegó el jurado.

y el pueblo Yanqui lo sentenció.

"Pena de muerte" pidieron todos,
y el abogado no protestó.
Veinte mil firmas de compatriotas
perdón pidieron al gobernador

toda la prensa también pedía

y hasta un mensaje mandó Obregón.
Todo fué inútil, las sociedades,
todas unidas pedían perdón.
La pobre madre, ya casi muerta,
también fué a ver al gobernador

And aroused poor Pompa.
The three friends advised him
To leave him alone and go his way,

And then the carpenter, with a hammer,

Very offensively threatened him.

Then Pompa, seeing the danger,
Fired in self-defense
With a revolver and face to face

As a man he killed him.
The case came to court, the jury arrived,

And the Yankee people sentenced him.

"The death penalty," they all demanded,
And the lawyer did not object.
Twenty thousand signatures of compatriots
Asked for his pardon from the Governor.

All the newspapers asked for it too,

And even Obregon sent a message.
All was useless; the societies,
All united, asked his pardon.
His poor mother, half-dead already,
Also went to see the Governor.

"Adios, amigos, adios, mi pueb-
    lo,
Querida madre, no llores más,
dice a mi raza que ya no venga
que aquí se sufre que no hay
    piedad."
El carcelero le preguntaba;
español eres? y el contestó

"soy mexicano y orgullo serlo

aunque me nieguen a mi el per-
    dón."
Esta es la historia de un com-
    patriota
que hace cuatro años allí llegó
y por desgracia en la misma
    fecha
en una cárcel muy mal murió.

Los Angeles, Calif.

"Farewell, my friends, farewell,
    my village;
Dear mother, cry no more.
Tell my race not to come here,
For here they will suffer; there
    is no pity here.
The jailor asked him:
"Were you Spanish?" and he
    answered,
"I am a Mexican and proud of
    being so
Although they deny me a par-
    don."
This is the story of a compa-
    triot
Who four years ago came there
And through misfortune on the
    same date
Died in a dreadful way in a
    prison.

Los Angeles, Calif.

CHAPTER VIII

RELIGION

From the point of view of religion and ethics there are in Mexico two social groups: First, that composed of persons who find themselves in accord with fundamental and universal ethical principles, and who do not need, or do not think they need, the moralizing influence of religion. This group is made up of an extremely small number of individuals, most of whom belong to the most cultured middle classes. Second, the group composed of those that possess varied special and characteristic religious concepts that they believe to be, or which in reality are, the motives of their ethical behavior. This group embraces almost all the population of Mexico.

This chapter considers various aspects of the religious ideas of the second group.

The pre-Columbian religions.—It is well known that the peoples that lived in Mexico in prehispanic days professed a great variety of religious conceptions, from the most rudimentary, such as the fetishism and animism of the savage tribes in the mountainous regions, to the most advanced systems, as in the case of the Aztecs and pre-Aztec tribes, who, it appears, came to believe in an impalpable supreme God called Tloque Nahuaque. Material objects, the stars, meteorological phenomena, plants and animals, the protecting spirits, heroes and leaders, gave origin to greater and lesser gods, adverse and favorable, visible or occult. The arrival of the Spaniards, and the Catholic religion, brought about a mixture of a large part of this polytheism with Catholicism to form a "mixed religion" or pagan-Catholic religion, of which we shall speak later. Nevertheless, as not all the indigenous groups of what was then

New Spain were conquered, many of them penetrating the mountain fastnesses or the virgin forests of the Tropics, it came about that a large section of the native population was uninfluenced by the religion and customs of the Spaniards. The missionaries, who were usually preceded by the conquerors, brought about during the colonial period either through skilful artifices or kindness the slow assimilation of some of these tribes into the Spanish colonies, with the result that the autochthonous and Catholic religions were found there.

The indigenous tribes that up to the present time preserve their autochthonous religions (such as the Lacandones, Seris, Mayas of Quintana Roo, etc.) offer great resistance to true incorporation into the Catholic church, even though they maintain relations with tribes subject to the government and to that church. We do not know the number of such Indians in existence, as no census has ever been taken of them. Their religion, as we have already said, is derived directly from various prehispanic local cultures, but for several reasons it has degenerated considerably. One of these reasons is the hostile pressure of civilized neighboring groups, which causes them to conceal and so to repress their religious ceremonies.

The Catholic mixed religion.—The pompous ritual of the Catholic church, its numerous images painted and carved, the tithes and tributes it imposed, the sacrifice of human beings that it effected through the Inquisition—all these characteristics made it more or less acceptable to the Indian, as the resemblance in rites, images, tributes, and sacrifices facilitates amalgamation of the Catholic and indigenous religions. The Spanish priests and laymen on their part did everything possible to accelerate that religious fusion. As examples we might cite the substitution of the cult of the Virgin of Guadalupe in place of the worship before given to the Aztec goddess Tonantzin on the same hill of Tepeyac; the dances "Moors and Christians," "Huehuenches," and others, that are nothing but a fusion of pagan dances and Spanish-Moorish dances then much in vogue in the peninsula and still danced in many sections of Spain. In Michoacan the mass of three priests developed into a comic folk dance, in which the natives wear the same embroidered ritual robes that the priests use.

To appreciate the general character of the mixed religion it is necessary only to witness some of the Christian-pagan ceremonies held during religious festivities, not only in villages and ranches, but in the vicinity of the capital, such as in the collegiate church of Guadalupe, or in the churches of Tacuba and Los Remedios.

The Indians of the mixed religion confirm their children, are married, and die in the bosom of the Catholic church. At the same time many ceremonies that are of great importance in their lives present distinct pagan tendencies. Thus, in parts of Mexico, when the cornfields begin to germinate and the tender stems are sprouting, the Indians hold it indispensable that some old Indian, guardian of mysterious charms, preserve the plantation from harmful animals, particularly from the deer that on silent moonlight nights come down from the hills. I have witnessed in the state of Veracruz a curious ritual. The devout Indian, true priest of his race, chants in Aztec tongue, in accents melancholy and devout, imploring the God of Deer not to bring his children, the deer of the forests, to graze in this consecrated *milpa*, or cornfield. Then under a large tree that shuts off the moonlight they burn on red embers sacrificed birds, scrapings of horns and hoofs of deer, strips of paper, and amber-like grains of copal, which the brown hand of the medicine-man throws on the fire, surrounding himself with clouds of white smoke. This basically is nothing else than the ancient prayer to the god of hunting—"the Heart of the Mountain" as he was called by the Aztecs.

We must also take into account the moral standards of the priests that mold the mentality of those pagan-Catholics. There are Catholic priests who truly comfort and aid with sincere Christian charity these unhappy beings that vegetate hopelessly and for whom the Christian faith is a mitigant that tempers their bitterness, and a beautiful mirage for the unknown future. Such priests, generally Indians or *mestizos*, are worthy of respect and consideration, for they not only contribute to the redemption of the Mexican masses from a moral point of view, but also from the educational and economic points of view. Unfortunately, their number is small, while there are many more so-called ministers of God, generally foreigners or *mestizos* and white Mexicans, that pervert the religion they should ennoble, exploit the populace like usurers, and dishonor with hypocrisy the poor people that form their parishes. These contemptible men have numerous offspring, and as matrimony is to them prohibited, it is easy to understand the stigma to which their descendants are fatally condemned. Baptism, matrimony, death, and the other sacraments that the parishioners consider indispensable must be paid for at prices which are excessive, considering their scanty resources. The threat of hell, lack of knowledge concerning the absolution of sins, and other similar measures are sufficient to convince the negligent. In addition these priests maintain constant opposition to the government and any liberal institutions established, making use of the pulpit and the confessional for their attacks.[1]

[1] As evidence that these statements are made in a spirit of absolute justice and equanimity, I cite a significant fact. When copies of the book *The Population of the Valley of Teotihuacan*—that contains among others the results of the investigation of the regional religious problems in their favorable as well as harmful aspects—were presented to the archbishop of Mexico and the Colombian prelate, Lopez y Llera, they wrote us letters in which they rejoiced that these investigations had been made, and encouraged us to continue them in the future. A copy presented to the parish priest of one of the principal towns in the valley, Señor José R. Alvarez, also evoked warm congratulations for the work done.

The Indians of autochthonous and Catholic mixed religions are now and will continue to be a field of contention between secular, governmental educators and representatives of the Catholic and Protestant churches. This conflict is beneficial, as it brings about competition between the three forces of enlightenment. It will be necessary, naturally, to respect the cultural characteristics of the Indians, their method of dress, habitations, legends, traditions, and language. The Catholic clergy should free the nation of the Catholic mixed religion and of the priests that today exploit and dishonor it. The Protestant clergy should make its influence felt in this section of the population so that by means of reasonable competition these evil Catholic elements will be corrected and eradicated.

The Catholic religion.—Mexican Catholicism is essentially the same as Roman Catholicism, but it presents differences in form imposed by historic causes. The peculiar conditions of the country and the characteristics of that part of the population that profess this religion—largely foreigners of Spanish origin and a small number of natives and *mestizos* that were able to break away from the mixed religion already described—have also effected certain changes.

The Catholic church during colonial times brought politics, riches, and art into its power. From the omnipotent archbishop-viceroy, who in one hand wielded the sword of the conqueror and with the other let loose the lighting of anathemas and excommunications, to the lowest parish priest, all were fighting for the growth of the church in its multiple aspects and tendencies. The religious orders, with tens of thousands of representatives, while they took part with nobles and courtiers of colonial political life, at the same time climbed the most distant mountains and penetrated the miasmic forests of the Tropics in search of souls that would augment the Catholic fold.

The energy that so powerful an institution spent in the accumulation of riches and power caused it to neglect what should have been its principal aim: to alleviate with Christian charity the material misery of the faithful and secure their spiritual welfare. The coming of independence little changed this situation, and, to a certain extent, brought advantages to the church. The reform laws, after many bloody battles, broke up the foundations of that gigantic structure.

The government of General Diaz was a retrogression from the victories achieved by Juarez and the reformers, as it permitted the church, under cover of law, to secure once more its old prerogative. Indirectly, through faithful representatives, the clergy once again became rich, and the numerous convents and monasteries multiplied rapidly throughout the republic, tolerated by the government.

Why is it that the Catholic clergy in Mexico has been an obstacle to progress, to the extent that many governments have found it necessary to restrict religious liberties? Why is it that in other countries, as, for example, in the United States, Catholicism freely grows and flourishes, and enjoys the respect of the state—and even that of churches of other creeds? The answer is not hard to find, and is based on what we have said: The Mexican clergy has usually fought for riches and power, holding only secondary its evangelical duties, whereas the American clergy has not meddled in dangerous politics, nor exploited the people, devoting itself to satisfying their spiritual necessities. This does not mean, naturally, that we consider all of the Mexican clergy as bad and all of the American clergy as good; there exist very honorable exceptions in the former case and reprehensible exceptions in the latter.

Those who, in Mexico, adhere to the Catholic faith in its more or less Roman form may be considered in two large groups: "Conscientious Catholics" and "Utilitarian Catholics." The former accept without reserve the Christian precepts of their religion, and they and their families and the clergy that they produce are truly moral forces. The latter, on the other hand, are highly noxious, as under the mask of Christianity they violate the precepts of Christianity and seek only riches and power. Everything that from them emanates menaces society, the government, and the church. These Pharisees should be fought by the conscientious Catholics in order to dignify their church—by society, by the state, and finally by the clergy of other creeds.

The Protestant religion.—Protestantism in Mexico flourishes principally among the middle classes. A majority of mixed race and a minority of white and Indians constitute the Protestant flock. This distribution is easily explained, as the Indian, because of his pagan dependence upon images and the irresistible pressure of four centuries of Catholicism imposed by the crucifix or the sword, will abandon only gradually the mixed religion already described. Those of white race, especially the well-to-do, do not adhere to Protestantism because of the traditional conservatism of their class, and because of the fact that their stock is Spanish, and therefore eminently Catholic. The middle classes, who have little of the conservative Spanish traditions, and who are too intelligent to accept the neo-paganism of the Indians, easily receive the Protestant creed, finding it simple, devoid of image cults, and demanding little pecuniary contributions.

Aside from the zeal with which the Protestant clergy has employed in swelling the number of its adherents in Mexico, another very important reason for their success is the large sums invested in missionary work. It is natural that, if the Protestant pastors aid the people materially, particularly the children, giving them food, shelter, clothing, and education, while the Catholic priests solicit from their parishioners aims and contributions, the Protestant work should bring proportionately better results than that of the Catholics.

One defect of Protestant propaganda is that frequently it is not limited merely to evangelization, but also seeks foreignization. That is, it tends to mold the mentality of the converts to alien northern patterns. This is undesirable. But fortunately those Mexicans of sane nationalist ideas who find in the Protestant activities foreign tendencies will probably reject Protestantism; or, if their consciences are elastic, will endeavor to accept the material advantages offered by the Protestants without accepting either the Protestant creed or the foreign tendencies.

Catholicism in the zones of emigration.—The nature and intensity of the religious spirit, or, rather, of the Catholicism of the inhabitants, has a characteristic geographic distribution. Perhaps it is because the pleasant climate and economic resources of certain regions made possible a greater number of churches, convents, and monasteries sometimes out of proportion to the number of inhabitants; but certainly it is a fact that it is precisely in the geographic zones that contribute most largely to immigration that Catholicism is more deep rooted and intense.

Jalisco, Michoacan, Guanajuato, and other regions in the central plateau are these zones. For this reason, Protestant missionaries have made less headway in the central plateau than in the north, with the exception of Mexico City, which is a peculiar and isolated case.

In the northern *mesa* and in Sonora, Lower California, and Tamaulipas, which contribute less to immigration, Catholicism has a general hold but it has not the fanatic character it exhibits in the central plateau. This might be explained partly by the proximity of the United States, which makes easier the work of Protestant missionaries. The coasts and escarpments, which contribute practically no immigrants at all, are regions in which Catholicism is least strong; popular attitude toward it almost reaches indifference, while native superstition and belief have an important place in the daily life of the inhabitants. This is probably to be explained by the fact that the extreme tropical climate, the malaria, fevers, and the poisonous insects of such places, have kept away both Catholic and Protestant missionaries. The small number of Catholic churches and convents in these regions confirms this fact. The recent religious conflict marked even more clearly the geographic division of religious spirit; what rebellion there was occurred almost entirely in Jalisco, Michoacan, and Guanajuato, in a few other places on the central plateau, and in scattered points in the north; but in the Tropics there was scarcely an echo.

Religion of the immigrant in the United States.—The change in religion undergone by the immigrant of intensely Catholic and even fanatic type is an interesting phenomena. It is certain that the burden of fanaticism which the immigrant carries from Mexico little by little slips away and often leaves him entirely. There are several reasons for this rapid change. In the first place he benefits economically because he no longer has to pay tithes or first fruit taxes, or any other of the many small contributions required of him in different forms by the church in Mexico.[1] This liberation does not bring the enmity of the priest nor the reproach of the community, which would be the case were he to do the same in Mexico.

[1] But in New Mexico, where there is a large population of Mexican-Americans long established in the country, there is greater tendency to remain faithful to the tenets and obligations of the church. The following paragraph is in the words of a New Mexican Catholic priest.

"Altho there is intense competition between religious sects, the majority of the inhabitants, especially in the small towns, are Catholic and keep up the religious customs of Old Mexico such as paying the priest a *peso* for every mass which they ask to be said, and bringing him offerings of eggs, bread, fruit, and candies. In some parts of the country Mexican-Americans, Mexicans, and American In-

Later the Protestant propaganda brings to his attention the weak points of the Catholic church. Furthermore, accustomed to respond to the highly vivid, colorful, pagan Catholicism of the small towns and rural districts in Mexico, American Catholicism seems to him almost colorless and standardized, and awakens in him no emotional response. One of three things happens: He becomes a normal, non-fanatic Catholic; indifferent or an unbeliever; or a Protestant.

The validity of this conversion to Protestantism appears to us in some cases doubtful. The Mexican immigrant may become a Protestant because he has been helped in some material way by Protestant organizations—almost out of gratitude, therefore. Or else, disillusioned as to the moral character of the Catholic priesthood, he expects to find in the Protestant clergy pure, moral, unselfish men. However, disillusioned in turn on this point—since especially in Texas and California public scandal has taken much prestige from the Protestant clergy—and also, unable to respond to the cold, intellectual, moralistic quality of Protestantism, and lack of color and artistic expression, his adherence to this religion is in some cases temporary, or if permanent, merely conventional.[1]

It is clear, however, that a large part of the Mexican immi-

---

dians act in harmony and with complete propriety in their attendance at church services, and at some *fiestas* they have picturesque processions in the plazas of the towns. The *fiestas* of St. Peter, St. Paul, St. John, and some others are unfortunately more times for merry-making for the faithful rather than occasions for religious ceremonials."

[1] As a curious example of the Catholic-Protestant conflict within the immigrant mass, we mention the fact that a version of the national Mexican hymn which circulated along the border when the religious conflict began in Mexico, in which the church is praised and its true sons are told to defend it. Shortly after it appeared another version, written by a Mexican Protestant minister who lives in the United States, went out in answer to the first version; in it the Catholic church is bitterly attacked.

grants abandon Catholicism. To this fact might be attributed the hostility of the American Catholic clergy toward the immigration. Such hostility is said by some to be the result of the recent political conflict in Mexico, but this seems hardly plausible, as obviously the immigrants had nothing to do with this conflict. That there is hostility, however, clearly appears from public statements of Catholic clergy.[1] The attitude of a Catho-

---

[1] "HANNA HITS FREE ENTRY OF MEXICANS.—Most Rev. Edward J. Hanna, Archbishop of San Francisco, President of the Commission on Immigration and Housing in California, has written a letter to the California delegation in Congress against unrestricted immigration from Mexico.

"Proposals are pending in the Senate and House Committee on Immigration to eliminate the head-tax and visa fee on Mexican immigrants for the purpose of bringing them to California to do seasonal labor.

GIVES REASONS

"Archbishop Hanna sets forth the following seven reasons why immigration should not be further encouraged:

"1. They drain our charities.
"2. They and their children become a large portion of our jail population.
"3. They affect the health of our community.
"4. They create a problem in our labor camps.
"5. They require special attention in our schools and are of low mentality.
"6. They diminish the percentage of our white population.
"7. They remain foreign.

GIVES FIGURES

"The San Francisco archbishop drew on statistics from all over California to show the extraordinarily large percentage of Mexicans benefited by charity organizations. In Los Angeles, where 7% of the population is Mexican, he said that 28% of all charity cases were Mexicans. 'The Bureau of Catholic charities in Los Angeles,' he continued, 'devotes more than 50% of its benefits to Mexican cases. One-fourth of the general hospital budget in Los Angeles is devoted to Mexican cases. The City Maternity Hospital devotes 73% of its budget to Mexican cases.'

"At a hearing held by the House Committee, California beet, sugar and cotton industry witnesses testified that they need Mexican labor in harvesting their crops and they asked that the expensive head-tax and visa fee be omitted. These interests also opposed the Box bill, which would put Mexican and Canadian immigration on a quota basis."—*San Francisco Chronicle.*

lic priest in a Mexican immigrant community and the reaction
of a Mexican member of that community are given in the following news story and accompany letter.

FATHER JOHN B. DE VILLE AGAINST
MEXICAN IMMIGRATION[1]

Laying aside his priestly authority and speaking straight from the
shoulder "as an American citizen," Father John B. de Ville, superintendent of the Gary-Alerding Settlement House, yesterday told Gary Rotarians a number of things that made them sit up and take notice.

Here are some of the high lights in his frank discourse upon many
subjects:

"Divorce has become a sort of progressive polygamy."

"Parents have abdicated their authority."

"Lack of children is a ghost that cannot be laid."

"It is dawning upon the people of the United States that prohibition
is a failure."

"We have shut out European immigrants and have accepted the uncivilized Mexican in his place."

"There are 560 organized communists in Gary and they consist almost wholly of Mexicans and Russians."

"You can americanize the man from the southeastern and southern
Europe, but can't americanize a Mexican."

"I stand with the Administration in its policy of protecting American
interests in Mexico, but I have no sympathy with the so-called religious
conflict in that country."

"I am not in sympathy with those who would intervene in Mexico to
protect Catholics. If the Catholic Church is good enough and influential
enough to govern Mexico it's all right, but if the Church is not good
enough and able enough, then it should not control."

Editor Post-Tribune:[2]

I am writing this few lines in answer to the speech you made before
the Rotarians in January 27. In reference to the uncivilized Mexican that
lives in Gary, I do not want to start or establish a controversy with you
for I want to respect you as you hold an honorable position and I as an

[1] *Gary Post-Tribune*, Gary, Ind., January 28, 1928.
[2] *An open letter to Father John B. de Ville.*

uncivilized Mexican it is my place to do so. I only want to comment on your unjust ideas concerning the Mexicans that we never become civilized American citizens.

To my conception the son should not be blamed for the father's failures. You evidently have no knowledge of our past history and that our conquerors had us under their power for 400 years. They just took us out of one idolatry and put us into another in all this length of time. Therefore we are uncivilized yet. Why don't you deny us? (because conscience justify it). The countries that are more behind and uncivilized are those controlled by fanaticism, including our own.

In regard to the title you give us as communist in your brilliant speech, I must say that if we were so undesirable the government of this country would not give us the hospitality and open the gates of this country for us. At the same time the U.S. is broad enough to see that we Mexicans come here to work and co-operate in the upbuilding of this nation.

Rev. Mr. de Ville, you also judge us to be criminals. Criminals exist in all kind of races not only among the Mexicans. No matter how great a nation or how small it is all they have their criminals from those who crucified Jesus Christ to the persons who insult a race.

As in reference to the Americanization, we do not have to become Americans because we are Americans bone and flesh, America is our country and we can not be otherwise. You should not contemplate the cactus by its thorns but by its blossoms. Furthermore you should remember that you have quite a number of Mexicans in your Sociedad de Nuestra Señora de Guadalupe who are liable to get offended. They should be treated equally to the Italian colony.

1309 MADISON ST., GARY, IND.   JOSÉ GALLARDO

These remarks induced the Mexican government to investigate through its consulates whether or not their publication had had a detrimental effect on Mexican immigrants. It did not appear, from the consular reports, that they had.

Not all the Catholic elements in the United States are opposed to Mexican immigration. A considerable number of immigrants receive help from American Catholic authorities when sick or in need. The Catholic Convention assembled in Los Angeles in 1927 warmly defended Mexican immigration from the attacks of those advocating the quota for such immigration.

The following document, written by a Catholic priest, represents this more lively interest of the church in the Mexican immigrants. It suggests that both the church-state conflict in Mexico, and competition with Protestants in the United States, have tended to stimulate the missionary interest of Catholics in the immigrants.

THE MEXICANS IN TEXAS AS SEEN BY A SPANISH CATHOLIC PRIEST

In every Texas small town one can see on one side the cleanliness of the moving pictures houses, the restaurants and the recreation centres, and on the other, beyond the railroad track, the poorer districts filled with filth, where the poor Mexicans live. If these Mexicans would join together to defend their interests they could attain great improvements. In many localities they completely dominate the vote—that is to say, they have a majority—for many of these Mexicans vote in the elections while still preserving their Mexican citizenship. They can elect as Sheriff whomever they wish, but they are often led astray by American politicians.

Orphans, out of touch both with religion and native land, they go wandering about from one place to another, seeking to earn their daily bread. It is in this situation that the missionary comes to them as a veritable blessing from Heaven, since he talks to them both of religion and of their country.

There are great masses of Mexicans thirsting to hear one word that they can understand. They are bursting with love for God and for their country. The tyranny which has enchained the liberty of conscience in Mexico has only succeeded in arousing religious sentiment in the Mexican towns of Texas. Formerly scarcely a man appeared at the missions; now there are more men than women.

In Skidmore, Fort Worth, Orange Grove, Beeville, Petlues, Georgewest, Three Rivers, towns which we visited, we saw that the Mexican congregations love the Catholic religion with a more intense and burning love than ever before.

As a sign of their faith and love for religion, one simple suggestion from a missionary has resulted in the formation in all these towns of the Holy Mexican Union, composed of men, women, and children and organized in order to defend the religious, civic, and social interests of the various groups of Mexicans.

The 12th of last December is a glorious date which will never be forgotten. More than two thousand Mexicans came into the streets with flags, with lighted tapers, with choruses of singers and a band, proclaiming together, under the *aegis* of the Virgin of Guadalupe, the birth of the Holy Union "Knights of Guadalupe." Twelve bonfires illumined this scene gay with the national colors and illumined with the light of faith, culture, and patriotism. Dominating it all was the radiant, pure white face of the Virgin of Guadalupe, mother of the Mexican religion and of the Mexican country.

Several "Protestants" have taken advantage of the absence of Catholic missionaries to disseminate their theories among the Mexicans.

Folk cults in immigrants communities.—In spite of the competition between Catholic and Protestant churches, and in spite of the tendency of the immigrant to lose the Catholicism which characterizes him in Mexico, folk cults survive or form anew even in the urban environment of cities of the United States. The following example illustrates this. A Mexican folk pattern—the pictorial votive offering commemorative of aid rendered by a saint—persists in a North American city outside the sanction of church authorities.

THE CHAPEL OF OUR LORD OF THE MIRACLES

In the intersection of ——— and ——— streets of San Antonio, there is a little chapel called "El Señor de los Milagros." To this chapel come every day many Mexicans, and not a few Americans, seeking cures for illnesses of the body or torments of the soul. With few exceptions they come seriously, filled with faith; many enter upon their knees, crawling to the foot of the Crucifix *El Señor de los Milagros*, that they are seeking. After offering their prayers and asking him for a cure for the ills which trouble them, believers leave alms in accordance with their means in a box inside the chapel. Sometimes they leave flowers, or burn a candle, and then leave sure that what they have asked will be granted to them.

The outside of the building is like that of a dwelling house; a climbing vine covers its walls. Above the little chapel there is a cross with an inscription bearing the date 1813, the year in which the chapel was constructed to shelter the image of *El Señor de los Milagros*. From time to time the little building is renovated as are also the three other images it contains in order that they may always present a new appearance.

The walls of the chapel are to a very large extent covered with *retablos*, pictures, and an immense number of photographs of those people to whom *El Señor de los Milagros* has granted some favor. In these *retablos*, —rude paintings often on boards—, the faithful express in simple sentences their gratitude, and tell the form which the miracle took, and the physical or moral suffering which they endured.

Many, not content with placing the description and their portrait on the *retablo*, paint a picture representing their illness at the moment at which the miracle was granted to them, in this way making clearer their gratitude for the favor done them. Among the *retablos* there are, for instance, some which record the thanks of parents whose sons went off to the Great War and returned unhurt from the field of battle. Generally the parents say that during the time that their son was in the war, they commended him to the care of *El Señor de los Milagros*. Another, for example, tells how some bales of cotton fell on a man but that he was not killed because at the moment of the accident he called upon the Holy Image of *El Señor de los Milagros*. In the *retablo* appears a truck loaded with bales of cotton which have collapsed and fallen on a man. Others tell how after suffering such and such a physical affliction for a long time, the votaries were finally cured because of the intervention of *El Señor de los Milagros*.

Since the *retablos* hung up in the chapel amount to thousands during the year, the woman who owns the chapel finds herself obliged to take down occasionally those that are old. These she puts away in boxes and ultimately destroys them. The money which the faithful leave in the alms-box or on the plate before the altar is removed by this woman, and upon these proceeds, which amount to a considerable income, she lives. Sundays and holidays the amount is greater since the number of people who visit the chapel is increased.

No religious rites are performed in this little chapel since it is private property, and the priests of San Antonio, as is well known, frown upon the cult and have attempted to have the image of *El Señor de los Milagros* conveyed to the Cathedral or to some other Catholic church within that jurisdiction.

The image of *El Señor de los Milagros* is actually the property of Señora X, who inherited it from her father and her grandfather. The latter saved the image from a fire which took place in the Cathedral of San Fernando. This man had to risk his life in the flames to remove this image and since that time it has been known as miraculous. It remained in the possession of its rescuer. A bishop of this city granted permission to the grandparents of Señora X to construct a chapel in order that people might come to pray to the image.

Recently, as has been said, certain Catholic priests have attempted to return the image to the keeping of the Cathedral of San Fernando, but the woman who owns it says she will not give it up and that at her death she will leave it to her favorite daughter or her granddaughter. The lot of land upon which the chapel is built is the property of Señora X and on the same lot there is a small house in which she lives with her family. The chapel remains open from early in the morning until nine at night, and is never empty, since devotees arrive continually not only from San Antonio but also from neighboring towns, to ask miracles and make vows.

The following instance, collected by one of our assistants, shows a folk cult developing apart from the formal symbols and institutions of the church.

EL TIRADITO[1]
("The One Laid Out")

"El Tiradito" is the name of a place situated on Main Street of this city at the south end; everyone knows it. This spot is an empty lot. Around it there are houses in which live Mexicans, for the most part, and a few Negroes. On this lot there is a space about eight metres square, more or less, in which there are many old tin cans, big and small; some hold earth and others are empty. In these cans there burn by day, and even more by night, wax or tallow candles placed there by many people, the great majority of whom are Mexicans, who burn these candles in fullfillment of vows previously made in praying for miracles.

Thousands and thousands of candles have been burned in this spot in a period of more than twenty years, and these candles in melting down have covered the earth with an enormous black layer of candle grease, which, some say, is more than a foot deep.

In the afternoons but especially in the evenings many people come to place here their candles which they leave burning until they go out of themselves.

[1] Tucson, Ariz.

This sacred spot is entirely in the open air; there is no chapel of any sort, nor any sort of roof. People come here freely to burn their candles; some of them make the sign of the cross and perhaps to pray silently, but they do not do so ostentatiously.

The persons whom I have questioned upon the legend of "El Tiradito" add further details of the cult. They declare that Monday is a particularly good day for miracles; at least, those who come to burn candles here believe so. For this reason on Mondays one can see a great number of candles and of people in the neighborhood. However, no one has been able to give me a reason why Monday has been the day selected to burn candles; believers come every evening to burn their candles, but Monday night is preferred.

Another detail is that people generally offer "six *reals*" [seventy-five cents] worth of candles. Why they have selected this particular amount is not known. The great majority of the people who seek for a miracle from "El Tiradito" offer in anticipation to burn "six *reals* worth of candles." Others offer more or less but the number considered ritually correct is six *reals* worth.

Most of the people with whom I talked concerning "El Tiradito" are Catholics and believe that "El Tiradito" is a spirit of a good man who suffered much in this world and for this reason is permitted to make miracles. There are people who have masses and other religious offices performed in his honor in the Catholic churches, and it seems that the priests support the worship of "El Tiradito." Others do not know the history of the place but know that it is miraculous and come here for their prayers and petitions.

Some of the explanations given for this curious shrine follow:

1. It happened one time that a famous criminal escaped from the penitentiary and the search party in pursuit came here where there at that time was a wood. The sheriffs soon met within the wood a man whom they believed to be the fugitive, and they fired at him and killed him in this spot although, as it turned out afterwards, the dead man was innocent.

2. A long time ago there lived in Tucson a man who was a woodcutter and had a little horse. The profligate son of this man wanted to sell the animal, come what might, in order to continue on his career of vice, but when his father opposed selling the horse, then his own son stabbed him to death.

3. El Tiradito was a man from Hermosillo who killed his wife and

then fled to Tucson. One of the sons of the woman swore vengeance, and when he grew up came to Tucson, sought out El Tiradito, by trickery got him to leave the place where he was working, and then stabbed him to death in the very place where now they pray to him.

4. Ramón Arbizo or Armigo of Hermosillo or Guaymas, the state of Soñora, Mexico, left his pregnant wife in one of these cities and came to Tucson. Arbizo had two stepsons. His wife gave birth to a child and died. Then one of her sons, enraged at what had happened, came to Tucson and sought out Arbizo. For many days they drank together in saloons until one day the boy stabbed him. And the place where he was laid out is to-day called "El Tiradito." And from that time on they began to say that he could perform miracles, and began to pray to him and built up the cult about him in the way that has been described. It appears that "El Tiradi-to" was a carter and traveled between Tucson and California transporting various sorts of goods.

In the spot where "El Tiradito" died a cross was placed, but this has already disappeared. However, since prayers have always been offered and candles burned here to him, the place has continued to be well known.

It is known that the owner of the lot of land on which "El Tiradito" is situated has conveyed it to the city in order that it may never be sold and may be always there for the practice of the cult. A few, so they say, tried to buy this lot and to build on it a chapel in order to exploit the legend as a business.

Some time ago they said that "El Tiradito" came out at midnight but other people living near the place say that they have never seen him or heard any noise.

They say that "El Tiradito" has great miraculous powers and that almost everything that is asked of him is granted, if the suppliant has faith.

They say that there are people who have come from California and even from Chicago especially to pray to "El Tiradito," and to make good their promises; there are people who have burned a whole box of candles to "El Tiradito."

"Mexicans, Mexican-Americans, Indians, Americans, Negroes, and those of every nationality come to 'El Tiradito' with their requests," a lady told us. "Chinese are the only people that I have never seen come to put down candles."

Another lady said that without any doubt "El Tiradito" was a man who suffered a great deal alive; at his death his spirit remained floating about in order to do good to all those who are suffering in the land and it is for this reason he is believed in.

One of the people who gave us the most information is a *curandera* [practitioner of folk medicine], generally known as "Doña Chonita." She says that down in Hermosillo, Sonora, a similar thing took place. She herself saw that over the spot where the dead Cienfuego had been killed, people did not want to drive cattle or carriages, and they closed it off, until the Government had to have put up here a kind of cenotaph, so that those who wished to pray there might do so.

The story is also told that on the spot where "El Tiradito" fell, a great many years ago, there was found a woman cohabiting with a dog, and a group of Mexicans, enraged at this degeneration, lynched her and the dog by hanging them to a tree.

It is said that the place in which "El Tiradito" is located and where the lynchings mentioned above occurred is called *El Ojito* ["The Little Eye"] because there is here a little *ojo de agua* ("eye of water") or spring.

CHAPTER IX

IMMIGRANT ATTITUDES AND IMMIGRANT INSTITUTIONS

Nationalism.—It has more than once been remarked that many inhabitants of rural districts in Mexico have little notion of their nationality or their country. They know their town and the region in which it is situated, and this is a "little country" for them. It is a notable fact that people of this type, when they become immigrants in the United States, learn immediately what their mother-country means, and they always think of it and speak of it with love. Indeed, it can be said that there is hardly an immigrant home in the United States where the Mexican flag is not found in a place of honor, as well as pictures of national Mexican heroes. Love of country sometimes goes so far that very often altars are made for saints and flag or hero, or both, giving patriotism thus an almost religious quality.

The original patriotism of the immigrant varies with different racial types. For several reasons, the white immigrant becomes American relatively quickly. First of all, there is no racial prejudice to keep him from intermarriage with Americans; and, in the second place, he is more often able to reach a position of economic parity with native-born Americans.

Generally, after the Mexican immigrant is nationalized the racial and other prejudice against him continues, and his social and economic conditions are scarcely changed. In Texas, California, and Arizona, the Mexican immigrant and the American of Mexican origin are more or less at a disadvantage beside the white American, who, consciously or unconsciously, classes them both as Mexicans and considers them more or less the same. From this situation two principal results follow: (1) The number of immigrants who become citizens of the United States is very small.[1] (2) The Mexican who becomes an American citizen does not think of this citizenship as does a native white American. With him it is regarded as a patriotism attached to the local Mexican-American culture such as prevails in many communities in the Southwest.

The attitude of the Mexicans who are American citizens toward the immigrants is a curious one. Sometimes they speak slightingly of the immigrants (possibly because the immigrants are their competitors in wages and jobs), and say that the immigrants should stay in Mexico. (The American-Mexicans consider Mexico a disorderly and rebellious country and native Mexicans as combative and aggressive.) Furthermore, they are displeased, possibly because of racial pride, at the miserable condition in which most of the immigrants arrive. They call these recent immigrants *cholos* or *chicamos*. The immigrant, on his part, considers the American of Mexican origin as a man without a country. He reminds him frequently of the inferior position to which he is relegated by the white American. He criticizes, as well, certain details of American material culture, above all the "Americanized" Mexican women who dress like Americans and have the customs and habits of American women. The American of Mexican origin is known as a *pocho*.

The American of Mexican race is really, so far as nationality is concerned, in a difficult and unfortunate position. Such a person, when he goes to Mexico, wearing American clothes

[1] The census for 1910 reported 102,009 Mexicans in the United States, of whom 10,932, or 10.77 per cent, had been naturalized; that of 1920 reported 478,383, of whom 22, 737, or 4.8 per cent, had been naturalized. The report of the Commission of Naturalization showed that during the year 1923–24, 92 Mexicans were naturalized; these constituted only 0.06 per cent of all immigrants naturalized that year. For the year 1924–25 the number was 101, or 0.07 per cent.

and speaking Spanish with a foreign accent, calls himself a Mexican because he is accustomed to being called a Mexican in the United States. Nevertheless, Mexicans in Mexico, knowing nothing of this, become indignant at the idea of such a person being a Mexican, while, on the other hand, Americans find it strange that he call himself an American, since in the United States he is always a Mexican or a Spanish-American.

Notwithstanding these differences in point of view between the Mexican immigrants and the Mexican-Americans—differences which in reality are of a purely superficial and formal nature—both groups consider themselves as together composing that body called by them "The Race"; both are called Mexicans by white Americans; they live together in the same districts; they belong to the same social stratum; they talk the same language; they wear the same clothes and possess the same needs and ideals; and, most significant of all, they frequently intermarry.

In New Mexico the Americans of Mexican origin are a case apart. The great majority are descendants of the first Spanish or indigenous colonists of the state; they have been American citizens for three quarters of a century, and yet they still have marked Mexican characteristics. They have been and probably still are the numerical majority in the state, and, for this reason, in spite of the racial prejudice against them, they have been able to achieve and maintain a position economically, culturally, and socially better than that of their brothers in the other states. They have even managed to hold political positions of some importance, a rather extraordinary case of this being that of Octaviano Larrazolo, a Mexican who came to the United States as a child, and who became governor of New Mexico—a thing that has never happened in any of the other states where there are many Mexican-Americans. This group has been isolated, as much because of its own characteristic aloofness as because the whites, officially and personally, draw apart from it. Naturally this isolation produced cultural and economic inferiority, which fact helps to explain in great part the general backwardness and poverty of this state, in comparison with others of the American union.

Lately there has been an influx from the East and Midwest to New Mexico, and this has helped it, as has also its position in the line of traffic between the eastern states, and western and southern California. The capital of this state and other cities, because of the climate, have become gigantic sanatoria for tubercular patients.

Politically, the racial division of the population of New Mexico is very marked. The majority of the Americans of Mexican origin, or Spanish-Americans, or simply Mexicans, are Republicans, while a minority, and all the whites, are Democrats. Owing to this division within the Mexican elements, the Democratic party controls, as a rule, for whites make a point of voting this ticket, though elsewhere they might have been by tradition and conviction Republicans. Mexicans seldom hold office, and rarely any office of importance. In many regions, they say, their needs are disregarded by the local government. Indeed, so bitter did the conflict become at one time that the Democratic party proposed legislation by means of which people who could not read, and those who could not speak English, would be disenfran‐hised. This would have affected forty thousand citizens of the state. In some local communities, in some parts of the state, Mexicans control the governments, though this is always where the population is entirely Mexican. In other regions (they say) they suffer indifferences, neglect, even political abuse. Their welfare in such cases is not taken seriously by public opinion, not even by Mexicans in other parts of the state where the political attitude may be less offensive.

Briefly, taking into account all that has been said in earlier chapters upon this point, one comes to the conclusion that in the United States the Mexican-American population or American population of Mexican descent, the source of origin of which has been and still is the Mexican immigration, does not constitute a different nation from the American but rather an isolated subnationality which has been clearly defined and integrated through historical, traditional, ethnic, social, economic, cultural, psychological, and linguistic factors.

Social organizations.—It is characteristic of the Mexican in his own country, especially in the small towns and rural regions, that he neither shows much individual enterprise nor readily forms co-operative organizations with his fellows for their mutual benefit. In this respect the immigrant in the United States changes radically. His social interests are aroused and develop markedly; the great number of Mexican societies in the United States are a witness to this.

These organizations are of all kinds; mutual welfare and relief, Masonic, purely social, literary, religious, or artistic. Of first importance are the four great organizations which are split up into hundreds of ancillary or local branches located in a great number of American towns in which there are Mexicans or Mexican-Americans: "The Honorary Commissions" (*Comisiónes Honoríficas*), "The Blue Cross" (*La Cruz Azul*), "The Spanish-American Alliance" (*La Alianza Hispano-Americano*), and "The Woodmen of the World" (*Los Leñadores del Mundo*).

The Honorary Commissions.—Almost everywhere where there is a group of Mexicans, no matter how humble, there is an "Honorary Commission" composed of the most respected members of the group. The object is mutual aid and protection. The Mexican consuls are generally honorary presidents of these commissions and collaborate with them in behalf of the welfare of the resident and immigrant Mexicans.

The Blue Cross.—This welfare organization was established for the same purposes and with the same sort of internal organization. It was once as widespread as the society just described, but recently its activities have decreased through causes which it is unnecessary to discuss here.

The Spanish-American Alliance.—The Spanish-American Alliance was founded by the Mexicans of Tucson, according to the information we have received. It is an association composed for the most part of immigrated Mexicans, but also to some extent of Mexican-Americans, Americans, and Latin-Americans in general. This society is semi-Masonic; the branches are called "lodges" and the governing center the "founder lodge," or the "supreme lodge." There are many "lodges" all over the South, and also in Chicago and in Mexico City. The laws or "rites" are concealed from all but members, according to the rank which they have attained. The organization also has some of the features of a mutual insurance society.

The "founder lodge," or central lodge, was founded in the last years of the nineteenth century; its aims were very clearly political since its object was to get control in the locality where all the men in power were native Texans. Most of the founders were Tucson Mexicans of Indian blood, but as some were of Spanish origin, in order to wound the sensibilities of no one they took the name "The Spanish-American Alliance," which includes all the native elements all over America. After this organization had attained more or less success in its political aims, it was changed into a mutual aid and fraternal society. In this guise it has attained strength and prestige and was recognized as a member in the "Union of Societies" in the United States.

The lodges are independent and have their own internal regulations, but all recognize the common constitution, which is subject to change in the annual congresses to which the lodges send delegates. This society has a weekly magazine printed in Spanish and published in Nogales, Arizona.

The Woodmen of the World.—The organizations of this name are composed of Mexicans and Mexican-Americans. They are derived or affiliated with the great American society of the same name, so that their constitution and activities are substantially alike.

The influence of the American Federation of Labor.—There has been an attempt to form associations devoted exclusively to labor problems among the Mexicans, and we believe one such was established in Los Angeles as a part of the American Federation of Labor. However, up to the present time the results have been of little importance. This may be easily explained since, if American labor organizations meet with difficulties in their development in the United States, one can imagine the obstacles interposed to the labor activities of a social group which, like the Mexican, occupies a position of inferior status and lives isolated from other groups, a victim of the prejudices and an object of more or less hostility from the side of the American laborers themselves who naturally do not enjoy the competition of Mexican labor. As for the employers, it is evident that they sometimes take a part in disorganizing, and destroying the attempts toward organization, of the Mexican laborers.

In chapter iii we referred to this hostility. Nevertheless, it must be recognized that although the American Federation of Labor includes very few Mexicans, the influence which through these few individuals has been exerted upon the organization of labor in Mexico is very important, as will be seen further on. On the other hand, the Mexican-American as an American citizen meets with no difficulties in his attempt to enter the American Federation of Labor, and since he and the Mexican live in intimate contact and almost all their other activities are identical, the Mexican is, as a result, inevitably influenced by these labor affiliations.

Influence of the Industrial Workers of the World.—The Mexican laborers have no difficulty whatsoever in entering this organization. The general opinion is that many of them are members. Actually the number of members who have really joined appears to be very slight, and their effect upon the entire immigrant group unimportant. In fact, when many of them do join, they afterward find themselves forced to resign. Instead of improving their situation thereby they usually injure it, since their affiliation arouses the hostility of both the employers and the American Federation of Labor. If the situation of radical Americans is difficult, that of Mexicans in the same position becomes so intolerable that soon they have to abandon the Industrial Workers of the World, conceal their affiliation, and become entirely inactive.

Other societies.—Besides these organizations and their branches, there are in the United States a great number of societies in every community containing Mexicans or Mexican-Americans. In the Appendixes we include a list of some of these as well as of the parts of the country in which they were located (at the time of this investigation), with the addition in some cases of the names of their presidents and their street addresses. Without fear of being mistaken, we may make the statement that there are many more organizations among the Mexican and Mexican-American population in the United States than in the republic of Mexico. Such a well-developed spirit of sociability, fraternalism, and mutual aid undoubtedly contributes much to the well-being and progress of the immigrants. Indirectly its beneficent influence, transmitted to Mexico through the repatriated immigrants, is of great importance there. It helps to modify the isolation of individuals in the country and small towns; it awakes the desire for social co-operation; it disciplines the character and the labor of the workman; and, in general, it stimulates many useful activities. An example of this is afforded by the labor organization in the capital of the republic and some industrial centers of the Mexican states. Although certain of their activities have been unnecessary and even prejudicial to labor itself, thanks to this organization the workingman becomes better disciplined, develops initiative, greater competence, and better moral character.

Press.—The development of a local press is another phenomenon, similar in many respects to the growth of clubs and societies, which characterizes the immigrant communities. Considering the number of individuals who compose the Mexican and Mexican-American population of the United States and the number of those who make up the total population of Mexico, it is clear that the number of newspapers published in the United States is proportionately greater than the number published in Mexico. As regards quality we cannot say as much, since excepting four or five Mexican newspapers edited in the United States which in character—though not in dimensions—can be compared with the newspapers of Mexico, they reflect the cultural deficiencies of the great masses of immigrants and of the Mexican-American laborers by whom and for whom this press is made. The columns of these periodicals, especially of the numerous humorous publications, are nevertheless filled with materials that constitute almost a type of folk literature. By their vigor, spontaneity, and originality they express the intellectual and spiritual characteristics of the group.

It would be a lengthy business to recount all the tendencies of this press, and we shall mention only a few: The principal characteristic is the tendency to hold up for admiration and even reverence Mexico and "The Race," or to defend the social conglomeration (of Mexicans and Mexican-Americans) from abuses of every sort of which they are made victims by white Americans. Political events in Mexico are felt to deserve great and continuous attention. In the second place appears the interest in local politics as bound up with the interest of "The Race." Politics which are strictly American or which pertain directly to the interests of the white Americans occupy less space. Preference is given in all these newspapers to the activities of the many Mexican or Mexican-American societies. Some of these societies have their own organs, as, for example, the official organ of the Spanish-American Alliance and that of the Blue Cross. Religious propaganda and the constant struggles carried on along this line of controversy are frequently the subject of articles in these papers, and some periodicals are devoted exclusively to religious propaganda.

It is evident that the foregoing observations cannot be accepted as the universal rule, for there are notable variations among these papers according to the localities, industrial or agricultural, urban or rural, in which they are published and in which they circulate. In New Mexico, for example, the press has a character of its own because the number of Mexican-Americans who have been a long time in this country is very great compared with the Mexican immigrants who have arrived comparatively recently. This explains why local politics take first place there and why there is more interest in American politics.

The newspapers of a truly popular nature are much more interesting than those which attempt to be serious, doctrinaire, or erudite. The former express in a genuine way the sagacity, the sentiments, the passions, and the intelligence of the Mexican; their style is pungent, brusque, and even incorrect, but, on the other hand, it is very picturesque and inventive. The more literary writing of the latter type generally suffers from the fact that it is simply an imitation rather than an expression; it is pedantic and full of antiquated romanticism, and on the whole its style is inferior to that of the former class since it lacks force, personality, and character.

Thus, a reading of this press, as well as of non-periodical productions in the nature of folk lore, confirms the statements made as to the nature of the influence which the American milieu exercises upon the Mexican. He thinks, feels, and expresses himself in the Mexican and not in the American way, although considering only material culture, he has absorbed, more or less fully, traits from the American environment.

A curious example of this fusion of culture elements is furnished by posters, so popular in Mexico, which announce the program of the greatest holiday in Mexico, the anniversary of national independence, a holiday which is celebrated on the sixteenth of September in every town in which there are people of Mexican blood. For the Mexican immigrant this is the most sacred and glorious day in the year, and it usually awakens more enthusiasm and emotion in the Mexican immigrant than does even the Fourth of July among Americans. Now, since it would be very expensive to print a poster for every town and a photo-engraving for the patriotic illustration which has to be on it, as is generally done in Mexico, here in the United States they have recourse to mass production (a characteristic of American material culture), and intrust all the printing to one printing office in San Antonio, Texas. The upper half of all the posters is printed just alike and consists of large red lettering which says: "Magnificent Celebration of the Independence of Mexico—1810–1926." In the center of the poster is the Mexican national emblem and surrounding this the portraits of five heroes of the Mexican struggle of independence with frames of laurel and acanthus: Hidalgo, Morelos, Allende, Josefa Ortiz de Dominguez, and Vicente Guerrero. This half of the poster which is common to all the posters represents the influence of American standardization. On the lower half of the poster are printed locally the name of each town or city, the program of each celebration, a short proclamation filled with the most ardent and sentimental patriotism, and finally the names of the members of the patriotic committees. This part of the poster represents the persistence of Mexican cultural traits.[1]

[1] The collection of Mexican periodicals and other publications of Mexicans in the United States on which this discussion is based has been deposited with the Social Science Research Council.

CHAPTER X

FOOD, CLOTHING, DWELLING

Antecedents and conditions in Mexico.—The food of the Mexicans in the prehispanic period, in the zones from which today come most of the immigrants, was largely vegetarian. There were no herds of domestic animals in America—no cattle, sheep, pigs, or fowl. Nor was there even the buffalo or bison of the United States. Neither were these Indians great fish-eaters. Occasionally they ate game; the only domestic animal which served as food was the turkey.[1] Their household utensils were made of beautifully shaped and decorated clay, wood, stone, and sometimes copper. Their houses were primitive, and as a whole their material and cultural development was not very advanced. Some of their architectural structures, such as those at Chalchihuites and La Quemada in Zacatecas, and the *yácatas* of Michoacan and Jalisco, are larger and more important survivals; but they do not represent a very advanced architecture, and, furthermore, were built exclusively for religious purposes or for their war lords and generals. It might be well to remark that the houses, primitive as they were and are—for today they preserve much of the type and character of the prehispanic dwellings—were intelligently adapted to the climate and the materials available for construction.

As to clothing, the women wore cotton tunics, more or less decorated. The men wore loincloths, sandals (*huaraches*), and wore or carried mantles which were the origin of the rectangular blanket with a hole in the center worn today, called *zarape*. The women generally dressed their hair very elaborately and wore earrings and necklaces, and the men also decorated their

[1] The Aztecs and related tribes ate dog flesh.

heads, especially on festive occasions, with feathers and other ornaments. Their love and use of color in clothing were especially notable.

The Spanish Conquest brought the clothing of a civilization more advanced and also of more extreme climate, and it effected changes in the manner of dressing of the native, but particularly did it influence the clothing of the mixed culture classes. The use of the hat became general, and the imported hat was changed from a narrow brim to a very broad brim, this being necessary, of course, to protect from the sun people less accustomed to its intensity. Dark trousers and coat were not adopted, although the natives changed from loincloth and mantle into a cotton suit of wide trousers and blouse, retaining the mantle and sandals. Leather was introduced in the use of "chaps" for horseback, and other objects or articles of clothing. Food was very little changed, continuing basically vegetarian. Household objects as to material remained almost the same. Houses remained much the same as to plan and material, though windows were sometimes adopted, and with them the iron-work, tools, weapons, balconies, and other objects of Spanish importation, as occasionally also furniture such as tables, and less frequently beds.

About the end of the nineteenth century Mexico opened its doors to new currents, and these affected the living conditions, houses, food, and clothing of Mexicans in the northern plains and much less so in the central plateau. With all this change, the essential characteristics of the old customs remained. For instance, food remained chiefly vegetarian, based on maize and its derivatives and by-products—*tortillas*, *pinole*, *gordas*, *tamales*, *atoles*, etc.

Besides maize, there are of course beans and other vegetables, such as several kinds of squash, also greens, tomatoes, the young leaves of cactus, rice, and potatoes. Indispensable to all meals is chili, of which there is a great variety. Occasionally, this diet is varied by fruit, chicken, eggs, turkey, veal, or pork, but often the regular rations of a family do not go beyond maize and beans, chili, and one or two vegetables.

As to clothing, although in the towns they have adopted the shoes and overalls and other things of the modern workman, in the country the majority of men still wear the cotton suit, sandals, and mantle of the colonial period, and the women, whose clothing has changed more, wear skirts, blouses, and shawls (*rebozos*) of more or less native derivation.

The houses have changed little in the rural districts, usually consisting of one or two rooms, and are made of material locally procurable, such as *adobe*, volcanic rock, trunks of trees or saplings, branches, palm-thatch, and grass. These houses generally have a small yard or *corral* for animals and fowl, and as a rule there are flowers in doors, windows, or yard. There are no toilets in the houses of the villages and rural districts, while in the small towns and in many houses of the cities the toilets generally are of the old-fashioned cess-pool type. The lighting in rural districts is done by candles or oil lamps.

As to furniture, there is very little, generally home made and primitive. There is always a saint or religious image on the wall for a small altar arranged with flowers, candles, and other decorations on a table in one corner against a wall. Modern domestic utensils, excepting the sewing machine, are rarely seen; there are no safety razors, electric irons, knives and forks, water filters, and also no modern agricultural machinery. In the poorest homes there is always an artistic touch: flowers, embroidered napkins and tablecloths, decorations made with native pottery, and artistically ornamented blankets. Often there are musical instruments, birds kept in cages, dogs, and cats.

In the villages each family generally has a house to itself, whatever the class of the house. In the cities, however, the typical dwelling of the poor classes is the *vecindad*. This is a building including many one- or two- room dwellings arranged around a court or *patio*, which serves as laundry place and playground. In this court there is generally a well or water pump, and in some parts of the court or opening off it, the community toilets, of the cess-pool type. The floors of the dwellings in the villages are usually of stamped earth; in the cities, of wood or brick. The sanitation in both is in general deficient, though, economic conditions being equal, as a rule the villages and rural houses are cleaner.

Such conditions are due, on the one hand, to the low wages received for centuries by members of the poor working class, and, on the other, to the very high price of even the simplest domestic or industrial modern objects, which are as a rule imported.

Better wages and lower prices of such articles cause an immediate change, as is demonstrated by the people of Indian or Mixed culture who have been able to get better wages in the city of Mexico and other industrial centers, and also by the average immigrant who has been in the United States or in and out for some time.

Food, clothing, and dwellings of immigrants in the United States.—The Mexican immigrant changes first and most in these three respects:

Food.—From being largely a vegetarian he becomes omnivorous, retaining, however, the style of Mexican cooking, and adding to it some American dishes. A report made by a member of our staff on the food of the Mexican immigrants living in various places of the United States will give an idea about to what extent this change is made. The report refers also to the food and prices charged in restaurants for Mexican immigrants:

El Paso, Texas.—The food among the Mexican residents in El Paso and the Mexicans born here is what is generally called "Mexican." It is made up of many dishes in which *chile* is used, both in meat and vegetable dishes. The great part of this *chile* is bought canned, which comes from California, already cleaned and toasted, therefore saving the cook much time. This *chile* is prepared with cheese, potatoes, and in other ways. It is called "Chile de Santa Isabel." Green pepper stuffed with meat is another dish. Other canned goods, sauces or Mexican dishes are sold in great quantities, as also canned tomatoes. Since vegetables are relatively cheap they are commonly eaten. The meat sold in nearby Ciudad Juarez is fresh and cheap, therefore it is commonly eaten, as are also eggs and ham. Fruit and salads also form part of the menu, and milk. Foodstuffs in general are very cheap in the Mexican quarter, it is said as much as 20% cheaper than in other parts of the city. Bread is more commonly eaten than *tortillas*, in the form of French rolls or *bolillos*.

Reports from other localities of Texas vary, but as a rule the basis of the diet is beans and rice, always with chili. Sometimes bread wholly or partly takes the place of *tortillas*, and sometimes wheat flour is used instead of maize to prepare these. Milk and meat are more generally part of the diet than in Mexico, and as a whole there is a marked change for the better, both in quantity and quality, though often these might be considered very poor.

As to kitchen and dining-room utensils, they are of the sort bought in the ten-cent stores. A certain kind of cooking pot, made of cement and iron, has been widely sold, because it cooks beans much more quickly than does any other vessel.

In the restaurants the "regular meal" costs twenty-five or thirty cents. Sometimes "lunch plates" are sold which cost twenty cents. Every sort of Mexican dish is sold—soups, beans, kid, scrambled eggs, sausage with eggs, rice, *mondongo*, or the famous Mexican tripe. Chili is added to almost every dish.

Tucson, Arizona.—In the Mexican restaurants there are no cards or menus. The waiters tell the customers what they have—almost always beans, rice, *enchiladas*, *chile con carne*, eggs in any style, *gorditas* and occasionally *mole*. These restaurants are poorer and dirtier than those in El Paso, San Antonio, and Los Angeles, for in these cities there are first-class Mexican restaurants with every sort of Mexican dish, especially *mole*, chicken with rice, and kid in sauce or *fritanga*. Kid is hardly eaten at all in this region, according to the information we acquired, nor is it served in the Mexican restaurants in California. Instead, tripe and *tamales* are favorite dishes in this part of the country.

The "regular meals" of the restaurants, including four or five courses, vegetable soup and coffee, cost twenty-five cents.

Miami, Arizona.—In the restaurants observed there were no menus. The regular meals cost forty cents, all the à la carte dishes are high priced. Beans, *enchiladas*, *tamales*, *chile con carne*, and pork chops are usually served.

In the two places just mentioned there are a great number of boarding houses. Also there are many signs reading "Boarders taken here." The least that is charged a boarder for his food is one dollar a day.

In almost all the restaurants which appear poor and dirty there are electric pianolas which play a piece of music every time five cents is put in. The music played is almost all Mexican.

In all these places contraband beer is sold. This is true of almost all the public places in these mining-towns.

Phoenix, Arizona.—There are many Mexican restaurants in which are sold *enchiladas*, *tamales*, and tripe. The Mexican dishes usually served are *chile con carne*, beans, soup, rice, meat with *chile verde*, *mole pipian*, *enchilada*, and *tamales*. The prices are generally 25% higher than in Texas and California. Almost none of these restaurants have printed menus. They generally have the lists of dishes chalked up on a slate on the door of the restaurant.

In Los Angeles, and in San Antonio, where the Mexican population includes, besides the poor immigrants who have just come, Mexicans and Mexican-Americans of comfortable means, the restaurants vary from humble places in which the regular meal costs twenty-five cents or less to those in which are served not only every sort of Mexican dish but also those typically American. In all these restaurants there are menus printed in bright colors. In Chicago, there are also many Mexican restaurants of a modest sort devoted exclusively to the Mexican immigrants. In New York City, Mexican restaurants have begun to grow up recently, but they are of another kind since they are not adapted to the needs of the poor Mexican immigrant, of whom there are very few in the city. Their custom comes from the Mexicans who work in offices or those who happen to visit the city.

Clothing.—With respect to costume the greatest change made is in the male immigrant, who immediately dons the shoes and overalls of the American workman. His shirts and hats are of the sort known as "workman," blue, black, or khaki. In cold weather he wears sweaters, woolen underwear, sometimes double clothing. For festive occasions he adopts something of the Texas cowboy style: brightly colored silk shirt, khaki breeches or dark trousers, and felt hat, more or less broad brimmed. Of course this varies according to the wages, the person, and the climate.

Dwelling.—The dwellings of the Mexicans in the United States can be, as a whole, divided into four types:

1. Small, modern, with several rooms, electric light, and modern sanitary conveniences; like the houses of American workers of middle class. These are rented or owned by the immigrants; sometimes they are bought on the instalment plan. The furniture is also of the type bought by American workmen, and nearly always there is a phonograph, a piano, or both.

2. Derived from the *vecindad* of Mexican cities.[1] This is a sort of tenement, or many one- or two-room dwellings around a court with common water supply and toilets. It is a type to be found especially in San Antonio. Sanitary conditions are generally bad, though sometimes individual dwellings are clean and fairly decently furnished. The furniture is of cheap Ameri-

[1] See Emory S. Bogardus, "The House-Court Problem," *American Journal of Sociology*, XXII, 391–99.

can manufacture, bought on the instalment plan, and very frequently even in a poor house there is a phonograph or even a piano. The decoration is usually of religious pictures and saints, Mexican pictures or postals, Mexican flags, portraits of Mexican heroes—Hidalgo, Juarez, and Madero.

3. One- or two-room house, usually wood, of the factory-worker type. It is usually equipped with electric light and running water, and toilet or use of toilet for two or three houses. This type is frequent where there are communities of laborers, as, for example, miners. They are poorly furnished, as a rule, but sometimes have a piano and more often a phonograph. Sometimes they are owned, and sometimes rented from employers at unreasonable rates.

4. Poor huts made of wood and tin, with thatch, canvas, or heterogeneous materials. Often they are built on rented land, but as a rule the hut itself is owned. Usually there is one room or two, occupied by one family or more. They are very poorly furnished, but on the whole better than the corresponding type in Mexico. Even here the phonograph is frequent. They are usually inhabited by transient labor.

CHAPTER XI

SOCIAL MOBILITY

Geographical mobility.—During the early part of the colonial period in Mexico, when the Spaniards were extending their political and social control to the peripheries of the realm, they brought Indian families with them from the south-central plateau ιo help subject and colonize these more distant regions. The mobility of the population thus brought about ceased, however, to characterize the Mexicans when the whole country had been dominated. Migrations ended until the close of the nineteenth century, when Mexican emigration to the United States began to develop.

It is notable that within his own territories the Mexican is not migratory in spite of the mobilizing effect of the revolutionary movements. This is probably due to the fact that there are no great and constant demands for labor by one zone upon another. In those regions where in former times labor was in great demand, as in the industrial centers of Northern Mexico and in the oil regions of the gulf, there is now a surplus.

On the other hand, the mobility of immigrants in the United States is extreme. As the majority are agricultural laborers, they have to go each year to many states of the Union, attracted by the seasonal demands which the various kinds of sowing and harvesting require. In the winter, when agricultural pursuits are interrupted and the climate is rigorous, large numbers of immigrants come back to Mexico and return once more to the United States at the beginning of spring.

Social mobility in Mexico.—During four centuries the structure of the Mexican social edifice has been and is still determined by a constant factor, the ethnic or racial. This has persisted whatever have been the variations of social organization. The highest strata or classes—economic, cultural, political, or occupational—have always been drawn principally from the white race, a lesser proportion from the *mestizos*, and an insignificant fraction from the Indians. In the intermediate strata the proportion of whites diminishes and that of the *mestizos* increases. In the lowest strata the Indians predominate; the *mestizos* follow; and the whites constitute an insignificant minority.[1]

Immediately after the conquest, when intermarriage began, the distribution of classes was very strict and definite. There was no means whereby the Indian might ascend to the highest strata reserved for the whites, but to belong to the very limited indigenous nobility recognized by the Spanish crown, and to have at his disposal the necessary economic means, which permitted him to equal the invading race and to enjoy their social privileges. The *mestizo*, on the other hand, was not often the product of a harmonious union and of recognized marriage, but rather of casual contacts, to which the Indian woman found herself driven on account of her condition of almost animal slavery. This mixture was naturally associated with the indigenous elements and increased the lower social strata.

Although, in general, this system persisted during the colonial period, certain means of social ascent, religious and scholastic, were open, and through these the *mestizo* and the Indian reached, although not usually, the intermediate strata, and very rarely the highest.

During the nineteenth century diverse circumstances tended to bring together the three strata cited, causing a more general mobility. Among these circumstances were the war for

[1] This generalization cannot be applied to Mexico City, which has a certain cosmopolitan character, or to various parts of the northern mesa or the south-central plateau where the number of Indians has often been much reduced.

independence and the other revolutions which followed it, and the resulting contact with foreign countries. Under special conditions the filtration of elements from one social stratum to another was made less difficult. Nevertheless, the ethnic grouping remained substantially the same. At that time, however, an interesting phenomenon became apparent. Although the Indians that formed the lower social classes continued to meet with obstacles which hindered their collective ascent and incorporation into the higher class, individual Indians came to fill the highest political, economic, and professional positions. Thus, for the first time in the history of the country, there appeared in public life presidents, generals, secretaries of state, archbishops, and capitalists from the Indian races. The most noteworthy example was Benito Juarez, a pure-blood Indian, who did not learn Spanish until he was twelve years old, and who nevertheless came to be the most conspicuous legislator and president that Mexico has ever had. He married into a family of the white race, and their descendants belong to the highest social classes, in the majority of whom no trace of Indian blood is distinguishable.

It might be supposed that this possibility which the individual Indian had to ascend socially in Mexico would decidedly and favorably influence the collective ascent of those of his race, as generally happens in other countries—for example, in the United States with the Irish and Jewish residents. In Mexico, however, this is not the case with respect to the Indian, for he who individually has succeeded in scaling the social heights becomes so penetrated with the habits, aspirations, and ideals of the white race and hypnotized to such a degree that he looks upon those of his own race with more indifference perhaps, and even with more disdain, than do those of the white race.

Among thousands of examples we may cite those of two illustrious Indians. One, a musical genius possessing ample culture and noble sentiments, who has recently been honored in various foreign countries and whose dark skin, hair, features, and other ethnical characteristics strongly proclaim him of the Indian race, serenely declared to the discomposure of the employees of the Mexican Department of Emigration that he was of the white race. The other, President Juarez, whom we have already mentioned, did magnificent work in his government; but in the last analysis the results were translated into advantages almost exclusively enjoyed by the high and intermediate social strata, that is to say, the whites and *mestizos*. With regard to the problem of the incorporation of the Indian masses into the public organism, Juarez did nothing or almost nothing. Accustomed to the aspirations and necessities of the classes with whom he was in contact, he honestly believed that he could improve conditions for the whole nation if he served those classes. This lack of racial conscience perhaps caused the musician mentioned before to devote himself to foreign classical music and look upon the real Mexican music, founded on the ideals and on the sorrows of his own race, with indifference.

This social distance between the whites of the highest strata and the Indians of the lowest is not due, as it may be supposed, to racial repugnance, for, as we have already pointed out, individually the Indian may associate with the highest aristocracy. White and Indian have interbred freely; the Mexican population is largely *mestizo*. Social distance is largely brought about by the different types of culture which characterize the whites and Indian. As indicated in previous chapters, the Mexican Indian possessed before the conquest a perfectly defined autochthonous culture, which in some of its ramifications had reached a very notable material and intellectual development. The whites represent the European type of culture, more or less influenced by the local environment. So, then, not only do the typical characteristics of both cultures differ, but some of their differences are positively antagonistic. The Spanish colonization did not harmoniously fuse these cultures, but tried, although uselessly, to destroy the indigenous and substitute the European.

The Indian defended and still defends his cultural heritage. It is this in reality that keeps him in the lower strata, for that culture, however picturesque and interesting it may be, is antiquated and inefficient for competition in the social struggle with the culture of the European type.

This has been a contributing cause of the Mexican revolutions, for when the Indians of the lower classes have wished to ascend in the social scale, they have resorted to armed rebellion, since they lacked modern cultural weapons with which peacefully to attain their object. For such a situation not the Indian but the whites are to blame. They did not know how to educate them efficiently; when they attempted to do so, they limited themselves to teaching them how to read and write, leaving them in the same miserable condition of life. The proper education for the Indians would be an integral education, which would contribute to their economic and physical improvement, in order to assure their cultural development. That is to say, they should be taught to take advantage of the natural resources of the country; to extract and transform industrially the raw materials that are within their reach; to modernize their agricultural methods, and to improve diet, dress, and housing. Afterward the aim might be to change their old cultural habits, but experience shows that in order to incorporate the Indian one should not systematically destroy the character of his autochthonous ideas.

Two conclusions derived from the foregoing may be stated: (1) The ethnic distribution of the diverse social strata does not correspond to the composition of the total population. A

majority of the people are Indians and *mestizos* and a minority
are whites. Yet the whites have always occupied most of the
places in the higher strata. (2) The white elements develop the
greatest social vertical mobility, next the *mestizo*, and last the
Indian. As the Mexican immigrants to the United States are
derived largely from the lower strata, it is the social mobility of
these groups, *mestizos* and Indians, that is of immediate interest.

The horizontal mobility of these classes, that is, the change
of positions and activities, within the same social level, seems
to be much less than that which is observed in other countries—
for example, in the United States. This may be due to the following causes:

a) There is little occupational specialization, especially in
the rural regions. The individual performs such a variety of
functions that a change of position in the same social level does
not necessarily imply a change of activities, because the new
activities of the second position were already traditionally
known by the individual and were already known to him. For
example, a *peón* can, inefficiently but indiscriminately, manage
mules, open and level a small irrigation canal, laboriously cultivate truck gardens, gather fruit, cut wood, or perform simple
carpentering jobs.

b) The small development of industry reduces the number
of possible jobs within the same social level.

c) The majority of Indians and *mestizos* are pagan-Catholic
and a very small minority Roman Catholic. Therefore the social organization lacks the large number of sects and religious
congregations which in other countries favor horizontal
mobility.

d) Political parties scarcely exist, and those who are affiliated with them are insignificant numerically; therefore there
can be no important social transfer from party to party.

Social mobility in the United States.—In the United States the large group which for practical purposes constitutes the nation is composed of white persons. They form social strata or classes in familiar proportions: a minority in the upper strata, a larger number in the intermediate strata, and a large mass in the lower strata. Mobility from one stratum to another is very great in this country as compared with that found in other countries. This is probably due, among other things, to the cosmopolitanism of the population and to a democratic system of government.

The modern industrial organization which requires a great number of specialized occupations, the broad and effective functioning of political parties, the existence of numerous religious sects, bring it about that the transverse or horizontal mobility is also very marked in each stratum.

Artificially incrusted upon the nation is the colored group constituting approximately one-tenth of the total population. This ethnic group is incorporated in the lower social strata, and its component elements exhibit their own horizontal mobility, like that of the white elements occupying similar strata. However, its vertical mobility is very slight, almost nil, considering not only the group as a whole but also the individuals. A Negro has never, in America, become president, secretary of state, governor, archbishop, or multimillionaire. Almost all the paths to social advancement are closed, particularly that of marriage since they cannot marry whites. To the low level to which the Negroes have always been kept there is not, however, a corresponding cultural difference; that is to say, the Negro population is not characterized by a Negro culture but by one clearly American and equivalent to that found among the whites at the same low social levels. This is undoubtedly due to the fact that the ancestors of the colored people came to the continent despoiled of all culture. For this reason it was relatively easy to educate them in accordance with American cultural principles.

A third ethnic group which amounts to approximately one-hundreth of the total population is composed of Mexican immigrants and their descendants. It also is incrusted upon the American nation, although much more artificially than is the colored group. This group considered in itself and in its relations with other groups is the object of this study. To the social mobility of this group we now turn.

Two closely linked factors have contributed principally to the great horizontal social mobility which characterizes the Mexican immigrant in the United States in contrast to the relatively slight mobility observed in Mexico: (1) the great number and variety of occupations which the organization and specialization of industry and American agriculture demands; (2) the periodicity of agricultural labor imposed by the changes in climatic conditions in the regions where the immigrant works. The scarcity of work in some parts of America are not always due to an absolute lack of work in all parts of the United States but to other causes. It has been demonstrated that while in certain cities and regions of the East and West there are a large number of unemployed, at the same time in the Southwest there is an urgent demand for labor. Nevertheless, the problem has not worked out as theoretically it should—that is to say, it has not been found possible to transport the excess of men from these regions to those in which they are needed. Possibly this unfortunate situation may be largely attributed to the specialization which is a characteristic of the American laborer, even unskilled labor. This specialization makes for efficiency in work but in some respects constitutes an obstacle when the workman endeavors to change from one occupation to another. Specialization, moreover, appears to produce certain sedentary tendencies in the individual. However, traditional generalized techniques of the Mexican immigrants, especially of those who come from the rural regions or small villages in Mexico, make possible a frequent change in occupations and frequent transfer from one region to another in the United States. Certainly the Mexican's efficiency in each of these occupations is less than that shown by the American workman who is specialized in a single occupation. Thus no matter how necessary and opportune the aid given by Mexican labor at certain periods and parts of the country, the pay which he receives is generally less than that given to the American workman who lives permanently in that part of the country and is experienced in performing tasks of the same sort and grade.

Let us now analyze the vertical social mobility of the immigrant, or the conditions of his rise from lower social strata to higher. From the time of their arrival in the United States the great majority of Mexican immigrants are automatically and inevitably incorporated into the lowest American social strata. In these strata they will remain until conditions in Mexico make possible and desirable their repatriation. The color of their skin, more or less dark, the small pay which they find themselves obliged to accept, their traditions of slavery and servitude which weighed upon them in the colonial period and even during the nineteenth century, the fact that in their own country they occupied the lower social strata—all these and many other factors bring it about that their social situation is in various respects similar to that of the colored race, though it should be recognized nevertheless that the race prejudice which exists toward the Mexican has never been so pronounced or exaggerated as that felt toward the Negro.

Previously we made the statement that the improvement which the Mexican immigrant in the United States experiences with regard to physical condition, food, clothing, and shelter, industrial and agricultural knowledge, is undeniable. In other words, his culture can rise to the level of the culture of the white Americans with whom he associates in the lower social strata of society. However, speaking generally, he cannot continue his vertical mobility. He is condemned to remain in the lower social strata in which he was incorporated from the time of his arrival in the country. This social situation does not only affect the non-nationalized immigrants, but also those who are nationalized, and even children who are, through birth, American citizens. This explains in part why the immigrant very rarely becomes naturalized, since he finds in this no social advantage, while it attracts the unfavorable criticism of those Mexicans who have kept their nationality. Let us examine what in actual fact are the chief means toward social improvement in the United States and what opportunities they offer to the nationalized immigrant and his children. Such persons cannot rise by means of intermarriage, or successive marriages with whites each time of a higher social stratum, since race prejudice prevents this. Political activity, and especially the filling of public offices won by this activity, are strictly forbidden to them. This is proved by the fact that although there are parts of America in which the Mexicans form a large majority of the population, very few public officers are of Mexican origins. The very few cases of Mexicans who are filling unimportant public offices are no more than a confirmation of the rule. In the army and the navy there have been no Mexican generals or admirals, and the number of Mexican officers has been very few. The churches have been more liberal since they accept Mexicans as ministers and priests, but these are generally destined for Mexican parishes which the white Americans probably would not be willing to take. The schools offer them a primary education, but they rarely enter high school or college and almost never the universities. The very few number of individuals who succeed in entering professions such as those of law or medicine find themselves forced to carry on their professions almost exclusively among the residents of Mexican origins. To bring out more clearly the state of horizontal social immobility of these social elements, one needs only to compare this situation with that presented by the immigrants from Europe and their children. These latter can ascend to the highest social strata of the nation.

In conclusion we should state that we are referring in these pages to Mexicans, principally *mestizos* or Indians, who are classified as unskilled labor and who have always constituted the great body of the immigration.

CHAPTER XII

IMMIGRATION AND REVOLUTION

Excepting Argentine, Uruguay, and perhaps Chile, the Latin-American countries are much alike in social, ethnic, and cultural structure, and their historic antecedents and traditions are more or less the same. This explains why their evolution has been in general parallel. Mexico, however, is an exception in so far as no other Latin-American country has had so many, such severe, and such almost continuous revolutions, especially in the last quarter of a century. Fundamentally, these revolutions, in Mexico as well as in similar Latin-American countries, are caused by the heterogeneous nature of these countries, economically, racially, culturally, socially, and linguistically. This heterogeneity is a characteristic of such nations, made up of Indians, *mestizos*, and whites, each with different needs and aspirations, divergent and sometimes antagonistic to each other. The laws and constitutions of these countries give the advantage, generally, to the culturally superior but numerically small white group.

Influence of migration on Mexican revolutions.—In the case of Mexico, an immediate and direct cause of revolution is also to be found in the states on the border, both Mexican and American. Owing to the cultural contact between Mexicans and Americans the immigrants and resident Mexicans in the United States are generally involuntary but effective agents of such revolutions. This statement does not have reference to the revolutions stirred up by Mexicans more or less supported by discontented American interests, nor to those created by Mexican politicians, immigrants in the United States—that is, professional conspirators or exiled political losers. Such uprisings are temporary and artificial, whereas those caused by the factors we just mentioned have had the character of continuous, real, and inevitable social movements.

Because of the heterogeneous nature of the Mexican people, the great masses have lived under tyranny and in misery—economic, physical, moral, and cultural. This has always produced serious social disorder. When there were no railroads, and only desert lay between Mexico and the United States, revolution was a purely domestic product, for the echoes of great social movements elsewhere were faint in Mexico and scarcely reached the people. When the railroads joined these two countries, however, and the people entered upon a period of more intimate contact, Mexican immigrants came to the United States and returned with ideas and memories of a better way of living. These ideas spread and developed in the masses, as it was from the *peón* class that the immigrants were usually derived. Since General Díaz began to build railroads to the United States this interesting reflex phenomenon has been developing. The ideas and longings of the Mexican masses crystallized with the return of immigrants who pictured another sort of life, comparing the advantages and liberties of the American workman with the terrible misery of the Mexican workman. Then followed demands for better living conditions, and since the officials—eternally unaware of social phenomena—did not satisfy these demands, the revolutions which have torn Mexico almost from the beginning of this century broke out.

This is proved by the fact that since the time of President Madero to the present date, the route of revolution has been from north to south, and the presidents and many of the ministers and high military powers have been born in the border states, and some of them have been educated in the United States or have lived in that country.[1]

[1] [The United States has also been a source of arms and money.—EDITOR.]

The central regions, on the other hand, have been far less revolutionary, more sluggish, more content with bad conditions, for they have had far less knowledge of the manner of living of the American masses, and therefore have had little grounds for comparison. This does not mean that in these regions the idea of revolution does not exist. As a rule, however, it has been sown there by men from the border or by ex-immigrants.

The capital of Mexico is an exception to the foregoing observations, for it is a modern cosmopolitan cultural center. It is situated in the central regions but its problems are different and peculiar to itself.

An example of revolution, though not by arms, rather an economic revolution, is the Mexican labor movement. Several of its leaders have been immigrants, and their big organizations are modeled directly upon the American Federation of Labor. This revolution has gained much ground in little time. The urban worker has a position from 100 to 300 per cent better—in dwelling, dress, food, and culture—than a short period ago. This influence of American labor ideas was to be expected, for the two groups of laborers, whose hands have been literally joined over the border line, could not have remained under utterly different conditions—one organized and developed, and the other, as a short time ago, in age-old misery and ignorance.

Another revolutionary movement which probably was imported from the United States to Mexico by the repatriated immigrants is the agrarian movement, which developed slowly and anonymously under the influence of such persons until their activities came to a head in the uprisings under Madero and later leaders. Certainly the circumstances of American social life which impressed the Mexican immigrant most was the existence of the homestead and the contrast between the comfortable and quiet life of the American workman and his own of perpetual misery and servitude upon the great *haciendas*, where he never realized the ancient and traditional desire for the possession of a piece of land of his own. Understanding this, although much too late, General Díaz, just before his fall from power, attempted to initiate measures leading toward the resolution of the agrarian problem. Another argument in defense of this hypothesis is the fact that until the immigration to the United States began to develop on a large scale and, in consequence, the repatriation of immigrants became great, the Mexican revolutions had a social, economic, or political character but never one fundamentally and exclusively agrarian. On the other hand, the revolutionary movements which succeeded, and coincided with the great development of immigration, were chiefly characterized by their agrarian tendencies, and the soldiers who fought in them were primarily from the rural regions. Perhaps it may be argued that the impulse of the immigrant to agrarian revolt ought not to be very great in view of the fact that the number of immigrants who own land in the United States is very small, as is even that of the tenant and share farmers. As a matter of fact, however, the reason that the number of immigrants who possess and rent land is small is first of all because the American landowners, and the American people in general, are not anxious that they should possess it; and, second, in other occupations such as industries, harvesting, and so on in which they are engaged, they are both needed more and probably more productive. Finally, the general desire of the immigrants to return to their native land is difficult to realize if they own or rent land.

Not all the revolutionary inspirations of American origin have produced happy results. Sometimes just the opposite has occurred, and this is because the factors that mean welfare to the American people do not necessarily mean welfare for the Mexican. The two are different, as we have said, historically, racially, culturally, and psychologically. The two countries are different geographically. However, these differences cannot be correctly and much less scientifically understood or interpreted by the average immigrant who returns to Mexico and influences or directly takes part in politics and government, for as a rule he has not sufficient cultural preparation to do so. Therefore, the revolutions he incites frequently incorporate exotic and impracticable and even harmful ideas, which have prevented or diverted more legitimate and important results. In the near future possibly the progressive but only partially efficient activity of the returned immigrant may be complemented by the activity of Mexican youth being educated at home according to modern scientific tendencies, or in centers of high culture in Europe and in the United States.

The influence of political upheavals on the coming and going of the Mexican immigrant.—Political upheavals appear to affect greatly the number of Mexicans who leave and come back to Mexico each year. In fact, as can be seen in chapter i, Table V, in the year 1920, in which the presidential succession was the occasion of political disorders, the number of immigrants that returned to Mexico only exceeded by 14,051 the number that had left for the United States (i.e., the number officially recorded as having left) during this same period of time. In other words, a certain proportion of the Mexicans who are accustomed to come back to Mexico each year remained in the United States. This probably explains the four-million-dollar increase in the 1920 money orders sent from the United States to Mexico as compared with those of 1919 shown in chapter i, Table III.

On the other hand, in 1921 when the political conditions were again quiet, the number of those who returned to Mexico exceeded by 97,077 the number that had left that same year (Table V). The small number of immigrants who went (officially) to the United States in 1920, namely, 9,165, is partly at least explained by the fact that in 1920 a comparatively small number, 14,051, of immigrants had come back. The exodus from the United States of such a large number of immigrants in 1921 reduced the value of the money orders sent to Mexico by immigrants to about half the amount it had been in 1920 (Table III).[1]

The political disturbances in 1923 which culminated in the De la Huerta rebellion coincided with the Mexican statistics, which indicate that only 5,032 more immigrants returned to Mexico than had left for the United States that same year, and that the value of money orders sent to Mexico by immigrants in 1923 was double the amount that had been sent during 1922, and that there was a return to normal conditions in 1924, when the number of those that returned to Mexico exceeded by 48,565 the number that had left for the United States during the same period. As a result, the value of money orders sent to Mexico in 1924 experienced a decrease of a little over five million dollars as compared with the amount sent in 1923.

Lastly, the rebellion with religious implications which reached a new intensity in the last months of 1926 was apparently the cause of the fact that an exceptionally large number of immigrants who had left for the United States since that time remained in that country during 1927, instead of coming back. This may be confirmed by means of data on migration between the United States and Mexico during 1927, which has just been furnished us by the Departamento de Migración of Mexico. In that year 76,209 Mexicans were re-

[1] [These fluctuations in the number of returning immigrants are in part due, not to Mexican political conditions, but to economic conditions in the United States. For example, in late 1919 and early 1920 American industry was operating at its peak, again in 1923 it heavily increased its demand for labor, including Mexican labor. In 1921, on the other hand, there was a severe depression in both industry and agriculture, which actually reduced for a time the number of Mexicans in the United States.—EDITOR.]

ported as departing for the United States, while during the same period 69,125 returned to Mexico from the United States. This is an exceptional condition in the migratory movement between the two countries, as shown in Table V, because the number (reported as) leaving the country is always lower than the number of entries. This is probably explained by the fact that the major part of Mexican immigration originates exactly in the regions where this religious rebellion developed, namely, Jalisco, Michoacan, and Guanajuato. The increase which the value of money orders sent to Mexico in 1927 shows over that of 1926 indicates also that the number of immigrants who remained in the United States in 1927 was larger than that in 1926. Moreover, the monthly amounts sent during the year 1927 are more regular and do not show the great seasonal decreases characteristic in winter and spring when great numbers of immigrants are accustomed to return to Mexico, as has been remarked before.

Lastly, Table XX, which refers to the second-class passenger traffic of the national railways of Mexico between various sections of Mexico and the border stations of the United States, shows that from July, 1926, to July, 1927, 94,725 persons left for the United States, while during the same time 58,204 returned. It is fair to assume that most of the second-class passengers going to frontier points are immigrants, for the small Mexican towns existing at these places could hardly employ such large groups of migrating workers. This table, besides verifying the conclusions just stated, shows where the railway concentration points are in the itinerary of the immigrants to the United States. At times contractors of Mexican labor operate at these concentration points.

TABLE XX

PASSENGERS CARRIED TO AND FROM FRONTIER PORTS, IN THE
PERIOD FROM JULY, 1926, TO JUNE, 1927

(Second Class)

Railway Station	State	To Frontier Ports	From Frontier Ports
Aguascalientes	Ags.	4,462	1,744
Rincón de Ramos	Ags.	51	15
San Gil	Ags.	1	11
Torreón	Coah.	7,910	1,886
Matamoros	Coah.	31	19
Viesca	Coah.	....	7
Parras	Coah.	20	11
Gral. Cepeda	Coah.	7	21
Jimenez	Coah.	1,006	485
Saltillo	Coah.	5,996	1,734
Ramos Arizpe	Coah.	56	67
Piedras Negras	Coah.	26	16
Rio Escondido	Coah.	414	386
Nava	Coah.	1,377	1,410
Allende	Coah.	4,106	4,142
Sabinas	Coah.	7,033	3,463
Monclova	Coah.	2,558	1,510
Agujita	Coah.	....	17
Cloete	Coah.	7	5
Rosita	Coah.	77	2,467
Las Esperanzas	Coah.	119	46
Muzquiz	Coah.	549	343
Nadadores	Coah.	4	1
San Pedro	Coah.	320	126
Santa Teresa	Coah.	3	1
Madero	Coah.	....	18
Colima	Col.	31	17
Manzanillo	Col.	3	....
Santa Rosalia	Chih.	700	592
La Cruz	Chih.	44	86
Concho	Chih.	222	146
Ortiz	Chih.	687	555
Chihuahua	Chih.	7,205	6,813
Ahuamada	Chih.	2,229	2,028
Lucero	Chih.	1,465	1,741
Ciudad Juarez	Chih.	26	18
Santa Bárbara	Chih.	208	392
Mexico City	D.F.	3,799	2,173
Tacubaya	D.F.	1	....
Simón	Dgo.	52	26
Gomez Palacio	Dgo.	1,677	599
Santa Clara	Dgo.	28	8
Bermejillo	Dgo.	331	114
Tlahualilo	Dgo.	8	5

TABLE XX—*Continued*

Railway Station	State	To Frontier Ports	From Frontier Ports
Rosario	Dgo.	27	34
Asarco	Dgo.	6	4
Canatlan	Dgo.	1	6
El Salto	Dgo.	....	1
Tepehuanes	Dgo.	5	34
Muleros	Dgo.	8	9
Velardeña	Dgo.	2	7
Loma	Dgo.	....	30
Pedriceña	Dgo.	13	12
Fco. I. Madero	Dgo.	6	13
Durango	Dgo.	1,034	645
Stgo. Papásquiaro	Dgo.	20	....
Celaya	Gto.	339	185
Cortazar	Gto.	15	14
Irapuato	Gto.	5,220	1,220
Villalobos	Gto.	4	4
Silao	Gto.	910	278
León	Gto.	1,131	415
Encarnación	Gto.	384	134
Guanajuato	Gto.	20	33
Valle de Santiago	Gto.	6	23
Jaral del Progreso	Gto.	28	2
Abasolo	Gto.	18	24
Pénjamo	Gto.	347	292
Palo Verde	Gto.	18	20
Rincón	Gto.	31	1
Comonfort	Gto.	....	1
Dolores Hgo	Gto.	13	23
San Felipe	Gto.	122	103
S. Miguel Allende	Gto.	31	15
Salvatierra	Gto.	720	446
Acámbaro	Gto.	273	118
Salamanca	Gto.	....	341
Tula	Hgo.	7	1
Pachuca	Hgo.	12	8
Lagos	Jal.	399	134
Santa María	Jal.	1,294	568
La Barca	Jal.	308	122
Ocotlán	Jal.	288	317
Poncitlán	Jal.	36	32
La Capilla	Jal.	6	5
El Castillo	Jal.	3	4
Guadalajara	Jal.	2,576	1,085
Catarina	Jal.	1	....
Zacoalco	Jal.	....	14
Sayula	Jal.	....	2
Ciudad Guzman	Jal.	13	3
Atotonilco	Jal.	15	6
Ameca	Jal.	6	3
Ahualulco	Jal.	....	1

TABLE XX—*Continued*

Railway Station	State	To Frontier Ports	From Frontier Ports
Tlalnepantla...............	Mex.	21	4
Cuautitlán................	Mex.	7	2
Toluca...................	Mex.	2	2
Tultenango...............	Mex.	3	2
La Piedad................	Mich.	594	494
Yurécuaro................	Mich.	892	366
Morelia..................	Mich.	179	301
Pátzcuaro................	Mich.	24	32
Ajuno...................	Mich.	....	6
Uruapan.................	Mich.	84	88
Maravatio................	Mich.	....	4
Villachuato..............	Mich.	169	80
Panindicuaro.............	Mich.	61	38
Zacapu..................	Mich.	46	57
Zamora..................	Mich.	299	402
Tinguindin...............	Mich.	....	26
Los Reyes...............	Mich.	....	16
Candela.................	N.L.	691	807
Bustamante..............	N.L.	676	754
Garcia..................	N.L.	27	39
Lampazos...............	N.L.	1,908	2,554
Monterrey...............	N.L.	16,324	13,425
Villaldama..............	N.L.	1,675	1,325
Salinas.................	N.L.	442	310
Linares.................	N.L.	81	76
Montemorelos............	N.L.	101	72
Teran...................	N.L.	5	14
Cadereyta...............	N.L.	....	4
Herreras................	N.L.	312	220
Oaxaca.................	Oax.	94	....
Puebla..................	Pue.	3	3
Bernal..................	Qro.	....	1
Hércules................	Qro.	1	....
Querétaro...............	Qro.	1,211	583
S. J. del Rio.............	Qro.	15	7
Bocas...................	S.L.P.	26	20
Catorce.................	S.L.P.	10	14
Cedral..................	S.L.P.	2	8
Charcas.................	S.L.P.	21	23
Moctezuma..............	S.L.P.	4	16
San Luis Potosi..........	S.L.P.	1,828	960
Venado.................	S.L.P.	10	21
Villa Reyes.............	S.L.P.	....	3
Peñon Blanco...........	S.L.P.	....	1
Cerritos................	S.L.P.	3	16
Cárdenas...............	S.L.P.	2	1
Reynosa................	Tamps.	2,237	975
Gonzales...............	Tamps.	35	4
Xicotencatl.............	Tamps.	34	11
Ciudad Victoria..........	Tamps.	210	88

TABLE XX—*Continued*

Railway Station	State	To Frontier Ports	From Frontier Ports
Tampico..................	Tamps.	791	476
Camargo.................	Tamps.	....	2
Guadalupe Victoria.........	Tamps.	....	4
Apaseo...................	Gto.	....	2
Matehuala................	S.L.P.	125	159
Rio Verde................	S.L.P.	1	....
Jalapa...................	Ver.	2	2
Veracruz.................	Ver.	9	....
Zacatecas................	Zac.	2,135	958
Calera...................	Zac.	69	35
Fresnillo.................	Zac.	439	224
Empalme Cañitas..........	Zac.	227	71
Rio Grande...............	Zac.	34	19
Sombrerete...............	Zac.	4	19
La Honda.................	Zac.	....	2
Total................	....	104,724	68,304

NOTE.—This table was compiled for us by the Contaduría de Ingresos de Pasajes of the Ferrocarriles Nacionales de México.

CHAPTER XIII

CONCLUSIONS: AN IMMIGRATION POLICY

Before turning to the question of what policy with respect to immigration promises to serve best the interests of the United States and of Mexico, we may sum up conclusions indicated in the foregoing chapters.

QUANTITATIVE ESTIMATE OF MEXICAN IMMIGRATION

1. The number of Mexican immigrants and non-immigrants in the United States in December, 1926, was, according to data supplied by the Department of Labor of Washington, 890,746, while the number obtained on the basis of the data of the Mexican Migration Service is 237,969. There is, therefore, an inadmissible difference of 632,777.

From the analysis and comparison of the American and Mexican data it is concluded that such statistical discrepancy is due to two principal causes:

a) Of the great number of Mexicans who yearly return from the United States to Mexico, only an insignificant number register at the American immigration offices, while a very large majority of these individuals register at the Mexican offices.

b) A certain number of Mexicans, a number we cannot estimate, even broadly, enter the United States and return to Mexico, without the knowledge of the American and Mexican migration authorities.

We reach the conclusion that the American data regarding Mexican immigration in the United States are not correct, whereas the Mexican information, though more nearly correct as to the number of returned immigrants, does not represent the actual number of immigrants in the United States.

2. *Origin and distribution.*—The greatest proportion of immigrants come from the high parts of Mexico, chiefly from the central mesa, where the economic conditions of the lower classes are traditionally bad, religion exaggerated to fanaticism, the earth extremely fertile, and the climate mild and healthy. The immigrants come from at least 552 Mexican cities, and are distributed in the United States in at least 1,555 American cities all over the Union, with the greatest number in California, Texas, and Arizona. In the last few years a large number of Mexicans have left agricultural occupations in the southern states for the North, or have gone directly from Mexico to the northern and eastern states, where they can get higher wages. This northward migration involves a harmful change of climate, for these immigrants come generally from regions in Mexico with a range of temperature of 20°, and go to regions in the United States with a range of 100°. Those who go from regions in Mexico where the climate is more extreme are distributed as a rule in the southwestern part of the United States.

3. *Economic aspect.*—The emigration of Mexican laborers is directly caused by the low wages and unemployment in the various parts of Mexico from which they come, indirectly by the political instability of the country, and secondarily through the desire for progress and the spirit of adventure.

The United States encourages Mexican immigration because employers have neither sufficient labor nor the right sort of American labor for the jobs which the Mexicans fill, and because the wages paid Mexicans are generally lower than those received by the American workman.

Mexican immigrants contribute directly and effectively to the operation and development of agricultural and industrial enterprises which represent nearly five billion dollars. In exchange, the immigrant receives wages which support him, and he also saves money to send back to his family in Mexico. According to the statistics of the last nine years, Mexican immigrants have sent to Mexico through postal money orders alone an average of five million dollars a year. The money from relief work among the Mexican immigrants is spent in regions where these are more numerous; therefore the agricultural and industrial enterprises of those regions which employ Mexican labor and benefit by it probably contribute a great part of this money.

4. *Physical conditions and ethnic factor.*—The Mexican immigrant, according to statistics we have at present, is as normal from physiological, anatomical, and pathological points of view as is the immigrant of other nationalities. As to his physical anthropology, his characteristics both before entering the United States and after are unknown. Nor is there such information upon American citizens of Mexican origin. There is therefore no scientific basis for an innate inferiority of the Mexican, nothing beyond the dark pigmentation of the Mexican to account for the racial prejudice against him and the sexual barrier between him and the American. There are practically no marriages between white Americans and Mexicans, though the latter may be American citizens, whereas between Mexicans who are American culturally and Mexican immigrants intermarriages occur constantly.

Contacts of civilization.—The influence of American civilization upon the immigrant is generally with respect to material culture, chiefly in the matter of dwelling, clothing, food, hygiene, and agricultural and industrial education. In lesser degree, the ethics and religion of the immigrant are also influenced. His folk-loric aspects persist almost unaltered. His patriotism—that is, his love for his native country—is strengthened; rarely does he become an American citizen, and he always wants to return to Mexico. This is shown clearly by the fact that very often Mexicans who have lived fifteen and more years in the United States are anxious to return, or have returned, to Mexico to colonize rural regions. The immigrants develop a marked social and co-operative impulse, and have developed a somewhat important Mexican press. As a whole, it can be said that the Mexican immigrants are bettered in the United States in various ways; but that although contact with American civilization is of benefit to them and they adopt some of its characteristics, the majority never become integrally assimilated to American civilization.

Influence of immigration on Mexican revolution.—When the people of the United States and Mexico became more closely linked by the railroads built during the last fifty years, the Mexican masses began to compare their own living conditions, their existence under tyranny, and their great misery with the liberty, and the intellectual and material well-being of the American masses. Since then many Mexicans who have emigrated to the United States have seen at first hand the favorable conditions under which the American laborer lives, and upon returning to Mexico they have attempted to better their own positions by whatever means were within their power. This was logical and natural. Reforms were first demanded from the government and lawmakers, in order to remedy the bad conditions immediately, but with these demands the conservative régimes did not comply. Then arose the most intense and widespread revolution in the history of Mexico. Confirmation of the course of events is to be found in the fact that most of the officials of revolutionary governments, as also the leaders of revolutionary movements, are natives of the border states where the contrast is more easily noted by the relative accessibility of the United States. Among these leaders are some ex-immigrants.

Influence of revolution on Mexican immigration.—The migration statistics for the last two migration periods indicate that the immediate effect of the revolutionary movements is to diminish considerably the large number of immigrants who usually return every year to Mexico. As a consequence of this, during the revolutionary periods the sums of money which are sent through the mail from the United States to Mexico by the immigrants are considerably increased.

We now turn to the matter of policy.

Public opinion and governmental policy.—The rapidity with which the Mexican immigration to the United States has developed accounts for the little study that has been made of the phenomenon, and for the absence of any official investigations. Nevertheless public opinion has provided itself with arguments both for and against the continuance of the immigration.

Opinion in the United States.—Knowledge and official opinion prevailing in the United States with regard to Mexican immigration are derived (besides from information obtained by departments and bureaus directly concerned) from the arguments made before Congress with regard to the question of establishing the quota for Mexican immigration. The proponents of unlimited immigration have attempted to show that Mexican labor is indispensable for the maintenance and growth of agriculture and industry in certain parts of the United States. Moreover, they have succeeded in making clear the good points and advantages that the Mexican immigrants, from the point of view of labor, present. These arguments have their origin exclusively in material interests and the profits which the presence of Mexican labor affords to certain American employers. Churches and social-welfare organizations have supported immigration from purely altruistic motives and are an exception to this rule.

The arguments for the limitation of immigration are inspired by the fear that the Mexicans now artificially incrusted upon the American nation will produce undesirable economic, racial, or cultural conflicts. In these arguments the political factor also enters, since in the border states unscrupulous political elements sometimes manipulate the Mexican vote in an improper way. Some church and social-welfare organizations are opposed to immigration principally for economic reasons.

The American Federation of Labor has come out against unlimited immigration because of the competition of Mexican labor with American Labor.

Unfortunately, official knowledge and opinion with regard to immigration are not satisfactory since they do not rest upon investigations of a thoroughly scientific nature. No such investigation has been made.

The American government and people, as a whole, are not in favor of Mexican immigration. There is a general belief that if this continues indefinitely it will create difficult problems—economic, racial, and cultural. However, since the agricultural and industrial development of important regions in the United States has been dependent upon Mexican immigration, and since the enterprises of these regions now rely upon Mexican labor, there is a struggle between these interests and the elements hostile to immigration.

Official attitude in Mexico.—Public opinion in Mexico is also at fault since it also is not based upon scientific investigation. However, the Mexican government has tried to learn the situation of the immigrants by consulting its consuls in the United States. This inquiry has been free from the bias of the material interest which inspires the attitude of American employers, and has not been concerned with the more or less serious social problem which the immigrant causes the United States. It was simply an investigation of the unfavorable conditions which hinder the honest activities of the immigrant and make his existence abnormal or miserable, and of how to better such a situation. With this in mind the Secretary of Foreign Relations and the Mexican Embassy in the United States have at various times sought information through the consuls concerning the conditions of life of the immigrant and the treatment which he receives on American soil.

With the consent of the President we were permitted to consult and to make use of the documents relative to Mexican immigration in the United States held by the Mexican Department of Foreign Relations. We have transcribed a number of these consular documents[1] sent to Mexico in 1926, which represent the judgments of Mexican consuls upon the conditions of life of the immigrant and the treatment that he receives in the United States. These documents present a wide range of opinion, from those in which the consul's judgment is highly favorable as to the situation and treatment of the Mexican in the United States, to those in which the immigrant's position is painted in very dark colors.

The Mexican government does not like to see the emigration, particularly that of a permanent character, become extensive, since this means a step backward in the progress of Mexico and a definite loss in useful energy for the development of the country. However, since it would not be constitutional to forbid emigration to those who wish to go, the government may only prevent as far as possible illegal departures and endeavor to better economic conditions in Mexico in order to decrease the number of those who go to other countries in search of labor.

The attitude of the immigrant.—The immigrant recognizes and proclaims the economic advantages offered to him by the United States as well as the favorable influence which the American environment has upon his physical, intellectual, and moral development. But at the same time he is offended by, and, whenever possible, protests against, the hostility or lack of racial or social appreciation which he frequently receives. He does not find in that country a true homeland even when he

[1] Now deposited with the Social Science Research Council.

becomes naturalized, while the love which he has for Mexico is greatly increased—a fact which explains the large number of immigrants who become repatriated every year. Since unfortunately the economic situation which he finds in his own country on returning is just as difficult as that which caused him to leave in the first place, he often finds himself obliged to depart once more to the United States. Beyond a doubt when the industrial exploitation of natural resources, the improvement of cultivation of land, the development of means of transportation and irrigation now undertaken by Mexico, as also the spreading industrial and agricultural education, begin to give visible result, the emigration to the United States will diminish progressively; for Mexico will need and use all her people in the development of the great lands which today lie fallow, in the transportation of their products, and in the industries which will arise around the great number of natural raw products. All this will of course suffice to raise wages and support the population, making it unnecessary to seek a livelihood elsewhere.

Undesirability of permanent immigration.—The permanent immigrant causes the problems to which we have referred, for generally he does not merge with the American population; he does not become an American, nor does he adapt himself to American life. He is prevented from doing so by the racial prejudice against him and also by the enormous difference in tradition and custom, and even the geographical difference— all important factors in his life in the United States. Often, as Mexican consulates can confirm, immigrants who have been in the United States for many years, as much as fifteen or even twenty years, ask for land in Mexico and colonize it. A case in point is provided by the immigrants we visited in Laguna, California, now established in Acámbaro, Guanajuato. Unfortunately, such colonization projects are not often successful because as a rule they are badly organized; and sometimes the ability and experience of the returned immigrant is absorbed and even blotted out by the culturally inferior environment to which he returns.

Transient immigration advantageous to both countries.—The transient immigrant adapts himself still less to American life; indeed, scarcely at all. He is not a permanent problem in any sense. He goes back and forth between Mexico and the United States continually, and in the United States travels from state to state, following the demand for labor of the sort which he performs.

Laissez faire.—We have heard it said that the best policy that can be adopted with regard to the immigration of Mexican workmen from Mexico to the United States is that of laissez faire, because its fluctuations are corrected automatically in accordance with the demand for labor in the United States and the supply of laborers in Mexico. We should be in accord with this suggestion if it were a matter of import and export of mere goods and chattels, machines, or animals, since it is possible that in such transactions economic laws rule exclusively. But it is "human material" that is being manipulated; the treatment required is very different, even setting aside paternalistic interests and purely sentimental abstract principles.

It is a fact that in the United States, from a strictly economic point of view, Mexican immigration benefits certain American interests. However, because of the profound difference which exists between the characters, the ideals, and the needs of the American and those of the Spanish-Indian elements which make up this immigration, this immigration into the United States often results in difficulties, and the Mexican population becomes an artificial imposition upon the American nation and, in so much, useless.

Mexico in her turn benefits economically through the emigration of laborers to the United States, since this emigration acts as a real safety-valve for men out of work. Moreover, the immigrants constantly send from the United States to Mexico the comparatively large sums of money which have been the subject of comment in other chapters. However, these benefits pale before the alarming outlook which the growing depopulation of the country presents and which is directly produced by the exaggerated development of permanent emigration. Moreover, it must be added that the disorganization and lack of system with which this immigration is effected brings with it injuries of every sort to the immigrants themselves. We shall give some examples. The Mexican laborers do not know exactly in advance in what parts of the United States, at what precise times, and in what precise numbers there is a demand for their services—a fact which frequently brings it about that in some parts of the country the supply of Mexican labor is insufficient, while in others it is excessive, and in some not needed at all. In the first case harvests are partly lost or industries are disturbed, while in the other two cases great numbers of men are thrown out of work. There should also be mentioned here the abuses of every sort of which the immigrants are victims and which help to make their own situation worse and their labor inefficient; for example, the attitude of employers who charge very high rents for small and dirty houses.

Briefly, the observations which we have made in those parts of the country where the Mexicans are congregating, as well as the observations we have made with regard to public opinion in both countries as to Mexican immigration to the United States, permit us to state that if this immigration is allowed to develop under the conditions prevailing at this writing there is no doubt but that it will become necessary to cut it off entirely or to diminish it to insignificant proportions. This would be done either by means of the quota, which the United States Congress would establish with respect to Mexico, or else by special legislation of the Mexican Congress.

However brought about, the sudden paralysis of immigration probably would bring with it the following unfavorable results for both countries:

First.—The present permanent immigrant population in the United States will definitely establish itself there, and the problem which it entails will thus remain unsolved.

Second.—Transient or temporary immigration will not be able to leave Mexico. Therefore the temporary problem which it involves in the United States will disappear. On the other hand, keeping such would-be immigrants in Mexico will possibly create grave problems for Mexico, in view of the economic difficulties of that country A problem of unemployment can thus arise. This can very easily develop into a social struggle, causing disorder and conflict. Furthermore, Mexico will suffer in so far as the education in agriculture and industry which thousands of people now receive in the United States will cease, thus bringing to an end the benefit which Mexico receives when they go back to that country and help to make of it a flourishing nation, agriculturally and industrially.

Third.—Those industrial and agricultural interests in the United States which depend on Mexican labor will suffer in direct proportion to the shortage of Mexican labor, and other interests will suffer indirectly.

Fourth.—The one hundred thousand, or perhaps more, Mexican immigrants who probably pass from Mexico to the United States and back again every year not only consume goods of American manufacture, but probably help the foreign trade of the United States, as on their return to Mexico they introduce these goods and create among their countrymen a demand for them. Should a quota be established for Mexico, this free advertising would cease. So far as American manufacturers are concerned, this advertising gives better results than one promoted by special agents, who could never reach the places where the repatriated Mexican lives.

CHAPTER XIV

THE CONTROL OF MEXICAN IMMIGRATION: SOME SUGGESTIONS

The considerations advanced in the preceding chapter suggest that interests and organizations concerned with the migration of Mexican laborers to the United States adopt as their fundamental aim the restriction of permanent migration and the encouragement of temporary or transient migration. In order to act effectively there should be harmonious collaboration of three groups: the official, the scientific, and the social.

The official group.—This is made up of the legislative bodies and the departments or executive bureaus of both countries, which, directly or indirectly, are concerned with questions relative to Mexican migration between Mexico and the United States. In the United States we believe the chief of these bodies are the Senate; the House of Representatives; and the Departments of Labor, State, Interior, and Agriculture. In Mexico they are the Chambers of Senators and Deputies; Secretariats of Government, Foreign Relations, Agriculture, and Industry and Commerce; and the Department of Health.

Action that Mexico might take.—Mexico might attack the question in two ways: (1) restrict permanent emigration directly and encourage temporary emigration through legal or administrative measures; (2) gradually repatriate the Mexican immigrants who are established in the United States.

1. *Legal and administrative measures.*—These might well include the determination, with greater exactness than has been possible in this study, of the cities and the zones from which come the principal groups of immigrants (the permanent as well as the transitory or temporary), the centers of concentra-

tion other than those already enumerated in chapter XII, and the routes and means of transportation used by the emigrants.

The authorities would then give frequent and timely information, in the frontier ports of entry and in these zones and centers of concentration, as to the demand for temporary or permanent Mexican labor prevailing in the United States, as well as to wages and conditions of labor. It should be made clear that the services of the laborer will be utilized only during certain periods of the year, and that the laborer will be obliged to return to Mexico after his work is ended. In his part of the contract the employer should be obliged to pay the transportation of the laborer from the frontier to his destination and return. It should be explained that it is as much in the interests of the laborer himself as for immigration in general to hold strictly to the limitation of temporary residence, and that violation of this provision would result in immediate deportation from the United States and would bar the violator out in the future. The laborer would be informed of the difficulties and penalties attending illegal entry into this country. In the frontier ports of entry identification tickets stamped "temporary labor" would be given out to all the laborers who agree to return to Mexico after the end of their seasonal work. Of those who have come to Mexico occasionally but who live in the United States, or who are going to the United States for the first time, proof of the circumstances bringing them in would be demanded. They would then be given a card stamped "permanent labor," and be allowed to establish themselves there permanently. On this card would be indicated the type of occupation in which the laborer has engaged in Mexico so as to assist him in finding like occupation in the United States.

It would be absolutely necessary to keep these tickets because they would be demanded in the American migration offices and would have to be presented when contracts were made or when the individual returned to Mexico. The laborers' tickets for departure would be frequently compared with their entrance tickets in order to find out what proportion are complying with earlier arrangements and what proportion are failing to comply.

The contracts for temporary labor would be made in the frontier ports of entry, on either side of the frontier, but would be visaed by the authorities of both countries. These would keep duplicates of the *visés*, and they would keep record of the proportion of contracts properly carried out and those which are broken by the one party or the other. The contractors would be registered in both countries and would pay a certain tax.

Another important step which could be taken by the Mexican authorities is the repatriation of the old permanent immigrants principally through the colonization of national lands. They should also place strong penalties upon the smuggling of immigrants. It would be well also to make upon the Mexican frontier a preparatory health examination of the immigrants, and to furnish them the necessary certificates so that the examination in the American offices would not have to be so severe.

To receive the above-mentioned tickets the immigrant would pay a small tax which would help to keep up the new service. This tax would not be burdensome because it would help to assure the holder of the ticket the performance of certain definite work, thus avoiding the loss of time and the expenses which at present a man entails who is waiting until a contractor decides to employ him.

2. *Repatriation of Mexican immigrants permanently established in the United States.*—The situation recommends a plan to diminish, through the measures described above, the number of emigrants who in the future may seek to establish them-

selves permanently in the United States. But it is of much greater importance to Mexico that the immigrants who have been already for some time established in the country be repatriated. In fact, these Mexicans have acquired during their stay in the United States valuable experience in agriculture or industry; they have learned to handle machinery and modern tools; they have discipline and steady habits of work. Moreover, their material and cultural requirements are generally greater than they were when they left Mexico. Having risen in the economic scale, they have been able to better themselves not only as to food, clothing, living-quarters, and acquisition of tools and furniture, but they have also abandoned, wholly or partly, fanatical religion; they tend to join together in co-operative or charitable organizations, and they have acquired the habit of reading the newspapers. They frequently have savings in the bank, and perhaps a small house and the lot upon which it stands.

Realizing the desirable qualities of these permanent immigrants, the government of General Obregon lent its support to a plan for the repatriation of various Mexican groups in the United States. With the same object the government of General Calles arranged that the lands of various *haciendas* which had been nationalized be divided and offered on easy conditions of sale and on long terms of payment not only to the rural inhabitants of Mexico but also to the Mexicans resident in the United States.

Unfortunately, almost all the attempts at repatriation and colonization have failed because the immigrants do not well organize themselves, and in general have sought to have the government consider such attempts in a paternalistic light. In the Appendixes we refer to the causes of these failures and present some suggestion for avoiding them.

Action that the United States might take.—The most important measure consistent with the policy we have indicated would be the modification of the Immigration Law in the following respects: (1) permitting unlimited entry of temporary labor that has been contracted for, provided that in these contracts the employers agree to furnish transportation to the laborer from the frontier to the point where he is to work and return; (2) permitting the entry of temporary laborers who cannot read and write; (3) fixing a maximum or quota with respect to immigrants intending to remain permanently, excluding all illiterates of this class, since these raise cultural problems in the United States while the temporary laborers do not; (4) providing that the sum for the consular *visé* and head-tax (eighteen dollars) be paid only by the permanent immigrants and exempting the temporary laborers from this provision or reducing the amount that they pay.

It would be desirable also to have better information than is now available as to the number and distribution of Mexicans in the United States. Any such estimates should be made at different times during the year, for the number of Mexicans fluctuates with the seasons. We are interested chiefly in knowing the number of agricultural workers, industrial laborers, and artisans (both skilled and unskilled labor). Most of these are found in comparatively few states. It would be advisable to request the state and municipal authorities and the Mexican consulates in the regions where Mexicans are numerous, as well as the employers of Mexican labor on a large scale, to furnish information as to the number of Mexicans in those places.

The employers should be required to give public notice of the dates when temporary laborers begin and end their work. The contractors will be under similar obligation with regard to the dates when temporary laborers enter and leave the United States and will always make accessible to the authorities the records and lists of laborers who have been contracted for.

The proper authorities will compare periodically these lists of the entry of temporary labor into the country with those of their departures in order to keep track of the favorable or unfavorable course that the experiment is taking; that is to say, to compare the proportion of temporary laborers who return annually to Mexico with those who, failing to keep their promises, remain in the United States. Study of these records would permit conclusions as to the economic effect which this experiment is having on the efficiency of labor, and the wage scale in the regions where temporary immigrants ordinarily work.

The tickets of temporary labor and permanent labor given out in Mexico would serve the American immigration authorities as well as employers and contracting laborers as useful sources of information for regulating the admission of laborers and classifying them, as well as selecting them and distributing their activities efficiently.

Joint action of both countries.—We believe that it is quite essential that the departments and bureaus mentioned above, which in both countries have direct or indirect contact with the movements of Mexican laborers, be constantly in contact with one another and exchange periodically data and information upon the migration. The wide discrepancy between Mexican and American statistics as to the number of Mexicans crossing the border testifies to the need for such co-operative collection of accurate information.

The scientific group.—The immigration of Mexican laborers between Mexico and the United States is one of the most interesting subjects of study to which both Mexican and American institutions of social science can devote themselves—such institutions, as for example, the Social Science Research Council in the United States and similar institutions in Mexico. Moreover, it would be well for the universities and colleges of both countries, principally those from the regions from which the immigration comes and those in which it generally establishes itself (such as the Universidad Nacional and the universities and professional schools of Jalisco, Michoacan, Guanajuato, Aguascalientes, Zacatecas, and Chihuahua in Mexico, and California, Texas, Arizona, Colorado, Illinois, and New Mexico in the United States), to aid in this work. It is necessary for the best success of certain of the investigations made in the United States that native Mexicans or those of other nationalities who are well acquainted with Spanish take part, since, granted the special psychological complex which, as we have indicated above, characterizes the Mexican immigrants and Mexican-American groups, many obstacles will be found if the investigators speak only English.

The fundamental causes of Mexican immigration to the United States are, as we have indicated, exclusively economic, but the concomitant phenomena are ethnic, social, cultural, psychological, and linguistic. Therefore, in order to come to a scientifically satisfactory conclusion upon the problem, we must investigate both the antecedents of the migration and its actual development in all aspects, not merely the economic.

Furthermore, this migratory movement affords an opportunity to make scientific studies on the frontiers of both countries on hundreds of thousands of individuals derived from many different Indian and *mestizo* groups. This could be done there far more cheaply and easily than it could be done in the regions of their provenance, in view of the time and expense that would be required to go to these different points of origin. Investigations can likewise be carried on of the contacts, of all sorts, which are made between these immigrants, representatives of the Spanish-Indian population of America, and the Anglo-Saxon element in the United States. In no other part of the continent are these contacts taking place so extensively.

We take the liberty of adding some further suggestions in line with the conclusions heretofore expressed.

We suggest that a study be made of the general economic conditions of the regions from which the Mexican comes, and thereafter a study of the economic situation in the regions of the United States to which the immigrant goes, and especially of the effect of the influx upon this situation.[1]

The data which we obtained and compiled from the records of the national Mexican post-office, giving the names, points of origin, and points of location in the United States of Mexican immigrants, together with the sums they sent back to Mexico by postal money order, cover only six months. It would be useful to collect and analyze all this available information covering a period of nine years. This would permit of reliable conclusions as to savings, movements, occupations, family anteced- ents, conditions, origin, and distribution of the immigrants. This information would include more than half-a-million indi- vidual cases, and from it one could derive a fairly accurate idea of the general trend of the life of the immigrant during those nine years.

The banking houses and life insurance companies, both in Mexico and the United States, can also supply some informa- tion as to the economic condition of the immigrants.

The anthropometric, physiological, and pathological inves- tigation of the Indians and *mestizos* of Mexico is more difficult to make in view of the obstacles we have mentioned before. It is chiefly for these reasons that no one of the ethnic groups of the indigenous Mexican population has been satisfactorily studied. To obtain positive results, that is, to establish the

[1] Two excellent recent studies of the economics of a region dependent on Mexican labor are Dr. Paul S. Taylor's *Mexican Labor in the United States: Imperial Valley*, "University of California Publications in Economics," VI, No. 1 (1928), 1–94, and his *Mexican Labor in the United States Valley of the South Platte, Colorado, ibid.*, No. 2, pp. 95–235.—EDITOR

characteristics of a given group, an anthropological bureau could be established at one of the ports of entry, for instance, Ciudad Juarez, El Paso. This bureau would function during the period of the year in which the entry or departure of Mexican labor is greatest. From among the immigrants could be chosen persons who have never been in the United States and who belong to the ethnic groups from which the immigration chiefly comes; from an examination of these samples the characteristics of the group could be established. The same method would be followed for immigrants returning from the United States after having lived for a certain length of time under the influence of the American environment. It would also be necessary to obtain, in various regions of the United States, the anthropological characteristics of Mexicans born in the United States, that is, of American Mexicans. This information, together with the geographic-climatic data of the regions in Mexico from which immigration comes, and the regions in the United States over which it is distributed, would be basis enough for scientific conclusions as to the manner of adjustment to the physical environment of the United States.

Little information is available upon the death- and birth-rates of the immigrants, their chief illnesses and the causes of these illnesses. To secure this information from the proper official and private sources such statistics should if possible be collected with separate lists of the Mexican immigrants; in most data available now they are considered together with Americans of Mexican origin and sometimes with immigrants of other nationalities.

An investigation should be made to determine the characteristics of the mixed Mexican culture to which most of the immigrants belong. An analysis should be made of its derivation and development from native and European culture; that is, the subjects which are barely outlined in chapter v should be given detailed attention. Similar but briefer investigation should be made of native culture, because a smaller proportion of the immigrants belong to it. We believe that it is essential to make these investigations first, as without this information it is impossible to describe and understand correctly the phenomena of contact between the Indian and mixed civilizations of the immigrants and modern American civilization. Without the results of such investigation, neither the immigrants nor the Mexican-American citizens can be properly studied.

The social group.—By "social group" we mean those organizations of both countries which have no official character and which directly or indirectly have or can have some connection with the migration of Mexican laborers between Mexico and the United States. These institutions can effectively aid in the regulation of temporary immigration, and in the restriction of permanent immigration, and at the same time see to it that the life of the immigrants during their stay in the United States is passed in accordance with the principles of true justice and humanity. Labor unions, chambers of commerce, churches, institutions of welfare and relief, scientific institutions, and lodges are groups of this character.

As examples we can mention certain organizations which are proceeding in this direction. Although the American Federation of Labor is against Mexican immigration because the Mexican competes with its members, its point of view is sympathetic with Mexican labor, as it has shown by lending a decided support to the organization of labor in Mexico, principally to the Confederación Regional Obrera Mexicana. Nevertheless we believe that this friendly attitude should manifest itself especially with regard to the Mexican laborers in the United States, since they are more in need of organization, of help, and above all of protection than are those living in Mexico. The American Federation of Labor can, first of all, help the Mexican workers to fight the abuses of which they are victims on the part of the employers, especially with regard to the very small wages—wages which are insufficient for the necessities of existence but which nevertheless the Mexican workers in some parts of the countries often find themselves obliged to accept. Another such abuse is the failure to carry out contracts of work or promises to pay the fare back to the frontier when seasonal work has ended. The plan here suggested to organize temporary immigration and restrict permanent immigration will be a good thing for the American workers, as it will diminish the competition of permanent Mexican immigrants and will lessen or even obviate altogether the competition brought about by temporary laborers in those periods of the year when they are needed in the United States. The labor situation which would probably result is that the permanent immigrants would confine themselves to the industries, since these use labor all year round. This would result in improvements in the skill and abilities of these immigrants—improvements which are difficult to attain when it is a matter of men who are working only for short periods of time in the factories. The temporary immigrants, on the other hand, would probably devote themselves exclusively to the agricultural work, which is seasonal.

The chambers of commerce.—These bodies, and other employers' organizations, might contribute to the solution of the problem by means of the following undertakings: (1) A classification of the immigrants upon their entry into the United States in accordance with the occupations which they have carried on in Mexico and into the following groups: skilled or unskilled; rural or urban; coming from the *tierra fría, templada,* or *tierra caliente.* A knowledge of these data will aid in making a rational geographical and occupational distribution of the laborers, and will further the efficiency of the work which they are carrying on. (2) The determination in advance of the parts of the United States where Mexican labor is needed, or what sort of labor is required, at what times of the year and what wages are there paid. (3) Securing the Mexican laborer wages equivalent to those paid an American laborer for the same work. This measure would not only be just but also be profitable for the employers, since thus would be avoided the conflicts which quite naturally occur between American and Mexican laborers because the latter accept lower wages—conflicts which are against the interests of the employer. The Mexican immigrant loudly proclaims that his work would be more efficient if he were rewarded with the same wages which, under the same conditions, the American laborer receives, since it would be logical to give him the opportunity to increase his capacity for production at the same time that his economic condition is bettered. (4) Combating in every way possible the evil activities and inhuman exploitation which all smugglers of immigrants carry on, and many contractors of immigrant labor as well. The bad treatment and deceit of which the immigrants are victims prejudice them in advance against the employers, and therefore they do not carry out their work with proper efficiency. Chambers of commerce could advise the employers to obtain the Mexican labor they need through the legal machinery we have suggested, and not through smugglers and criminal contractors. It will be to the interests of the employers if temporary immigration is encouraged and organized and permanent immigration is restricted for the following reasons: First of all, the threat of serious danger from the application of the quota to Mexican immigration will disappear, for there will be no reason for the quota when the serious problems which the development of permanent immigration carries with it are lessened or almost entirely removed. Second, temporary laborers can then be obtained and distributed at just those times of the year when they are needed; in this way the injuries which excess or lack of labor brings both to the employer and the employed will be avoided. Third, it will no longer be the case that some regions will have an excess of laborers while others will not have enough, because there will be no reason for unnecessary labor competition. Fourth, as railway traffic will increase largely because of the continual transport of temporary laborers from the Mexican frontier to their destination in the United States and return, the chambers of commerce can ask from the railroads a decrease in the cost of transportation for laborers, and moreover they can demand that the conditions under which travel is carried on conform with the elementary requirements of health and comfort.

Churches.—The Mexican immigrant is in a curious psychological state in so far as his religious ideas are concerned. For many years he has been a witness and even an actor in the conflict, which recently became a sanguinary conflict, between the lawfully constituted civil authorities and the Catholic clergy of Mexico. Upon arriving in the United States he frequently takes part in another struggle, that which is going on between Catholicism and Protestantism—a struggle which occasionally assumes a combative and even bitter character. In the preceding chapter on religious ideas we could not include some of the occasionally defamatory controversial literature of propaganda which circulates in some regions where there are many Mexicans. The religions and churches of both parties will not accomplish the spiritual and ethical betterment of the Mexican immigrants if in place of inculcating noble and lofty precepts of true Christianity they turn them into spoils of war. Undoubtedly the members of both churches who have a genuinely apostolic spirit have observed the existence of this harmful situation and will endeavor to combat it, but nevertheless we have felt ourselves obliged to refer to it emphatically in the interests of the moral well-being of the immigrant. On the other hand, it should be recalled that both churches, and principally the Protestant, strive generously to supply with material necessities poor or sick immigrants.

Press.—We have already said that one of the principal aims of the Mexican press published in the United States is to make itself heard by the general public and the American authorities in the defense of the interests and rights of the Mexican population. This press has arisen, among other reasons, because the American press regards the Mexican element as of very small importance or ignores it completely. In fact, with the exception of some few American periodicals in parts of the country in which there are hundreds of thousands of Mexicans, so that they necessarily must be taken into account since they form part of the reading public of these papers, the majority of papers know nothing and for that reason say nothing in their columns of a social group, the growth of which within the American nation is beginning to show how contacts between Spanish-Indian and Anglo-Saxon elements of this continent result. As an example we may cite the contrast between the manner in which the American press treats the offenses, the crimes, and the abuses of Americans and the way in which it treats similar events when Mexicans are involved. When an American citizen is assassinated in Mexico, both the Mexican and American presses demand unanimously and loudly that justice be secured, while in the United States when a Mexican is killed by an American and the latter remains unpunished the Mexican press immediately protests but the American press generally makes no mention of the case.

Organizations for welfare and relief, clinics, etc.—We can really make no suggestion with regard to the activities of these organizations. The truly disinterested character of the humanitarian work which is growing up on behalf of the immigrants who need help and council compels the gratitude not only of the immigrants but also of all the Mexicans who live in Mexico.

Artistic organizations.—The presence of the Mexican immigrant in the United States is a most important factor which will contribute powerfully to the establishment of an art which is genuinely American, granted that the aptitudes of the Mexican are as far as possible encouraged and utilized. Unfortunately, until recently the innate artistic gifts of the immigrant have been checked and even destroyed through the competition of machine production and the indifference of the public. Anybody can prove this assertion by means of the following experiment. If of a group of immigrants recently come in the United States a certain number of adults and children are selected, and, following the system adopted in the primary schools of Mexico, they are asked to paint, to draw, or even to carve in wood some object or theme of their surroundings, it will be very probable that they will produce works of an undeniable artistic value. If they are asked to make a song and to compose the music to accompany it, the results will be the same. However, if the same experiment were tried with Mexican-Americans, it would be seen that the artistic results were insignificant and always inferior to those which could be obtained from immigrants just come from Mexico.

This applies to the immigrants in general, but if among these were selected some who besides possessing artistic ability have had some technical training in Mexico, the result would be more important than the common labor which they generally perform as unskilled workers.

We should suggest, then, that American institutions of art select a group of immigrant artists: musicians, sculptors, painters, designers, carvers in wood and stone, leather-workers, weavers of *zarapes* in many colored designs, workers in precious metals and stones, and allow them to develop their work without attempting of course to impose any artistic rules upon the nature of the productions, which should be absolutely spontaneous. It is very probable that after a certain period of observing, selecting, and assimilating beautiful motives from the American environment, they would produce works of art more or less freed of European aesthetic influences, which would contribute to the formation of a genuinely American art.

With reference to the artistic industries it would be necessary to investigate in Mexico which are the most interesting in order to choose, and adapt them for development in those parts of the United States where materials are obtainable easily and markets are accessible. We are aware that the artistic crafts can hardly compete in matter of price with machine-made products, but the problem is of great enough importance to deserve special attention in order to discover some solution.

Lodges, associations, and societies.—It is very commendable that the Mexican immigrants and the Mexican-Americans develop their spirit of sociability and establish many organizations, but it would be a very good thing if in their formation and administration they would be influenced by the steadiness, efficiency, and practical considerations which characterize similar American organizations. Thus unreasonable emotionalism, depressing sentimentalism, combative impulses, impatient enthusiasms, fickle efforts, easy and quick pretenses, and other characteristics which often appear inherent in the character of the immigrants when they form associations and in less degree are found in the Mexican-Americans will always block the progress of their organizations.

It would be well if the organizations of which we have spoken above be in contact with similar organizations in Mexico, since these in their turn can develop like activities before the immigrants leave Mexico and after they return to this country.

APPENDIX I

GUIDE FOR FIELD-WORKERS USED IN CONNECTION WITH THIS PRELIMINARY STUDY

AN OUTLINE OF POINTS TO BE CONSIDERED, BOTH OBJECTIVELY
AND SUBJECTIVELY, WITH REGARD TO THE MEXICAN IMMI-
GRANTS: THOSE WHO PRESERVE THEIR OWN NATIONALITY,
THOSE WHO BECOME NATIONALIZED AMERICANS, AND THOSE
WHO ARE AMERICANS BY BIRTH BUT OF MEXICAN DESCENT

Attention should be directed principally toward those individuals who
are typical representatives of the Mexican immigration—that is to say,
the *mestizos* and full-blooded Indians who make up the greater part of
both unskilled and skilled labor and the tenant and share farmers.

Objective observation.—In general, information should be obtained by
direct observation rather than by the questioning of individuals, families,
or groups upon whose way of behaving and manner of living information
is sought. When interrogation is necessary, outsiders should be questioned
rather than those who are under observation. All the material and non-
material aspects presented by the subjects of investigation should be observed, but particularly the following:

Food.—Do they eat American foods exclusively or also articles of food
imported from Mexico? Is their diet varied or does it continue to be
basically vegetarian, as it was in Mexico? Are the methods of cooking and
seasoning predominantly American or Mexican, or are they a mixture of
both? The use of the various sorts of chili? Do they make *tortillas* of corn
or wheat or of both? How do they feed small children?

Housing.—What about the number of people who live in each house
and in each room, and the number of cubic meters of air which each individual can breathe? What sort of toilets have they? Do they wash clothing by hand or by washing-machine? In what does personal cleanliness
consist? Do they keep their clothing in closets or in wardrobes? What
sort of furniture have they? (Special attention should be given to pictures and *objets d'art*, to portraits of famous Mexicans or Americans, to
American or Mexican flags, and to little altars or tables which are placed
before a holy image or historical hero and which bear flowers or other

offerings.) The dining-room and kitchen furnishings, are they American or are there a number of objects brought from Mexico? Is there a similarity between their houses and those which they occupied in Mexico?

Clothing.—An enumeration of the wearing apparel of all sorts should be made. What are the work clothes and what the street clothes? The difference between the clothes worn by field laborers and city and factory workers? Is there a preference for lively colors? For which? Is there a preference shown for the cowboy costume? Do they generally use the Texan *sombrero* in the fields? Can the Mexican influence be seen in their way of dressing? In what does this influence consist?

Religion.—What is the character of the churches which they attend in comparison with the churches which they attended in Mexico? Are there many images of saints and mural decorations? Do the images appear wasted and bleeding? Are there offerings at the "miraculous" images of gold and silver, wax candles, flowers, and so on? Do they wear around their necks small chains or cords bearing medals, scapularies, or reliquaries? In what do these latter consist and to what saints do they belong? Which are the favorite saints among the images of the church?

Amusements.—Do they attend theaters, circuses, moving pictures, or dance halls? Do they own radios, phonographs, pianos, or any other musical instruments? What sorts are they? Do they have picnics and excursions to the country? Are Mexican influences shown in their amusements?

Sports.—Are they fond of athletics, including baseball, football, boxing, swimming, hunting, etc.?

Press.—Do they read newspapers written in English or in Spanish or in both? What are the newspapers and where are they published? Is there a Mexican influence discernible in the press?

Ceremonial.—Relative to birth, marriage, and death: What Mexican influences can be observed here?

Work.—In what occupations do they engage? How many hours daily? What occupations do they prefer? Do they belong to the American Federation of Labor? Have they accident insurance? How well do they perform their work?

Birth control.—What is an average of the number of children in the family of the immigrant before coming to the United States and after a long stay in this country? An average of the number of children in the Mexican-American family? Is birth control practiced? What means are used?

Economic situation.—As to wages, expenditures, savings, life insurance: Do they own the houses in which they live or the land which they cultivate, or do they pay rent? Do they buy their clothes, food, furniture, and other objects by cash or credit payments? Do they send money to Mexico?

Education.—What sort of schools do they attend? What do they pursue and how far do they go? What are their natural aptitudes? Compare with the situation among white Americans.

Vices.—Are they abstemious or very fond of alcoholic drinks? Of what sorts? Do they use *marihuana* and other narcotic drugs? Does prostitution exist? Of what sort? Is there a tendency to gamble?

Crimes.—Which are the principal types of crime? Is the imposition of the death penalty frequent? What type of sentence is most common? What is the attitude of the jails with regard to prisoners of other races? What are the effects of American justice upon the morality of the Mexican?

Race prejudice.—In what does the race prejudice to which they are subjected by the white man consist? Compare with the attitude of the whites in regard to the Negro, and vice versa. How do the Mexicans and Americans of Mexican origin react to the race prejudice of which they are the objects?

Subjective observations.—Since direct and inopportune interrogation of individuals who are being studied does not always give satisfactory results, it is often a good thing to stimulate reactions and to excite the memories of individuals studied in an indirect way. One of the best ways to accomplish this is to establish contacts with a group to which the individual belongs and to listen to his spontaneous conversation. Then, since this conversation generally makes reference to certain special aspects of his experience, the observer put questions upon the subject under discussion to the individuals engaged in conversation and thus brings it about that not only the latter but also the person under observation will reply, even though he has not been directly interrogated. Finally, if the attitude of the individual under observation appears to be confiding and spontaneous and his reactions are uninhibited, he also may be questioned. If the observer possesses a good memory and especially if he has good assistants, a number of individuals in each conversing group may be observed. The questions should not be formulated exactly like those suggested, but the wording and ideology should be adapted to the grade of mentality and culture of the individual under observation. The following questions are to serve as no more than a help or guide for a just approach to the methods of drawing out the individual with special attention to the social medium and the psychological environment in which he lives.

QUESTIONS FOR MEXICAN-AMERICANS AND NATURALIZED MEXICANS

PATRIOTISM

Are you a Mexican who has become a naturalized American or are you American by birth and nationality, but Mexican in origin?

Do you celebrate the Mexican civic festivals, such as Independence Day on September 16, or the American, such as the Fourth of July, or both? Which stirs you more, the former or the latter?

Do you know who were Washington, Hidalgo, Lincoln, Juarez?

Do you feel equally sympathetic with Americans as with Mexican-Americans?

Do the Americans show sympathy with you?

Do you have the same opportunities that the Americans have?

Do you feel sympathy or antipathy for the Mexican immigrants, and to what are your feelings due?

Do you think it is a good thing to apply the immigration quota to them so that they are restricted in coming to the United States?

Whom do you include within the general term "The Race"?

Do you include only the descendants of Mexicans or also the Central and South Americans or the so-called Latins, such as the French, Italians, etc., as well?

Do you believe that those who constitute "The Race" are destined to a happier future or to be absorbed by the Anglo-Saxon race on this continent?

In case of war with the United States, would you take the side of the Americans and fight the Mexicans?

Do you have the same idea of your native land as the Americans do?

RACE

Would you prefer to marry a Mexican-American, a Mexican, or an American?

Do you like American women on account of their white skin, because they are more beautiful than the women you know, or because you think your social position would be improved?

Do Americans like to marry Mexican-Americans or not? What is the reason for their attitude in this regard?

Do Negroes like to marry Mexican-Americans or vice versa? Is this case an exception to the general rule?

Do you like to have many children or few?

Do you enjoy a good economic situation, political liberties, and social harmony in the part of the country in which you live?

Do you live in a district composed exclusively of Mexican-Americans or is it composed of both these and Americans?

Are there also Mexican immigrants living in the district with the Mexican-Americans? Is there harmony between both groups?

Are the American people with whom you have to do kind-hearted, honorable, and generous with regard to the Mexican-Americans or rather selfish and proud, or very indifferent?

DOMESTIC TENDENCIES

Do you have Mexican cooking in your house?

Do you read Mexican or American newspapers or both?

Do you use the modern American implements in your farming and industrial work; in your home do you have sewing, washing, ironing machines, etc.?

Do you like American or Mexican music or both?

Would you like to establish yourself in Mexico if you had there the means for a livelihood similar to those you have here?

In Texas and other parts of the United States the Mexican immigrants are called *cholos* and *chicamos*, the Mexican-Americans *pochos*, the American men are *bolillos*, and the American women *cristalinas;* are similar or different names used here?

RELIGION

Are you a Catholic?

Do you confess, partake of communion, have your children baptized, go to mass?

What festivals of the church do you keep?

Have you made requests of the saints and fulfilled the vows and offerings if your petition was granted? Give examples of some of these.

Have you a special predilection or feeling of devotion for God, the Virgin Mary, for Jesus Christ, or for a special saint?

How do you feel about the Protestants?

Have you ever considered changing your religion?

Do you think that you can be a Catholic and a Mason at the same time?

If you are a Protestant, and always have been one, what do you think of the Catholics and the Masons?

Are you a Mason?

What do you think in this case of the Catholics and the Protestants and of their churches?

Are there in your lodge Americans, Mexicans, and Mexican-Americans?

AFFILIATIONS

Are you in sympathy with the American Federation of Labor or the Industrial Workers of the World, or neither of these?

Do you belong to clubs, political parties, religious or philanthropic organizations, or associations devoted to sport?

SUPERSTITIONS

Do you consult witches or herb doctors when you are sick, when you wish to get good luck, to harm anyone, or to seek defense from someone, to obtain a good harvest, or to better your position, etc.?

What illness do you know can be cured by herb doctors, and in what activities and circumstances of life are witches effective?

What remedies, methods, and ritual do both of these employ?

Have you been a victim of the "evil eye," the "spirits of the air," or have you been bewitched?

Have you had recourse to witches or herb doctors?

The nature of the occupation exerts a great influence upon the life, the customs, and the language of the individual. Thus the questions must be adapted to the sort of occupation engaged in. For example, the workman on the railroad generally lives in isolated encampments where the principal recreation is playing and listening to popular music. As a result, in these places original compositions of merit frequently appear. In the cattle ranches, which are usually remote from the city, traditions, legends, and folk lore of all sorts are abundant. The cotton-picker also has a distinct character as has the laborer on the railroads, the bricklayer, the sheep herder, etc.

Many of the questions given above can also be applied to the Mexican immigrants, since in many respects they resemble the Mexican-Americans, especially the naturalized Mexicans. Exception should of course be made of those questions which require that the individual either had been born in the United States or had had a long stay in this country.

QUESTIONS FOR MEXICAN IMMIGRANTS

ATTITUDE TOWARD AMERICAN LIFE

Why did you leave Mexico?

How long have you been in the United States and how many times have you returned to Mexico?

Do you find the life you lead in the United States pleasant or unpleasant, or pleasant in some aspects and unpleasant in others?

How does this life appear to you in comparison with that which you led in Mexico? What effect does the excessive snow and cold of the winters and heat of the summers produce upon your mind and health?

What impression do the big buildings, the trains, the many automobiles, the factories, the moving-picture houses, and schools of this country make upon you?

How do you find the systems of farming and the fruits and cereals produced here?

Do you like the appearance of the houses, their furnishing and arrangement?

In general, what do you think of what you saw here in comparison with what you saw in Mexico?

Do you wish to adopt American customs or do you prefer to preserve Mexican customs as far as possible?

Do you intend to become nationalized or to nationalize your children?

Have you a definite wish to return to Mexico? Why have you not done so? When do you hope to do so?

Do the laws of this country appear to you more or less strict than those in Mexico?

Do you think you have in this country the freedom that you had in Mexico? What idea have you of freedom?

Have you the same chance to rise in the economic and social scale here as in Mexico? In case this does not occur, to what do you suppose this fact is due?

APPENDIX II

LEGAL AND ILLEGAL ENTRY OF MEXICANS INTO THE UNITED STATES

Legal entry and general information.—A great number of Mexican laborers enter the United States illegally. Those who go through official channels, however, follow this procedure: As soon as they arrive in Ciudad Juarez (this information, secured there, nevertheless holds good for the other ports of entry on the Rio Grande border) they go to some little hotel or boarding-house, and then to the Mexican Migration Office. Since many arrive daily, each one is given a number and waits his turn, sometimes three or four days. Bringing to the Mexican office the documents, photographs, etc., required, the immigrant is given a passport, which he takes to the American consular authorities for a *visé*. This takes a varying time, sometimes even several days. After this he goes to the offices on the international bridge, where he is examined and questioned again, is given literacy tests, and asked how much money he has. Here he pays his head-tax (eight dollars), after which he is given a medical examination and bathed, sometimes with gasoline, while his clothing is disinfected. Women go through the same process. The total cost, head-tax plus visé, is eighteen dollars. On both sides of the border there are "coyotes" who for five dollars arrange that the documents be attained very quickly. The American officials speak Spanish to the immigrants, but often very coarsely and roughly; to this the immigrants as a rule submit quietly, sometimes smilingly.

While waiting for the documents to be put in shape, the immigrants stay in poor hotels and boarding-houses. At this time they change from their peasant's white-cotton clothing or whatever other garment they are wearing into the overalls and jumpers of the laborer. They also buy and wear shoes, instead of the Mexican sandals or *huaraches*. They generally arrive in Ciudad Juarez in groups of three or four, and sometimes stay together even after they have crossed, managing to go to work for the same enterprise. The hotels and boarding-houses where they stay are near the railroad station in Ciudad Juarez. The regular price in these places is fifty cents, Mexican gold, for each person. Four or five individuals generally share one room, and in this case they make a discount to perhaps thirty cents a day; for this reason sometimes as many as ten share one room. They have wide beds, in which two or even three men sleep at once. There is, of course, no bath. Throughout this period of wait, they spend their spare time singing, playing cards, etc., and some even learn to read in those few days, in order to pass the American literacy test. They eat in the markets and cheap restaurants, for about twenty-five *centavos* a meal. Here, also, they begin to change their money, and this often places them in the hands of unscrupulous speculators, who charge high rates both ways. Near by are many photographers, who make a specialty of passport photographs, and professional letter-writers.

Illegal entry.—Because passing through these official channels entails a great deal of bother and delay, and also expense (for besides the money of the head-tax and *visé* there are the living expenses of the days spent in waiting), and since many laborers, furthermore, are not able to pass the literacy tests of the American authorities, a great number of them enter illegally into American territory. It is relatively easy and quite common to smuggle or be smuggled across the border, and there are many people who make a profession of this. The number of illegal entries has recently been materially reduced by the growing effectiveness of the border patrol.

There are several ways of doing this. One of the most frequent in Ciudad Juarez is to take the immigrants to little towns near the official port of entry, which are as a rule scarcely watched. These towns are San Ignacio, San Augustin, Guadalupe, and La Colorada. Here, especially at La Colorada, the border line is little more than a barbed-wire fence, which is easily passed. La Colorada is full of saloons, cheap dance halls, and gambling dens, where come many cowboys and adventures from the American side, to drink, gamble, and cut loose generally. Many of these go to the line in cars, leave the cars at the fence, and jump over into Mexico. This is very easy and not very risky, since there are few officials on the watch, and those few there merely to prevent contraband of munitions or valuable goods. Busses loaded with laborers leave Ciudad Juarez daily for La Colorada, not far away. The trip costs three Mexican *pesos*. These men jump the fence, usually at night, and get work on nearby ranches. Their employers, taking advantage of their risky position, as a rule pay very low wages and treat them almost like slaves.

There are many other ways of crossing, most of them engineered by professional smugglers, called "coyotes," who hang around the *plaza*, hotels, restaurants, and even offices where the laborers must go, and suggest that a lower price—from five to ten dollars—and less trouble, they can go over the border. Sometimes they take them in automobiles across the shallow places in the river, or in carts and trucks. Others are taken in boats, and some even swim across, a dangerous thing to do because the river is treacherous.

The smugglers, or "coyotes," who manage the illegal crossing of the immigrants work as individuals and also in gangs. These people know their ground thoroughly, and the habits of both American and Mexican authorities, and sometimes they even have an arrangement with some district official; therefore they are generally successful in taking their human cargo over. They charge as a rule from five to ten dollars apiece, and more if there is baggage or in unusual cases. Sometimes instead of taking the person over they sell or rent a forged head-tax receipt and passport. Such a receipt costs from two to five dollars, and often it is not sold outright for this price, but merely rented, to be returned once the immigrant using it is safely in American territory. The passports generally belong to people in the United States, who "rent" their document to the smugglers, and they in turn to the immigrants. When the smugglers form a gang, they have men on both sides, either in the offices or along the banks of the river—depending on their system—and they employ a set of signals to avoid an armed clash with the authorities, which nevertheless sometimes occurs.

The smugglers are at times employed by big commercial, industrial, or agricultural enterprises in the border states and even in the interior of the United States, which have need of Mexican labor. When labor is scarce, they pay to the smuggler so much for each laborer imported, and when labor is plentiful, they maintain the smuggler on a salary basis. Most of the immigrants are under contract before they cross, although this is against the American laws, and therefore they are instructed to say that they are going in search of labor. Soliciting labor from one side to the other is likewise against the Mexican laws, but this goes on under cover. Just on the other side of the river are stationed the offices of the contractors, or *enganchistas*, who either make or clinch the bargain. From these offices men are sent to ranches, railroads, factories, or wherever labor is needed and has been asked for. The contractors get, generally, from fifty cents to a dollar for each man they supply. Sometimes the enterprises themselves smuggle their own labor over, but as a rule they prefer to "contract" for it; married men are preferred to single.

There are a great many abuses and many ways in which the immigrants are exploited. From the beginning they are absolutely in the hands of the contractor, and even more so if they have been smuggled by him. One of the most common abuses is the "camp store," the concession for which is sold to the contractor, who makes enough out of the store—living expenses and traveling expenses of the laborers, charged to them according to his own will—to repay him well for the trouble. Immigrants contracted for and taken to their place of work are often overcharged greatly for food and incidental expenses on the road, and in the camp. Since the wages of the men are kept in the hands of the contractor until the debt to him is paid, generally for the first two or three weeks the laborer gets nothing, and sometimes it results that he is in debt to the contractor at the end of that time.

In spite of American and Mexican laws, the smuggling agents are numerous, for the demand for labor pays them well, and even when caught and fined they do not suffer greatly because, since the fine is about a hundred *pesos*, and since a "coyote" sometimes earns that much in one day, two or even more such fines a month can well be borne.

APPENDIX III[1]

RACE RELATIONS IN NEW MEXICO

In connection with the studies of the Commission on International and Interracial Factors in the Mexican problem in the Southwest, Superintendent Donaldson, of Menaul School, Albuquerque, has secured twenty-seven full and careful replies to a questionnaire he prepared referring directly to the Spanish-American native-born inhabitants of New Mexico and Colorado as distinguished from the Mexican immigrant. These replies came from some of these Spanish-Americans, from Anglo-Americans long time residents in New Mexico, and from missionaries whose experience had been largely with this group.

A very considerable proportion of the population of New Mexico and southern Colorado is Spanish-American, the descendants of those who pushed across the Rio Grande and settled in the midst of the hostile Indian country long before this territory was detached from Old Mexico. They left Mexico to be free from the oppression of the great landowners, preferring the struggle with Apaches and Navajos for land and a home to the condition of practical peonage which they must accept if they remained after the loss of the communal holdings of their villages. Gradually even in this country they were forced off the richest valley lands and into the mountains where they maintain a simple village life, poor but independent.

For more than thirty years the needs of these people have been the concern of several mission boards. But the advance of the typical American business and agricultural life into this territory has revealed a social problem of racial adjustment as well as a missionary problem. Missionary workers are studying this social problem, and the personal reports of seventeen Anglo-American missionaries and business men and ten Spanish-Americans is the basis of this report.

Seventeen of the twenty-seven who have reported feel that there is a definite racial question between Spanish-Americans and Anglo-Americans, eight would not be inclined to emphasize its significance, and only two feel

[1] [Mr. Donaldson informs us that this document embodies a brief study made under the Commission referred to. Dr. George Cady was chairman of this Commission, and Dr. George Hinman secretary.—EDITOR.]

there is no serious interracial difficulty. The Spanish-Americans who reported are themselves divided in about the same proportion on the subject, six out of ten feeling that the racial question must be faced, and only one that there is no significant feeling between the groups.

Practically all agree that the situation is very little affected by relations between the United States and Mexico. One or two indicate that the problem of schools and economic conditions is made somewhat more difficult by the presence of Mexican immigrants, and another indicates that difficulties result because the Spanish-Americans are confused in popular thinking with the Mexicans. One reports, "There is a more deeply seated prejudice between the Spanish-Americans and the Old Mexico Mexicans than there is between the Anglo- and the Spanish-American." Another says the coming of the Mexican immigrant renders the problem a three-sided one, since the Mexican immigrants do not identify themselves with the Spanish-Americans. But in very many sections where there is a large Spanish-American population there are no Mexican immigrants. They are beginning to come for railroad work and in industrial centers, and are, as elsewhere, largely migrants. The Spanish-Americans are generally farmers owning their own land. They get on well with these Mexicans with whom they come into contact, through a similarity of language and tradition, but evidently resent being confused with them, as is so often done by Anglo-Americans.

The racial problem between the Spanish-American and the Anglo-American is therefore quite distinct from the general problem of relations with Mexico and the Mexican immigrants. Some think the misunderstanding and jealousies between the Spanish-Americans are largely the result of political rivalry and intrigue, which always finds race prejudice a conventional tool to serve its interest. One writer of long experience in New Mexico says, "If partisan politics were eliminated the question would cease to be an issue." Others say in some sections only a Spanish-American can be elected to office, and in other sections only an Anglo-American. The fact that all the Spanish-American groups are native-born citizens of three or four generations makes the competitive relations between the two groups less one-sided than when one group is not naturalized or is ineligible to citizenship. The situation has many points of similarity with that in the territory of Hawaii between the native Hawaiians and the American elements in the population.

Making all allowance possible for the exploitation of racial prejudices as a political method, there remains a very general conviction among those who have reported that Anglo-American snobbishness, ignorance of the Spanish language and traditions, shrewdness and often unfairness in dealing with the Spanish-Americans, and the general habit of classing them with the Mexicans are the causes for what is admitted to be a very considerable amount of friction between the groups. Many of the Spanish-Americans themselves admit, however, that the unwillingness of their people to give up the old Spanish traditions and ways of living, their slowness in learning English and becoming assimilated to American ideals, and their uncleanly habits have given some excuse for prejudice. It is admitted that the dark skin has had a great deal to do with the development of prejudice, especially among the Anglo-Americans who come from Texas and the other southern states. It is notable that in a number of different racial situations it has been observed that southern prejudice against Negroes has been transferred to any other group whose color approached the Negro, although the historic and economic relations of that group with the white group has been entirely different.

The historic basis for racial feeling between Spanish-Americans and Anglo-Americans is somewhat different from what might naturally be assumed. There is no reason to suppose that the Spanish-Americans resent the taking of the Southwest from Mexico, or have the slightest feeling for the land of their ancestors. What they object to is taking the land from them, when the Anglo-American traders and settlers began to push into the "land of *poco tiempo*" which they wished to preserve in its primitive condition. They did not want to be disturbed. They are able to match all our American traditions of Spanish ruthlessness in the occupation of Mexico with traditions of American ruthlessness in the invasion of the new territory. Anglo-Americans have been brought up to believe, through our school histories, our dime novels, and now our movies, that the Spanish-speaking people are all cruel and treacherous bandits. The simple, polite, naturally friendly Spanish-American people of New Mexico have had to bear this traditional reputation. Nearly a hundred years of Anglo-American aggressiveness, always influenced by this assumption of the Spanish-American, has tended to produce a certain amount of chronic distrust and bitterness.

It is extremely significant that two or three thoughtful Spanish-Americans put the blame for a great deal of the present situation on the federal government and neglected the Spanish-speaking inhabitants of the territory of New Mexico. Indians were always a concern of the federal government, but no attention was paid to the great need of the Spanish-speaking inhabitants for education and protection. Even today one is impressed with the elaborate provision by government and mission agencies for the care of the Indians of New Mexico as compared with the little that is done to help the Spanish-Americans in their *plaza* towns. The state of New Mexico is in recent years planning intelligently and with energy in the interest of these communities, but there is no doubt of the neglect of the federal-government from the time of annexation, until, as one Spanish-American says, the territory "fell into the hands of politicians and crooks."

In striking contrast with the Mexican immigrant the Spanish-American natives of New Mexico are thoroughly loyal to the United States. Their voluntary enlistment in the Spanish-American War and World War were greater in proportion than among other races. Many think the Spanish-Americans have been slow to appreciate the public school and some of the other institutions of American life, and explain this by the adverse influence of the Catholic church. Some feel that their loyalty to American ideals is not always intelligent, sometimes only formal, but it is plain that the public schools are, as everywhere, making great changes along this line.

There is universal agreement that the younger Spanish-American people are much more intelligently sympathetic with American ideals as a result of education in the mission schools and the public schools, by new business and social contacts with Anglo-Americans and to a very considerable extent by the experiences of the World War. There is much reason to suppose that the state public-school policy and the development of more business contacts between Spanish-American and Anglo-Americans, with the training of leaders of the Spanish-Americans by the mission schools, will, as one correspondence says, greatly improve the situation for the next generation.

There is considerable difference of opinion as to the relations in which there is most evidence of racial feeling. Very many think it comes out most definitely in political relations, though one discriminating writer points out that this feeling in political relations has a background in the differences of religion. Only a very few think there is much evidence of race feeling in the economic field, though one of the best-informed men in the missionary group makes this the chief source of friction. Several of the Spanish-Americans indicate the most intense feeling in social relations, and practically all include this as one of the major fields for the exhibition of racial feelings, since differing brands of politics and religion are only convenient standards under which to rally different racial groups, and the factor of economic competition between the groups in New Mexico does not seem to be conspicuous. One should give special attention to this evident racial feeling in social relations.

Racial feeling between Spanish-Americans and Anglo-Americans does not appear to be a blazing hate, rather a smoldering resentment. One Spanish-American describes it very accurately as indifference. There are four types of racial prejudice: hatred, contempt, indifference, patronage. Any one of these is bad enough. In this case there seems to be a lack of common interest to bind the Spanish-American and Anglo-American together rather than any ineradicable racial difference. The fact that the World War did so much to break down the separation and indifference indicates that there is need for a more challenging co-operation in some common interest if the process is to go on. Undoubtedly, the artificial barriers created by the priests greatly obstruct the natural social movements which would draw the groups together. One correspondent laments the absence of brotherhood in the relations between Spanish-Americans and Anglo-Americans. Brotherhood is created through the sharing of some big social task. When the groups are prevented from co-operating, brotherhood cannot be worked up merely by religious appeals.

The racial prejudice toward the Spanish-American is generally regarded as quite different from that felt toward the Negro or Oriental, though these races are not much in evidence in the territory occupied by Spanish-Americans. It is more like that toward the Pueblo Indians, whose village life has much similarity to that of the Spanish-Americans in the *plaza* towns. In fact, the Spanish-American and the Indian are in the great majority in the rural sections. The contacts with the few Anglo-Americans, teachers, and ranchers in these rural sections are more likely to be friendly, according to the view of most who have reported, than in the cities. Some think that racial lines are more sharply drawn in the country, though ordinary contacts may be friendly. However, there is possible a more complete segregation in urban communities. Each group can live its own life. This segregation keeps up racial alienation. Even the business contacts that are made cause more friction. Mere association, no matter how close, will not produce brotherliness.

While some think it will require one or many generations to bridge completely the differences between the Spanish-Americans and the Anglo-Americans, only a very few feel that there are permanent racial characteristics which will keep them apart. The strongly opposed types of religious allegiance will long separate them, and some feel that the Anglo-Saxon superiority complex is a very stubborn disease. Several think the question of intermarriage will be a permanent bar to close and sympathetic association. Apparently the only ineradicable difference in the mind of anyone is that which makes intermarriage undesirable. But there are a great many who feel that the intermarriage of Spanish-Americans and Anglo-Americans would be helpful. Three Anglo-Americans positively and two with reservations approve of such intermarriage; six Spanish-Americans approve it quite positively, believing that those who come together in such marriages are interpreters and peacemakers. But two young Spanish-American students are very positive that such marriages are never helpful, and other Spanish-American correspondents also disapprove. By far the majority disapprove of intermarriage as a means of racial adjustment, though few would claim biological differences as a reason.

One mission school-teacher insists on the old argument of distinct races, which ought to be kept pure—whatever "racial purity" may mean. Those who explain their objection refer to the social consequences, the social ostracism, and the tendency of the Anglo-American husband who has married a Spanish-American wife to accept the less advanced standards of living.

Many of those who recognize a feeling of strain between Spanish-Americans and Anglo-Americans are not able to point to particular instances of unfair treatment. But one reports a case in which the prejudice was visited even on the Anglo-American teacher who taught a Spanish-American school. There are several reports of Spanish-Americans being refused service in restaurants; even in Santa Fé the signs of "No Mexicans" are up, though probably scarcely one of the Spanish-speaking inhabitants of Santa Fé was born in Mexico. Spanish-American correspondents report refusal of service in restaurants and barber shops discriminating in hotels and public conveyances; one Spanish-American was taken out of a theater at the point of a pistol, and one was lynched in Colorado. Most of these cases seem to have occurred from outside of New Mexico, where the Spanish-Americans have not been distinguished from the Mexicans.

In the Spanish-speaking *plaza* towns men have been paid with fake checks and have been heavily overcharged for professional services. In the southeastern section of Colorado large tracts of land occupied for generations by Spanish-Americans have been seized by large companies. Spanish-Americans have been systematically defrauded by Anglo-American warehousemen when they brought in their lettuce crop in one section of Colorado. In many ways they are taken advantage of in commercial transactions, just as the Indians have been. But they have lacked even the dubious advantage of government protection which the Indians are supposed to have had. Union labor has opposed the Spanish-American labor the same as the Mexican. Probably the largest number of instances of unfair treatment toward either racial group can be found in political life, and probably many cases on each side. It is unfortunate but not necessarily a serious racial problem when, temporarily at least, racial groups are aligned against each other in politics. That difficulty can be overcome much more easily than some others.

The instances of personal prejudice against Spanish-Americans even in churches are the most serious consideration. Two splendid mission schools reported objections to the presence of their pupils in the Anglo-American churches. Whatever may be said as to the desirability of separate Spanish-American churches to give opportunity for spiritual expression and development, one ought to be able to expect in the churches a welcome to those who have chosen the church's invitation to its mission school.

One Spanish-American reminds us that New Mexico sided with the Union in the Civil War and the Spanish-American inhabitants drove out the Confederates. He thinks the southerners have not forgotten that, as he has not. And yet, some people think the Spanish-Americans and the Mexican peasants know nothing and care nothing about history.

Analyzing the attitude of Spanish-Americans and Anglo-Americans, most of those who have reported find that the Spanish-Americans would be friendly if it were not for the evident superiority attitude of the Anglo-Americans. Some Spanish-Americans say they appreciate what the Anglo-Americans have accomplished for the development of the country, but are inclined to be envious. Others refuse to admit the superiority which the Anglo-American assumes, and adopt a policy of passive resistance.

One writer analyzes the situation in this way:

The Anglo works too hard, loves money too much and plays too little. The other goes to the other extreme, perhaps, but can teach us something about enjoying simple, inexpensive pleasures. He meditates and reflects more than the Anglo, is more artistic, has a greater inherent love of beauty. These qualities if developed properly are very valuable. In education the Spanish-American should not be run through the ideals of government, of office-holding, freedom of opinion and speech, of religious life, etc. In that respect he must conform to Anglo no-tions. In other respects the best education for him is one which will show him how to grow as far as he can according to his abilities. His racial heritage after all makes him somewhat different from the Anglo-Saxon.

This is certainly not an idealistic missionary presentation of the situation, but probably represents the feeling of many kindly intentioned Anglo-Americans.

In some respects the situation of the Spanish-Americans in New Mexico and Colorado resembles that of the southern mountaineers of Kentucky and Tennessee. They are almost as resentful of the aggressiveness of outsiders coming into their country, and the apparent assumption of these outsiders that material prosperity means superiority. New Mexico has been captured completely by the outsiders as the southern mountains have not been, and probably the adjustment between these diverse viewpoints has progressed farther in New Mexico. If it were not for a particularly intolerant religious control of the Spanish-American group and a rather exceptional amount of superstition, the prospect of assimilation would be much more encouraging. At present there seems to be little real co-operation between the two groups, and a great deal of political and religious competition. The notable progress that has been made in the development of education and general social conditions appears to be in spite of much intergroup friction. No reports have been received of any notable co-operation between the two groups for the advancement of the general or local community.

When it comes to a question of solution for the local problem of maladjustment between Anglo-Americans and Spanish-Americans, most of those who have reported very properly insist on education and Christianity. Some have made really helpful suggestions by specific applications of education and Christianity in concrete plans. A Spanish-American very wisely suggests teaching of Spanish to Anglo-Americans, lectures in the schools and the churches on friendship between the races, and a public opinion which would condemn the mutual criticism between the groups in public meetings, especially by politicians who kept the prejudice alive for their selfish gains. Although the constitution of New Mexico forbids discrimination against Spanish-Americans, yet few Spanish-American students go through the high schools and the university. They should be encouraged to take higher training as leaders of their people. Several insist on religious freedom and tolerance as a condition of the solution. There is little doubt that religious intolerance uses racial attitudes as a means of maintaining its dominance. While Spanish was used in the public schools of certain sections of New Mexico and priests taught the catechism in the public schools during school hours, there was sure to be racial friction. A very practical and simple method is being used in one of the mission boarding-schools and is being considered in others, the mingling of a small proportion of Anglo-American children with the Spanish-American children in the elementary grades. This works in the public schools. Why should it not be even more effective in the home life of a mission boarding-school?

One missionary teacher says frankly that the Spanish-American must be given higher moral and sanitary standards. If the priests who dominate the life of the Spanish-American communities do not help them to these higher standards, the state government can do so in many ways, by better enforcement of prohibition, better health regulations, and better education and control in the matter of sex relations. It is evident that progress along all these lines will be stimulated and encouraged by the intelligent co-operation of all missionary teachers with the department concerned of the state government.

This report is not supposed to consider the contribution of missionary schools to the adjustment of race relations between Spanish-American and Anglo-Americans in New Mexico and the assimilation into a homogeneous community of these two cultural or racial groups. One can hardly say that this contribution has been as great as might have been hoped. However, the combination of direct missionary agencies with a growingly conscientious spirit in the administration of justice and the care of public health and the promotion of an American type of education has made it possible to foresee in New Mexico a comparatively speedy and satisfactory ending of the present racial friction and misunderstanding.

APPENDIX IV[1]

FOLK LORE FROM MICHOACAN AND JALISCO

Near Cuitzeo there is a stone serpent, and the inhabitants of the place believe that it turns into a drum, a ball, or a pig. They believe that if this stone were taken away, misfortunes would come, such as hailstorms, drought, or some other calamity.

In Cherán they venerate the ancient idols called *tarés* (a venerable old man). Each native has an idol buried in his field, in his house, and in his granary, because they think it watches over the corn. They believe it is bad luck to show the idols, and that misfortune would result if the *yácatas* (archaeological mounds) should be explored.

The *fiesta* of Cristo de los Milagros in Parangaricutiro takes place on the fourteenth of September. Booths are constructed in the *plaza* for vendors of wines, toys, etc. Within the church the people dance with lighted candles up to the foot of the image. They hand over the candle-ends as offerings to the church. The pilgrims crawl on their knees up to the church and then stand up to begin dancing. Many people spread out for them blankets of *rebozos*, not so much to mitigate their discomfort as to win indulgences for themselves. Some pilgrims arrive dressed in fine clothes and adorned with flowers, ribbons, pieces of many-colored cloths, and so on; some come with bells sewed on to their clothing; others with crowns of gilded cardboard (that is to say, the costume of the *matachines;*[2] and some few wear masks. Each little procession approaches the church to the sound of a martial hymn sung by two voices. At the head of each group is carried the patron saint of their community, inclosed in a wooden box covered with a piece of glass. As the procession passes, the Indians kiss the holy niches in which the saints are placed. Before entering the church, the procession stops and the men dance a little. They play music of flutes and violins, and the *matachines* are admired. Pictures referring to the miracles of Santo Cristo and many kinds of printed pictures and prayers are sold.

In Paracho they tell the legend of the well. There was once a girl

---

[1] This material is included to illustrate the primitive customs prevalent in many villages in that part of Mexico from which come many of the immigrants to the United States.

[2] Religious dancers.

named Tzitzic[1] who was the priestess of the Sun. Since she was very beautiful, she was much admired by the young men. Sometimes when she went alone to draw water, she would happen to meet her betrothed and would delay with him so long that her parent chided her. In spite of it all, the lovers continued meeting, and on one occasion they were so forgetful of the time that it was too late for the girl to reach the spring. Greatly distressed, she began to invoke Father Sun, begging him to permit her to find water near at hand in order to avoid the anger of her parents. Then she saw issue from the grass on which she stood a bird, shaking its wings as if it had just taken a bath, and sprinkling drops of water around about; she understood immediately that Father Sun had granted her request, and had put in her path a spring; and overflowing with joy she filled her *lirimacua*, or jug, and set off at full speed for her home. Her parents were surprised to see her return so soon and supposed that her betrothed had helped her with the pitcher; but she told them that such was not the case but that on the same path over which for many years the women had gone for water she had found a new spring. All the principal people hastened to come and hear the marvelous tale and went to visit the place of miracles where a well twelve yards deep had opened. To this day it is the principal source of water for the city. It is situated to the east of Paracho, at least a mile from the center of town, and the inhabitants call it Queritziaro.[2]

In Ihuatzio (coyote) *pueblo*, situated near the lake of Patzcuaro, the young men observe the following custom. When some young fellow has been courting a girl for some time and believes that his feeling is reciprocated, he catches hold of her by the *rebozo* at the fountain and will not let go until she says "yes." Then, with an oaken stick which he carries hidden in his blanket, he breaks the pitcher so that the water falls over her. The companions of the girl come up hastily; they take off her clothes, leaving her barely more than her necklace and earrings, and lend her other clothing and another pitcher with which to carry the water home. She returns then to her home with a pitcher and clothing not belonging to her, and the wet clothing is retained by her admirer. In order to get back the clothing the father of the girl must pay a half a *real* for each piece. The next day the youth comes and puts a load of firewood near the door of his betrothed, and immediately goes away. He does not return until three days have elapsed, and then, if he sees that the wood has been accepted, he knows that his fiancée is disposed to follow him to his house. She in fact

[1] Flower.

[2] *Quer*, "large"; *itzic*, "water"; *aro*, "where there is"—in other words, "The Great Spring."

does go to his house, collects her clothes, gives him the money, and also a present of some flowers, of which the yellow ones have a special importance.

In Zirahuen and Santa Clara the custom is to prove the good qualities of the bride by opening before her face a cloth filled with bees. If she retreats fearfully, she is undesirable; but if she remains quietly without defending herself, it is certain that she possesses the fortitude necessary to bear the burden of matrimony.

In Angagua, a *pueblo* near Parangaricutiro, there is still practiced the ancient marriage ceremony of the Tarascans, which is, in its essentials, that of the Aztecs of Tuxpan and other nearby places. It consists in examining the sheet on which the bridal couple have slept; if this appears stained with blood it is a sure sign that the bride was a virgin. Some old woman, ordinarily the aunt of the groom, is selected as godmother to the bridal couple, and when evening comes this old woman spreads a sheet over the *petate* which is to serve as the marriage bed and discreetly retires. In the morning she enters and performs her delicate office, which, even among the Indians, is considered a very serious duty, since on her announcement depends the continuation of the *fiesta* and the happiness of the bride for all the rest of her life. If she finds the proof that she is seeking, she appears joyfully to the company and triumphantly holding up the sheet exclaims, "She is a virgin." All hearts are filled with happiness and all repeat the glad news. The groom orders the music to play. Rockets are set off, they walk around the sheet, and all express their reverence for it, kissing it as if it were the image of a saint. They lavish upon the bride all sorts of attentions, offer her chocolate and whatever else there is, and all give themselves over to dancing, eating, and drinking. On the second day they execute a dance called *canara*, which has a special musical accompaniment. The women dance with the spindle whorl, their loom, or even their *metate*, and the men with their agricultural implements. One of the women makes a rag doll, dances with it, and immediately passes it over to the groom and to the bride, who holds it in her arms as if it were a child. The parents of the bridal pair dance with bread and chocolate in their hands which they hold close to the hands of the bride, but when she opens her mouth to receive this food, they turn away quickly and they themselves eat it. If the inspection of the sheet results unfavorably, the godmother communicates this unfortunate news first of all to the parents-in-law, saying, "We are ruined! We don't even deserve water! Now there will be no *fiesta!*" They put out the lights and all the guests go home very sadly, not without first showing their disapproval by destroying all the bride's presents, which consist entirely of pottery. To punish and cast scorn upon her, they crack and make holes in the *ollas* so that the unfortunate girl can only use them by giving them much laborious mending. She prepares, as a cement for this process, a mixture of the milky juice from certain trees, cow's milk, clay, cotton, ground beans, and the white of an egg. The pottery must be reburnt, but even so it does not appear as before. The worst consequence of all is that the poor girl, who lives with her mother, is the object of general ill will. She is not shown the least consideration; she is obliged to work hard, and her burden is not lightened until she is close to becoming a mother.

San Isidro directs the clouds and makes the seeds grow.

Santo Santiago is a crafty rascal and has enriched himself at the expense of the people, and they are afraid of him.

San Mateo sends the wind and the frosts.

They spend all their savings on the *fiestas* of the saints. By taking part in a *fiesta*, health and happiness are assured, thus it is better to give up money than to miss one.

No business is carried on after dusk. No corn is shelled when the sun has set, nor is it taken from the granary once it has begun to grow dark because it is thought that the corn is sleeping and does not want to be waked.

If a pregnant woman looks at an eclipse of the moon, her child will be born lame—a common idea among the natives of Central Mexico.

In every house is found the image of the saint, placed in the best room, which is given up to it, the people of the house sleeping in the kitchen in order not to disturb it. Only strangers may occupy the same room. At noon the wife and her husband place before the saint a small dish of *copal* to offer the incense which serves the saint as food. The visitors who come in the house go to see the image first of all. If it hails, the people take out the saint from the church early in the morning and punish it by ducking it in cold water; but if the harvests are good, they carry it in a procession, make a great *fiesta* for it which they celebrate with liberal drinking of *mezcal* and eating of quantities of *tamales*. Every year an old man is selected to represent San Mateo. On the Day of the Dead the people fasten flowers, especially yellow ones, to the doors of their houses to invite the souls of their friends to enter, and they pay with some offering for every paternoster which is said for the dead. For their own special parties they send invitations by word of mouth of a messenger who carries a flower to each invited guest—flowers which are collected again on the arrival of the guests.

A woman crossing a river with her baby on her back is afraid of the evil spirits of the water, and so she never stops calling her child by name and crying, "Come, come, don't stay behind!"

A woman who is soon to bear a child does not carry salt, chili, or lime for fear her child will be born deaf or blind.

They look reverently at twin ears of corn and are very careful of them. It is bad to step over a man who is lying down.

They do not like people whom they do not know to fondle their children for fear of the "evil eye." The mothers beg their visitors rather to tease and arouse the anger of the child because this keeps the child well. Any sickness which occurs afterward they attribute to the "evil eye," since they recognize no other causes for the sicknesses of infancy. To avoid such evil effects, many Indians tie twists of red thread on the wrists and ankles of their children, and fasten in their hair a red feather from the woodpecker, with the idea that this color obscures the vision of the witch.

When two people are quarreling, they will say, "I will make you die within four or five *petates*," meaning by this the amount of time necessary to wear out five of the mats on which they sleep. Those who believe they have been bewitched put *nopal* thorns in the corners of the houses and outside them. In order to learn witchcraft, some go to *pueblos* like Characuaro or Tzirandaro.

In order to learn the whereabouts of some object which has been stolen or lost, they place a tallow candle inside an *olla* and divine the direction in which the missing object will be found by means of the movements of the flame; and by the way that the candle melts they foretell whether the lost object will be found in the woods or in the fields.

Owls are considered unlucky, so whenever they see one, they curse it and threaten it with their *machetes*. When an owl passes over the house, the master of the house takes it for an omen that his death is not far off and begins to pray.

No one should touch a snake, much less kill it.

The mothers of Jilotlán are accustomed to pull the noses of their children during the first two or three months after birth in order that they may not become pug-nosed.

When a cat licks its chops, visitors are going to come. Another sign of this is the crackling of the fire; in this case a little water should be thrown on the flame.

When a hen crows like a cock, it must be killed because it has the devil in it.

A girl should allow no one to eat from the same plate in which the food was cooked if she does not wish it to rain very much on the day of her wedding.

If a woman leaves rubbish beside the door the devil will hide in it.

When something has become lost in the house, it is well to light a candle at the tip or lower end and let it burn.

When someone has affected a child with the "evil eye," one must overcome him by arranging the hair in the form of a topknot.

If someone treads on the saliva of a twin child, a tumor appears in the groin.

It is a popular belief that only a male tree can injure a woman, and a female tree a man. Poison does not harm people who are drunk, nor does the stinging of scorpions and *turicatas*.

When three coyotes howl in the night there will be a dispute the next day.

To meet a white dove is good luck; a black one, bad.

A swallow might bring good or bad news to a woman whose husband is away.

Holy Thursday a bell rings in the middle of Lake Patzcuaro by order of King Calzontzin.

On the day of Santa Cruz, where one sees the ground burning there is money.

When one dreams of peaches or pears it is a sign of misfortune.

The inhabitants of this region enjoy good health and generally attain a very advanced age. However, in the Sierra, owing to the cold climate, coughs, pneumonia, and pleurisy are very common; but the sickness which is most of all prevalent in Paracho is jaundice. This attacks both old and young, at times lasting for several years before it attains a fatal result. Also very common is typhoid fever, which, although it is not very malignant, is usually fatal because they do not know how to treat it and there are no preventive or curative serums.

Every kind of sickness is called "Father Evil," and is spoken of with great respect as if it were a real person. When there is an epidemic of smallpox they come out of their houses burning incense in order that the sickness may come in a good humor; but if the illness results fatally, the relatives of its victims are irritated with the pestilence and beat the corners of the room to drive it out. When they suppose that the patient has twisted his body through having put too heavy a burden on his back when a boy, they bring bundles of ten or a dozen cords of different colors, and fastening the feet of the patient to some stakes stuck in the ground, they strike him from top to bottom with the bundles of cords. If someone shows symptoms of leprosy or syphilis, they give him dried and powdered snake's flesh to eat.

They possess some knowledge of medicinal herbs and of surgery. The women of Parangaricutiro assert that they know a remedy for sterility and have a knowledge of something that produces abortions. They also know how to bleed and how to put back into place dislocated bones. They cure fractures perfectly, applying a dry herb and corn husks as bandages and disinfectant. All over the region syphilis is cured by using certain herbs to produce excessive perspiration, in combination with a system of dieting including milk, rice, chicken, potatoes, and *atole blanco*. This treatment lasts nine days but the diet continues for some forty more. There are women who make such cures their business and charge moderately for their services.

Ordinarily families spend nothing for doctors or medicine, but spend large sums on funerals. They kill a head of cattle, grind as much as four bushels of corn, and provide a barrel of *aguardiente*. The celebration lasts about three days, during which the Indians dance all night and part of the day beside the corpse stretched out between four candles. Violins and guitars are played and songs sung in honor of the dead man; the family continues to live in the same room as the corpse, and all get drunk. Until the last morsel is gone the *fiesta* does not come to an end.

In parts of the *tierra caliente* live the spotted Indians whose bodies are more or less covered with blotches—red, blue, white, and black—which gives them a very repulsive appearance. Even the *mestizos* avoid eating anything cooked by a woman with such spots. It is thought by some that these discolorations of the skin are due to syphilis, but others attribute it to the water of these localities. The cases occur generally among the *mestizos*, although their children are frequently born quite without blemish. It is not thought that the sickness is contagious. Goiter is another sickness which is common in certain parts of the *tierra caliente* of Michoacan.

The men move more slowly than the women, who always walk along quickly, with short steps, often turning out their toes. The women are cleaner than the men, who only bathe once a year, while they do it at least every two weeks. Both sexes wash their faces and feet every day at daybreak, for which purpose they have in Uruapan special troughs. In some parts, as in Arantepacua, only the women observe this custom, which appears to have a certain ritualistic character.

APPENDIX V

OBJECTS BROUGHT INTO MEXICO FREE OF CUSTOM DUTY BY 2,104 RETURNED IMMIGRANTS IN THE YEAR 1927, ACCORDING TO PERMIT NO. 202 OF THE DEPARTMENT OF FOREIGN RELATIONS ISSUED DECEMBER 14, 1926

CLASSIFICATION OF OBJECTS	FRONTIER PORTS AND NUMBER OF RETURNED MEXICANS											RATIO OF NO. OF OBJECTS LISTED TO EVERY 100 IMMIGRANTS RETURNING
	C. Guerrero—12	Sásabe—24	Ojinaga—50	Naco—35	Reynosa—178	Matamoros—88	Agua Prieta—60	Piedras Negras—318	Laredo—700	Ciudad Juarez—639	Total—2,104	
Agricultural and industrial implements:	NUMBER OF OBJECTS											
Ploughs	1	....	15	.....	15	10	4	16	34	87	182	8.64
Hoes	....	....	14	.....	45	....	6	4	6	37	112	5.32
Disinfecting pumps	....	....	....	1	....	....	....	....	....	....	1	0.04
Machinery bands	....	....	....	....	....	....	....	1	....	....	1	.04
Drills	....	....	....	....	1	....	....	....	....	....	1	.04
Levers	....	....	....	....	2	....	....	....	1	3	6	.28
Air pumps	....	....	....	....	2	....	....	....	....	....	2	.09
Chisels	....	....	4	....	....	....	....	....	....	....	4	.19
Mowers	....	....	1	....	....	....	....	....	....	....	1	.04
Beehives (boxes)	....	....	....	....	1	....	....	....	....	....	1	.04
Iron boilers	....	....	....	....	....	....	....	....	1	....	1	0.04
Cultivator ploughs	....	....	5	....	1	3	1	5	3	7	25	1.18
Grain shakers	....	....	1	....	1	2	1	2	....	9	16	0.76
Emery wheels	....	....	1	....	....	....	....	....	....	....	1	.04
Weeding machines	....	....	1	....	....	3	....	....	....	....	4	0.19
Sets of tools	1	1	12	6	29	36	....	18	117	69	289	13.72
Agricultural tools	1	....	....	....	....	2	....	....	1	4	8	0.38
Axes	3	....	12	....	44	10	....	26	19	42	156	7.38
Carpenter tools	....	....	....	....	2	1	4	4	2	1	14	0.76
Barber utensils	....	....	....	....	2	....	....	....	6	....	8	.38
Shoemaker's tools	....	....	....	....	....	....	....	....	3	....	3	.14
Hammers	....	....	....	....	1	....	....	1	....	3	5	0.23
Corn mill	....	2	3	....	16	4	3	9	3	7	49	2.32
Motors	....	....	1	1	....	....	1	1	....	....	4	0.19
Machetes	....	....	....	....	3	....	....	....	....	....	3	0.14
Shovels	....	....	5	....	10	4	2	10	41	57	129	6.12
Punches	....	....	3	....	....	....	....	....	....	....	3	0.14
Pulleys	....	....	....	....	5	....	....	1	....	....	6	.28
Rakes	....	....	5	....	3	1	2	....	....	2	13	0.61

CLASSIFICATION OF OBJECTS	FRONTIER PORTS AND NUMBER OF RETURNED MEXICANS											RATIO OF NO. OF OBJECTS LISTED TO EVERY 100 IMMIGRANTS RETURNING
	C. Guerrero—12	Sásabe—24	Ojinaga—50	Naco—35	Reynosa—178	Matamoros—88	Agua Prieta—60	Piedras Negras—318	Laredo—700	Ciudad Juarez—639	Total—2,104	
	Number of Objects											
Hand saws					4	2	4	9			19	0.90
Sowers			4		6	3	1	4		4	22	1.04
Wheels								1			1	0.04
Small axes					1						1	.04
Anvils		1	1								2	0.09
Pickaxes					4				13	7	24	1.14
Automobiles and trucks:												
"Oakland"				1				1	5	4	11	0.52
"Dodge"		2		1	1		9	6	11	16	46	2.18
"Ford"	5	6	13	7	26	20	2	76	112	99	366	17.38
"Ford" (truck)	1	3	9	1	5	8	2	40	75	64	208	9.88
"Chevrolet"		3		1		6		4	9	13	36	1.71
"Star"		1	1	1			2	2		1	8	0.38
"Overland"				1				1	9	4	15	0.71
"Buick"		1		1		1	6		7	9	25	1.18
"Willys-Knight"				1							1	0.04
"Rollin"									1		1	.04
"Oldsmobile"		1						3		2	6	.28
"Nash"					1			2		2	5	.27
"Durant"									4		4	0.19
"Studebaker"		1		3			1		12	16	33	1.56
"Paige"				1					5	1	7	0.33
"Westmotor"					1						1	.04
"Pontiac"					1						1	.04
"Hudson"					1			2	13	3	19	.90
Carburetors									3		3	0.14
Inner tubes									431	118	549	26.05
Cranks					1						1	0.04
Tools (bundles)								5	83	23	111	5.27
Tires	5	6	14	13	36	12	16	122	341	227	792	37.62
Wheels	2		8		1	2	1	2	36	31	83	3.94
Domestic animals:												
Donkeys			14		8	2		6	2	9	41	1.94
Horses	1	3	10		13	7	1	18	32	4	89	4.22
Goats			332		1						333	15.81
Chickens	26		110		31	52	12	187	1,212	817	2,447	116.23
Hens (cages)	1				6						7	0.33
Cocks									131		131	6.12
Mules	3		58		20	4		14	8	4	111	5.27
Chickens (cages)	1									3	4	0.19
Colts		3	1		3	1					8	.38
Dogs					2	1		4	8		15	.71
Pigs							9		6		15	.71
Cows				5							5	.23
Mares		6	12		12	5			3		38	0.80
Household implements:												
Pillows (bundles)	2		3		20	16	4	10	20	109	184	8.83
Cupboards		2		1	1				9	3	16	0.76

Classification of Objects	Frontier Ports and Number of Returned Mexicans											Ratio of No. of Objects Listed to Every 100 Immigrants Returning
	C. Guerrero—12	Sásabe—24	Ojinaga—50	Naco—35	Reynosa—178	Matamoros—88	Agua Prieta—60	Piedras Negras—318	Laredo—700	Ciudad Juarez—639	Total—2,104	
	Number of Objects											
Rugs		2	1	7	3	9	20	14	30	16	102	4.84
Fence wire (rolls)			12	1				8	160	23	204	9.69
Night tables			1							3	4	0.19
Sheets	4				136	60	10	40	335	222	807	38.19
Trunks	2										2	0.09
Barrels	1				9	5			226		41	1.94
Buggies for children	1		3	1	1	5	12	4	13	7	47	2.23
Bags	1										1	0.04
Buckets		2	8		95	30	26		85	113	359	17.05
Buggies			1		1	4		2	13	3	24	1.14
Iron barrels			10								10	0.47
Cutler's sets									15	7	22	1.04
Dining-room sets									23	16	39	1.85
Cradles		1	1		4	8	4	9	6	19	52	2.47
Baby buggies		1									1	0.04
Empty boxes					11						11	.32
Carriage covers	1							15			16	0.70
Beds	8	23	50	26	135	95	60	230	615	563	1,745	82.88
Coverlets	10		6		9	9	5				39	1.85
Mattresses	9	4	47	16	144	106	53	170	516	419	1,484	70.53
Curtains (pairs)	3			1	2					16	22	1.04
Carriages	2	4	27		29	9	1	48	9	6	135	6.41
Bedsteads	2		12		32	10	18	40	9	23	146	6.93
Drawers and chests	1	7	2	5	8	2	16	1	9	6	52	2.47
Comales	1										1	0.04
Bed covers (bundles)			5		8	4	3				20	0.95
Chifferobes				1		6	4	9	52	26	98	4.65
Coal (sacks)							9				9	0.42
Phonograph records		40	128	32	363	198	160	518	580	687	2,706	118.53
Furniture and domestic implements:												
Stoves	10	7	36	7	51	45	23	130	61	211	581	27.58
Mirrors		2	3	1	7	10	6	10	42	67	148	7.03
Brooms					4	2	2	2	12	10	32	1.52
Plaster statues					1				5	1	7	0.33
Cuspidors						2					2	0.09
Phonographs	1	2	9	2	33	12	20	40	67	84	270	12.82
Filters			1				2		3	2	8	0.38
Electric globes					2						2	.09
Kitchen cabinets								8		6	14	.76
Pitchers					2						2	.09
Hall (sets)										1	1	0.04
Table oilcloths (yds.)	5		4						17	6	32	1.52

Classification of Objects	C. Guerrero—12	Sásabe—24	Ojinaga—50	Naco—35	Reynosa—178	Matamoros—88	Agua Prieta—60	Piedras Negras—318	Laredo—700	Ciudad Juarez—639	Total—2,104	Ratio of No. of Objects Listed to Every 100 Immigrants Returning
					Number of Objects							
Floor oilcloths (pieces)			12			3				23	2	40	1.90
Portable oven						1					1	2	0.09
Bookstands				1				7		1	3	12	0.57
Books (boxes)	1	1	1		7	1	18	6	·23		7	65	3.08
Hand lamps	1		1									2	0.09
Lanterns					14	4						18	.85
Gasoline lamps		1			1	2		2			2	8	0.38
Oil lamps			12	2	33			20	28		18	113	5.36
Laundry sets			7	1	62	35	19		61		83	268	12.73
Washing-stands			3		5	4		8	1			21	0.99
Wood (box)							1					1	.09
Metates					8	6						14	0.76
Sewing machines	4	8	15	9	44	42	36	50	59		82	349	16.57
Tables	5	10	37	9	54	81	90	80	121		109	596	28.21
Parlor furniture (sets)				1		1			4		7	13	0.61
Photo. frames		4	62	1	72	15	38	20	131		98	441	20.94
Washing-machines					1		2		2		3	8	0.38
Coffee mills			2		4	1	1	2	1		6	17	.80
Chocolate mills									1			1	.04
Hoses				1		3						4	.19
Iron pots					1	1						2	.09
Trunks					4							4	0.19
Hand bags	3	2	9	1	12	4						31	1.47
Wooden doors	2					1						3	0.14
Hairdressers		1		1			3	2	33		15	55	2.61
Pressing-irons			13		15	4	14	4	16		41	107	5.08
Pianos				2	1	1	2	5	19		9	39	1.85
Pianolas				1				2	13		6	22	1.04
Wallpaper (rolls)						1						1	0.04
Perches								1				1	0.04
Bedroom (sets)									33		22	55	2.67
Bed clothing (bundles)	5	8	23	12	82	16		72	229		187	634	30.00
Wardrobes		1	4		2	6		16	16		6	41	1.94
Refrigerators		1	3	2	3	13	12	15	22		9	80	3.80
Clocks			7		3		4		4		4	22	1.04
Sofa				1	1							2	0.09
Couches					1	1	3		1			6	.28
Sheets	5		4									9	0.42
Chairs	12	85	70	41	183	99	114	620	513		419	2,156	112.31
Armchairs	3	4	5	5	33	21	46	138	122		92	469	22.27
Curtains (bundles)							10					10	0.47
Curtains (pieces)									16		16	32	1.52
Vacuum bottles					1							1	0.04
Rugs	1		2	1	1		4	16	13		8	46	2.18
Kitchen utensils	17	14	54	23	172	93	54	204	598		413	1,642	77.99
Kitchen utensils (stands)	2	3	13	2		12	2	18	32		4	88	4.18
Dressing-tables	2	1	7	1	1	4	4	9	23		18	69	3.27

Classification of Objects	C. Guerrero—12	Sásabe—24	Ojinaga—50	Naco—35	Reynosa—178	Matamoros—88	Agua Prieta—60	Piedras Negras—318	Laredo—700	Ciudad Juarez—639	Total—2,104	Ratio of No. of Objects Listed to Every 100 Immigrants Returning
					Number of Objects							
Toilet stuff									1		1	0.04
Bath tubs	4	9	15	10	15	12	48		56	49	218	10.36
Boards					6						6	0.28
Pressing-boards	2		2			5	2		20	43	74	3.51
Dining-room utensils					43	4	6		7	18	78	3.70
Dining-room utensils (sets)		2	8		1				13	11	35	1.66
Washing-tubs			23	1	4	6	16	63	87	57	257	12.20
Carving-table						1	1				2	0.09
Vessels (bundles)	2				97	10					109	5.17
Windows				4	2	2					8	0.38
Sheep fur					1						1	.04
Musical instruments:												
Accordions				1	5	9		1		1	17	.80
Clarinet				1							1	.04
Cornet			1								1	.04
Counterbass			1							1	2	0.09
Guitars			2		5	1		2	17	4	31	1.47
Music. instm. (soprano)				1							1	0.04
Music. instm.					1						1	.04
Mandolin	1					1	1	1	9	6	19	.90
Organs			1						3		4	.19
Trumpet			2								2	.09
Drum					1						1	.04
Timbrel					1						1	.04
Violins	1				2				4	3	10	0.47
Miscellaneous:												
Overcoats					1	1	1				2	0.09
Saddle						1					1	0.04
Food (bundles)	3		14	1	36	22	14	5	188	215	489	23.66
Seed (bundles)					3			2			5	0.23
Cane seed (bundles)			2		3						5	.23
Harnesses (sets)	1							6	4	9	20	.95
Infant safety strap								1			1	0.04
Bicyclettes					2	1	2	1	27	19	52	2.47
Cameras				4		3	1	4	6	18	36	1.71
Tents		2	2		2		4		1	4	15	0.71
Guns	1	1	3	1	4	6	3	30	3	7	56	2.66
Gasoline (reservoir)									91	67	158	7.50
Crampiron (bags)	1										1	0.04
Horse gears (sets)			29		25	12	3	90	3	2	164	7.79
Incubators					1				40	14	55	2.61
Toys	1				1	2			10	7	21	0.99
Toys (boxes)		1		1	1		12	2	23	14	54	2.56

CLASSIFICATION OF OBJECTS	FRONTIER PORTS AND NUMBER OF RETURNED MEXICANS											RATIO OF NO. OF OBJECTS LISTED TO EVERY 100 IMMIGRANTS RETURNING
	C. Guerrero—12	Sasabe—24	Ojinaga—50	Naco—35	Reynosa—178	Matamoros—88	Agua Prieta—60	Piedras Negras—318	Laredo—700	Ciudad Juarez—639	Total 2,104	
	Number of Objects											
Second-hand lámina					37	6					43	2.04
Empty cans					6						6	0.28
Zinc cans	3										3	.14
Barber-shop counter						1					1	.09
Hair-cutting machine						2					2	0.09
Typewriters				1	2	3	6	1	13	4	30	1.42
Saddles	1	3	15		8	7	1	20	2	6	63	2.99
Wooden counters		2							1		3	0.14
Motorcycles							1		1	1	3	.14
Crutches					2						2	0.09
Clothes (bundles)	1	2	11	6	157	90	13	92	271	185	828	39.33
Clothes (trunks)	12	10	9	13	128	42	49	76	460	392	1,191	56.57
Clothes (cases)	5	1			14	2		10	35		67	3.28
Clothes (suitcases)	4	10	70	13	154	103	57	163	645	415	1,634	77.61
Radioapparatus						1			3		4	0.19
Parts for saddles	1										1	0.04
Men's hats				2		10			19	3	34	1.61
Women's hats			2		3				2		7	0.33
Parasols					1						1	.04
Clothes (bundles)					1						1	.04
Tricycles					4		4	3	1		12	0.57
Ventilators	1					3		6	19		29	1.37
Shoes (pairs)	20		2		1	8		16		32	79	3.75
Shoes (bundles)			4		35		2		9	16	66	3.13

APPENDIX VI

THE LINGUISTIC CONTACT

The three invasions, racial, cultural, and linguistic, which characterized the conquest of the aborigines of Mexico by Spain were not carried
out with equal thoroughness, nor did they cover the same ground. The
racial fusion developed very slowly, as the relatively high proportion in
the population of Indians of pure blood or very slightly mixed blood
proves. The substitution of unmodified Spanish cultural traits for native
traits was fairly extensive, but was affected only in the case of certain cultural elements in the chief urban centers; on the other hand, the fusion of
these traits—that is to say, the creation of a mixed culture—was more
important, since this mixed culture embraced more than half of the population in the field of linguistic contact. Finally, there was the substitution
of the Spanish language for the native languages and dialects which was
widely accomplished, as shown by the relatively small number of Indians,
perhaps less than two millions, who still do not speak Spanish. It should
be noted, however, on the other hand, that among those who speak Spanish there are many who preserve and continue to use the Indian languages. The Spanish which is spoken in Mexico exhibits probably much
greater local diversity than that spoken elsewhere in Latin America,
since it has been and still is strongly influenced by the hundred and one
languages and dialects of Indian Mexico. Anticipating the protests of
compatriots jealous for the prestige of their native Spanish, we may state
that in our opinion this local diversity does not signify incorrectness or
imperfection; the "Mexican Spanish" of the present time and the "Span-
ishes" in all the phases in which the language of Cervantes has passed are
equally correct and deserving of respect so long as usage, the supreme and
irrefutable authority, imposes it.

The Aztec language was the language which probably covered the
widest area in Mexico at the time of the arrival of the conquerors, who for
their part aided in spreading the language through the colonizing movements and wars which they carried on in order to subjugate other parts of
the country. From this it resulted that the majority of Indianisms incorporated in Mexican Spanish are Aztecisms, some of which in their turn
through the Mexican immigrant have been incorporated into the English

language as spoken in the United States. Such words are "chili," "tomato," "chocolate," and "avocado," derived from the Spanish words *chile, chocolate,* and *ahuacate,* and indirectly from the Aztec words *chilli, chocolatl, tomatl, ahuacatl.* Some few Spanish words in English may be derived from "tarasquisms," "otomisms," "zapotequisms," and "mayisms."[1]

The number of immigrants who learn the English language in the United States appears to be rather small, due to the fact that during their hours of work they do not have opportunities to learn it, and during their free time they constantly talk Spanish with other immigrants, or with naturalized Mexicans or Americans of old Mexican stock. Moreover, in the hotels, clubs, societies, shops, and restaurants which they frequent Spanish is spoken also. The newspapers that the immigrants read, of which there are a great many, are written in Spanish.

The majority of the immigrants, then, continue to talk Spanish, but since they generally belong to the lower classes of Mexico and since in the United States they come in contact with the same grade of people, their poor Spanish becomes deformed and incrusted with English words, and the result is a barbarous jargon which could not be understood in any Spanish-speaking country. For example, this dialogue: *"Guasamara* valedor, que estas *guachando?"* "Espero que abran la *lundrera* para sacar mis *yompas* y luego ir a la *marqueta."* Neither educated Mexican nor American can understand this strange patois, which in Spanish would be: "Que sucede amigo, que estas mirando?" "Espero que abran la lavanderia para sacar mis blusas y luego ir al mercado." And in English: "What's the matter, kid, what're you looking for?" "I am waiting for the laundry to open so I can get my overalls and then I'm going to the market."

This incorporation of English words in the language[2] is necessitated by life in a foreign country in general, and in particular by the technical terms used in the tasks in which the immigrants are engaged, such as work on the railroads, harvesting of fruit, iron, cement, or brick construction.

[1] On Mexican contributions to American English see Victoriano Salado Alvarez and Federico Gamboa, *Mejico Peregrino: Mejicanisms supervivientes en el Inglés de Norte-América.* Mexico: Talleres Gráficos del Museo Nacional, 1924.

[2] On the influence of English upon Spanish spoken in the United States see Aurelio M. Espinosa, "Speech Mixture in New Mexico," in *The Pacific Ocean in History,* by H. Morse Stephens and Herbert E. Bolton (New York, 1917). Also Espinosa, *The Spanish Language in New Mexico and Southern Colorado* (Santa Fé, 1911), and *Studies in New Mexican Spanish.*—EDITOR

Any immigrant, however, understands the following words, typical of the mixture and showing clearly the manner in which this occurs:

Daime..............	Dime	*Ahcerapate*............	Shut up
Nicle..............	Nickel	*Aromovil*[1]	Automobile
Traque............	Track	*Suera*................	Sweater
Borde.............	Board	*Injuriado*.............	Injured
Abordado..........	Boarder	*Yompa*................	Jump(skirt)
Casa de borde.......	Boarding-house	*Trampear*.............	To tramp
Yardas............	Yards	*Chirife*..............	Sheriff
Pinta..............	Pint	*Jaun*.................	Hound
Bos...............	Boss	*Guore*................	Water
Aiscrin............	Ice-cream	*Guorear*[2].............	To rain
Escrines...........	Screens		

Piquiniqui..............	Picnic
Llaqui.................	Jack
Lundrera..............	Laundry
Parquear mi coche........	To park an automobile
Tallas.................	Ties
Mechas................	Matches
Estoque yardas...........	Stock Yards
Bancosteados............	Bunco steerer
Guasamara?.............	What's the matter?
Guachando.............	Watching
Groserias...............	Groceries
Punchar...............	Punch
Lonchar...............	Lunch
Tiquetes...............	Tickets
Dipo..................	Depot
Chansa................	Chance
Tiempo................	Time-check
Troca.................	Truck
Troquero..............	Truck-driver
Biles.................	Bills
Bonch.................	Bunch
Chante................	Shanty
Bisquete..............	Biscuit
Omeleta...............	Omelette
Bulega................	Bootlegger
Chain.................	Shine
Taxas.................	Taxes
Marqueta..............	Market

[1] In passing over from Spanish to English *t* is frequently substituted for *r*; *aromovil* for "automobile"; *guore* for "water"; *ciri* for "city."

[2] Verb derived from the patois noun *guore*, which means "water," Span. *agua*.

The transformation is made somewhat amusing by the fact that some of the words which have been derived from English, and used with the meaning of the original word in English, have nevertheless a Spanish meaning far different; for instance, *pinta* which in border patois means "pint," in good Spanish means "spotted"; *mechas*, supposedly "matches," is in Mexican everyday speech "tufts" or "tangles of hair"; *grocerías*, border version of "groceries," in Mexico means "foul or insulting epithets."

A similar influence is to be seen in the poems, songs, ballads, and plays of which we have spoken in the section on folk lore, and among the autobiographies we find twists of speech and thought of this peculiar Mexican-American category. It is to be noted that though in the speech of the immigrants there is evident influence, the English-Mexican hybrid words do not pass over into Spanish, spoken and written in Mexico, whereas some of the Spanish or Indo-Spanish words adopted into the English of these regions where Mexican influence has been most marked eventually pass over into English, spoken and written in the United States: *plaza, bronco, reata, suave,* etc.

Of special interest in this patois are the curious terms of racial meaning. For instance, white Americans are called *bolillos,* a word which coincides with the name given in Mexico to the French roll, the white bread generally eaten in Mexico, though whether the term originated in this or in some other twist of thought we cannot say. In the same way, American women are called *cristalinas,* which might be translated "crystallines"; but the reason for this term, also, we do not know. Mexican natives of New Mexico are called *manitos,* an affectionate slang version of *hermanitos,* "little brothers." Half-Mexicans and half-Americans, that is, a child of Mexican-American union, are called *coyotes,* in Texas and New Mexico and elsewhere, generally *encartados.* Immigrants are called *cholos* or *chicamos,* the last probably derived from *mexicanos.* One of the first surnames applied to Mexican immigrants was *Surumato.* A *haciendo* in Michoacan wherefrom a great number of immigrants came and still come is named *Zurumate,* which is the origin of the surname.

Besides the flagrant grammatical error of incorporation of English words, the Spanish spoken by the immigrants has a great many Spanish words incorrectly used. For instance:

Lumbreros (bomberos)—Firemen
Taurria (Atauderia)—Undertaking establishment
Carranclan—A very cheap grade of cotton cloth or a certain sort of dress trimming

Galenton (Estufa)—Stove

Papel (periodico)—Newspaper (lit., paper)

Establo—A group of boxers; corruption of the English word "stable." They say *el establo de Juan*, or "John's group of boxers."

Guerco—Boy, little fellow

Aseguranza—Insurance, especially life insurance

Conductor—For the director of an orchestra, from the English usage

Aluzar—They use this word for *alumbrar*, "to light." They say *aluzame* for *alumbrame; estoy aluzando* for *estoy alumbrando*

Arriar—Run an automobile

Colector (for *cobrador*)—Collector

Rision—A word which means that something is ridiculous or comic. *Ese individuo se ve muy rision*, "This person looks very *rision*," say the Texas Mexicans.

Changuira (Engaño)—Deceit

La ley—A phrase signifying the representatives of authority, particularly the police

Mueble—The name for a *guayin* or wagon drawn by a horse

Ouba—High silk hat

Chota (la policia)—The police

Bisona (fea, ridicula)—Ugly, ridiculous

APPENDIX VII

CAUSES FOR THE FAILURE OF REPATRIATION AND COLONIZATION ENTERPRISES AND SUGGESTIONS BY WHICH THIS MAY BE AVOIDED

Frequently there attach themselves to groups that are attempting to become repatriated and to form colonies in Mexico exploiters who, profiting by the ingenuousness of the future colonists, succeed in having themselves made representatives of the group and charged with the work of organization and with taking the necessary steps of a private and public nature, without its being seen that they lack both the abilities and the good faith indispensable for this. Individuals of this sort come to Mexico to examine and consider the lands upon which the people they represent might settle, and as it is to their interest to attract the latter there at any cost in order to obtain for themselves advantages and profits in their transportation, their establishment, in the distribution of the lands, etc., their reports are always optimistic and flattering even when the general outlook of the situation is certain failure.

Sometimes these representatives are persons of entirely good faith and enthusiasm, especially when they have risen from the ranks of those seeking to be repatriated themselves, but through their very generosity and their lack of practical abilities for carrying out such a difficult task they try to make of this a pilgrimage and of the repatriation and colonization works of charity, which is not possible since the government could not even if it would adopt a paternalistic policy of transporting, ceding lands, and establishing gratuitously hundreds of thousands of immigrants, at the cost of tens of millions of *pesos*.

Among the groups who attempt to become repatriated through establishing agricultural colonies there are not only individuals who have some acquaintance with tilling the earth and other farm-labor practices in Mexico, and who possess some money and tools, at least enough to establish themselves and to begin their work, but there are some who join themselves to the true farm colonists relying upon good luck alone. When such individuals make up a good proportion of the group they constitute a great danger to the success of the colonization, since they cannot cultivate the land, nor can they pay the sums of money necessary for buying or renting the latter.

There may be groups in which the majority of the supposed repatriates are not skilled in agriculture but in industrial occupations: road construction, railroad work, cement, iron, or steel-construction work, or making of automobiles, etc. If these individuals, who possess the mere rudiments of agricultural knowledge, ask help in colonizing, the problem will have to be considered from a different point of view than if it is a question of repatriating real agriculturalists, since it would appear reasonable that the country profit by the previous industrial experience that has been acquired in the United States. The ideal situation is that in which the majority of the group is made up of cultivators of the soil and a minority of industrialists since this would make for an efficient division of labor.

When the lands destined for colonizing are close to towns which are small or of secondary importance agriculturally, the colonists make their homes here; there the danger threatens that this colony will not attain a state of high development, but that it will decline until it reaches a state close to ruin. In a word, the would-be colonists return to Mexico impressed, as was said above, with the favorable characteristics which the painful struggle for existence in the United States has imparted to them. In exchange, the majority of the inhabitants of the small hamlets of the type described are characterized by their out-of-date methods of farming, poor tools, imperfect hygiene, religious fanaticism, and in general a lower standard of living than those of the new colonists. Moreover, the bitter exile which these latter have undergone has developed and raised to a high pitch in them a lofty and broad conception of their fatherland—as can be observed in thousands of them—while the people who have never seen beyond the hills of their own little village still possess a completely absurd conception of nationalism. For this reason there arises at times a natural antagonism which is often even unconscious between the characters, automatic attitudes, and tendencies of the reactionary majority and the progressive minority of those who are being repatriated, who are charged with being "Yankified" innovators, Masons or pagans, destroyers of the old customs, freakish, intruders, etc. If the colonists are few, they immediately separate themselves from the group settlement or else yield without a struggle, remodeling their customs, habits, and aspirations upon the standards which the retarded majority impose. If their number is relatively large, they offer resistance by carrying on a useless struggle which impedes their work and chills their enthusiasm until it ends by their submitting to the yoke or perhaps emigrating to the United States never again to return.

Foresight is a factor which is almost always lacking in the organization of the colonizations and repatriations. For example, many individuals or groups who were planning their repatriation when we were in the United States in 1927 lacked exact and positive information upon the following points: the geographic, agricultural, and economic conditions of the lands which they were thinking of colonizing as well as of the regions in which they were situated; the neighborhood of railroads and stations; the importation of freight. Are there roads for automobiles, carts, or horses? What about the character of the markets, of the topography of the soil, and of the local products, and the nature of the pastures, etc.? From lack of such knowledge it comes about, for example, that the automobiles and tractors which the colonists are so inclined to bring with them are useless since gasoline cannot be bought except at a very high price in the region as well as because the lands are very rough and not suited to cars or to cultivation by tractor; the gas and coal stoves which have been acquired in the United States in accordance with the demands of the climate and the easy access to these fuels are of little or no value in this country in which the only fuel which can be got at a low price is wood; the old and workworn animals which they possessed in the other country do not become acclimatized, and they die in a short time.

Among the principal consequences of the unsuccessful repatriations and colonizations for the reasons described above mention may be made of the following: (1) Their last resources spent, the colonists abandon the lands and go to the capital of the republic or to other principal cities, the result being that men who might have been ideal cultivators of the soil are turned into mediocre laborers, or as urban serfs make labor competition more acute, and add to the number of those without work. (2) The exploiters, parasites, and other harmful elements who came with the unsuccessful colonists are either added to the criminal element in the cities or turn bandits and often rebels in the country, their activities being all the worse in that they have been instructed in the modern school of American crime. (3) Many unsuccessful colonists return to the United States never to return to Mexico. In this country they continually fiercely condemn the repatriations and colonizations, citing their own bitter experience as a proof, which makes for a large reduction in the number of serious colonizing groups, possessing the necessary knowledge and the desire to work, who venture to come, while the number of indigent, lazy, or mischievous elements is relatively high. These, confiding in paternalistic aid from the government, join themselves in the repatriations and colonizations as if to a last refuge.

The foregoing analysis is the result of thousands of personal observations which we have made in the United States upon individuals who were about to become repatriated, others already repatriated in Mexico, and finally with those who, after their project of colonization had been broken up, had decided to establish themselves definitely in the United States. As a typical example of this we may take the three hundred or so people who were organizing their repatriation in Laguna, California, and whose situation and living conditions we examined in detail in April of 1927. Some of this group had already heard of the lack of success of other efforts at repatriation and finally decided not to go along, but the remainder did so, in spite of the fact that we made plain to them the lacks in their organization and the dangerous aspects of the enterprise in some respects. In August, 1927, we again made a study of the living conditions and general situation of the aforementioned repatriated laborers who were living in Acámbaro, Guanajuato, the spot where they had settled, and we perceived that unfortunately our prophecies had been fully confirmed; after wandering through various parts of the republic they had stopped and taken up work on the Hacienda de la Encarnación in Acámbaro. Land was insufficient, hygienic conditions terrible, tractors and automobiles rusted and practically useless.

Taking into consideration the conclusions reached above, it would perhaps be well to form a commission composed of a few competent persons which, proceeding in accordance with suggestions like those which were suggested earlier, may proceed to organize efficiently the repatriation of permanent immigrants and the colonization of the lands which can be given over to them. In this project is not included the repatriation of the immigrants destined to work in the industries of the capital or large cities of the republic, since the relatively small capacity of Mexican industries does not need labor. On the contrary, in these manufacturing centers there is an oversupply of labor, although the rural regions still offer chances of success to the repatriated citizen.

The commission would dedicate its activities to some such schemes as this:

1. The investigation of the following facts: prices and conditions of sale of the land; the amount of federal and local taxes; the cost of deeds of sale; the character of the land, pastures, woods, types of cultivation, and

irrigation; local raw materials, materials for construction, fuels economically purchasable; the general topography of the fields and of the surrounding country; freight and passenger rates by railroad and other means of transportation from the nearest frontier port of entry to the place where the land to be settled on is situated; the cost of freight and the location of the railroad station and of the most convenient markets; conditions of the automobile and cart roads and trails for horses. Moreover, gradually the *haciendas* which were being sold would have to be visited in order to discover the aspects of secondary importance which perhaps would not be mentioned in the reports but which might be of the greatest use to the colonists in enabling them to make a success of their repatriation.

2. Having acquired such information and made such observations, the next thing would be to go to those American states in which not only are the Mexican immigrants most numerous but chiefly to those regions in which there are any Mexican settlements of a permanent character engaged in agriculture, such as Texas, Arizona, California, Colorado, and New Mexico. At once contacts should be established with the consuls as a cheap and easy way of spreading the report of the lands offered for colonization by the Mexican government, indicating at the same time that inquiries and advice for those interested might be obtained from the consular offices. Copies of this announcement should then be sent to the person or persons charged with the permanent direction of immigration, in order that he may be informed, while the originals should be preserved at the disposal of the consul and the commission.

3. When inquiries from single individuals are received, steps taken will be limited to sending to the interested parties pamphlets containing the facts mentioned above, and supplementary information will be given in case of verbal queries. The advantages in forming a group will be suggested, since it is difficult or even impossible as well as expensive to carry on complete investigations for individual cases.

4. When inquiries are received from a well-established group—for example, from fifty or more individuals—the commission will go to the part of the country in which these people live in order to regulate or, better, to collaborate with them in the organization and arrangements for their repatriation, proceeding immediately to obtain and so far as possible classify through personal investigators of a proved character the following facts: name, age, and place of origin in Mexico of the intended colonists and their dependents; amount of money that they are planning to invest in land; occupations in which they were employed in Mexico and those

which they had in the United States, classifying these last in agriculture (various sorts of cultivation, picking of fruit and cotton, of tending cattle, sheep, etc.) and industrial occupations (bricklayer, laborers in cement, iron and steel construction, or upon the roads, etc.). Does the individual intend to devote himself entirely to farming in Mexico or to farming and some other trade which he has acquired as well, or to the latter only? What and how many vehicles, machinery and tools, furniture, animals of various sorts, etc., is he planning to transport to Mexico?

In the light of this information and the observations brought from Mexico, the future colonization will be discussed with the group of intended colonists and it will be pointed out to them just what the condition of the land and its possibilities are. The suggestion will be made not to bring automobiles, tractors, stoves, etc., if there are no roads or suitable land or the necessary fuel; that they rid themselves of their old farm animals and acquire in their place others that are young and able to become acclimatized, as well as fertilizers, serums, medicines, and drugs, which are very cheap in the United States and will aid them to increase their harvests and to fight epidemics and crop diseases. If certain of the colonists have some special trade, the necessity for obtaining his special tool equipment in the United States should be indicated, in order that he may practice his trade for the benefit of the colony. Although the would-be colonists possess a broader nationalistic conception than that possessed by certain of their countrymen in Mexico, it should be pointed out to them the harm which a foolish display of unnecessary egotism acquired in the United States may do them, although of course this does not mean that the habits of progress and culture acquired there should be abandoned. Other suggestions will be made for which there is not space here, and, to sum up, the commission will collaborate with the future colonists in order to organize their repatriation efficiently.

Finally, the commission will direct and aid the colonists to communicate with the proper Mexican and American authorities in order that the steps toward the departure from the United States, entry into Mexico, convenient and economical transportation, and establishment of the colonists upon their lands be correlated and carried out quickly, since it often happens that the colonists and their representatives do not know what steps to take, or to what bureaus to apply, as a result of which their efforts are irregular, inefficient, or unproductive and wasted from the standpoint of time and effort.

The commission of which we have been speaking will not limit its activities here, but once the colony is established, it will consider whether it is proper to give bank credits to the colonists. The development of the colony will be investigated annually in order to improve conditions and to gain experience which will help perfect methods of organizing future repatriations and colonizations.

In order to support, in part at least, the commission, each one of the repatriated citizens would pay a certain fixed sum to the Mexican government for the service which he receives.

APPENDIX VIII

LIST OF SOME MEXICAN SOCIETIES IN THE UNITED STATES

CALIFORNIA

LOS ANGELES

Logia "Benito Juarez".....................Señor Bernardo Barraza
1938 Atlantic St.
Logia Superena de la Alianza Protectora de Obreros
1322 Stanford Ave.   Señor Esteban C. Arredondo
Logia Anahuac 14.........................Señor Elbaerto C. Bravo
Sociedad Mexicana Benéfico-Recreativa.........Señor Ismael Guzman
Logia Hispano-Americana, Log. 110...............Señor E. Martinez
Club Automovilista Mexicano...............Señor Pascual Echevete
5117 Brooklyn Ave.
Sociedad Ignacio Zaragoza.....................Señor Luis Escobar
4217 Leigh St.
Sociedad Benéfico-Mutualista, Log. 2.........Señor Leocadio Martinez
611 Bunkerhill St.
Cruz Azul Mexicana......................Señora Elena de la Llata
802 California St.
Unión Nacionalista Mexicana..............Señor Francisco Contreras
715 N. Moyy St.
Club Victoria Mutualista.....................Señor Porfirio Padilla
929 E. Twenty-fifth St.
Logia Socrates 12............................Señor Jesús Estrada
228 N. Hope St.
Sociedad Moctezuma de Señoritas...........Señorita Angela González
1470 N. Soto St.
Union Cultural Pro-Mexico..............Señor A. Moncada Villarreal
628 N. Main St.
Logia 88 de la Alianza Hispano-Americana Señor Grancisco G. y Lozano
129 Clarence St.
Club Cuauhtemoc........................Señor Guadalupe Franco
741 Clover St.

El Malcriado (periódico).....................Señor Daniel Vanegas
128 N. Main St.
Club Morelos Mutualista.....................Señor Remigio Nilás
1107 Effie St.
Club de Damas Benito Juarez..............Señora Esperanza Sanchez
1720 Bishop Road
Asociación Cooperativa Mexicana................Señor M. S. Salinas
4219 Regent St.
Logia Dante 34.................................Señor Santescoy
627 N. Main St.
Sociedad Benéfica Mutualista...................Señor Emilio Flores
611 Bunkerhill St. N.
Obreros Aliados Mexicanos, Log. Suprema.....Señor Dionisio Mercado
341 N. Chicago St.
Club Juvenil Mexicano Pro-Raza..................Señor José Torres
518 N. Alameda St.
Logia Cuauhtemoc 1.....................Señora M. C. A. Mercado
Logia Hidalgo...............................Señora Antonia Solís
4104 Brooklyn Ave.
Sociedad Mexicana Benefico-Recreativa...........Señor Fausto Vega
649 Castelas St.
Aliados Mexicanos, Log. 2.....................Señor Cristobal Ortiz
Y.W.C.A. Instituto Internacional
                    Señoritas Gloria Bonales y Susuna Bonales
Circulo Social Deportivo.................Señor Jesús Portillo Escobar
Banda de Tambores.......................Señor Ezequiel B. Avilés
Sociedad Benéfico-Mutualista, Gran Logia.........Señor Emilio Flores
Sociedad Benéfico-Mutualista, Log. 1..............Señor L. Martinez
Club Victoria Mutualista.................Señor Francisco O. Gurrola
"Benito Juarez," Log. 2 de la Alianza Protectora de Obreros
                              Señor Gerardo Barraza
Logia Suprema de la Alianza Protectora de Obreros
                              Señor E. G. Arredondo
Club de Damas "Benito Juarez".............Señora Nemesia Ruacho
Cuerpo Ejecutivo de Obreros Aliados...........Señor D. E. Mercado
Sociedad Benéfica Recreativa Mexicana, Log. 2.......Señor T. Frausto
Obreros Aliados Mexicanos, Log. 2...........Señor Jesús P. Gesijerlez
Asociación Cooperativa de Belvedere.........Señor Pedro M. Salinas
Club Automovilista Mexicano...............Senor Pascual Echeceste

Camara de Comercio Mexicana de Belvedere......................

Brigada de la Cruz Azul de Glendale.........Señorita Ana de Mancilla
42 Magnolia St., Glendale, Calif.

Sociedad Benéfico-Recreativa....................Señor Adolfo Castro
2069 Louis Ave., Long Beach, Calif.

ILLINOIS AND INDIANA

CHICAGO

Sociedad Mexicana "Benito Juarez"; *Presidente:* Señor José de la Mora, 609 Woodland Park, 1022 S. Ashland Ave.

Centro Cultural, "Manuel Acuña"; *Secretario:* Señor José G. Lovera, 219 S. Throop St.

Sociedad Mexicana "Miguel Hidalgo y Costilla"; *Presidente:* Señor Pedro M. Gutierrez, 906 W. Forquer St.

Club Recreativo "Anahuac"; *Presidente:* Señor José Rivera, 4630 Gross Ave.

Club Atlético "Cuauhtemoc"; *Presidente:* Señor Carlos R. Mora, 1016 S. Bloomis St.

Sociedad Mutualista "Ignacio Zaragoza"; *Secretario:* Señor R. Barba, 1615 S. Newberry Ave.

Sociedad Mutuo-Recreativa "José M. Morelos"; *Presidente:* Señor José Rodriguez, 3585 Pennsylvania Ave., Indiana Harbor, Ind.

Sociedad Mutuo-Recreativa "Azteca"; *Presidente:* Señor Antonio Ortiz P., 1010 Blue Island Ave.

Sociedad Fraternal Mexicana; *Presidente:* Señor José V. Sosa, 626 S. Sholto St.

Sociedad de Obreros Libres Mexicanos; *Secretario:* Señor Julio Limón, 8837 Houston Ave., South Chicago

Asociación "Caballeros de Guadalupe," 9024 Mackinaw Ave., South Chicago, Ill.

Confederación de Sociedades Mexicanas; *Presidente:* Señor Manuel Peña, 3783 Main St., Indiana Harbor

Sociedad Protectora Mexicana; *Presidente:* Señor J. Morales, 1208 Adams St., Gary, Ind.

Sociedad Mexicana "Benito Juarez"; *Presidente:* Señor Manuel Peña, P.O. Box 774, Indiana Harbor, Ind.

MICHIGAN

In a Mexican population of little more than six thousand individuals there are more than twenty societies. Unfortunately we do not have this list.

NEW MEXICO
ALBUQUERQUE

Circulo Cultural de Albuquerque
Sociedad Hidalgo y Morelos (de Gallup)

Comisiones Honoríficas (en Gibson, Mentmore, Gallup, Breece, Grant, Madrid, Dowson, y Raton)
Cruz Azul Mexicana (en Gallup)
Alianza Hispano Americana

OHIO
TOLEDO

Sociedad Mutualista Mexicana

MISSOURI
KANSAS CITY

Comisiones Honoríficas (in Independence, Coffeyville, Garden City, Topeka, Parsóns, y Horton)
Sociedad Mutualista de State Line
Sociedad Mexicana (de Wichita)
Sociedad Mutualista Benito Juarez (de Topeka)

Sociedad Mutualista Mexicana (de Horton)
Union Cultural (en Kansas City)
Brigadas de la Cruz Azul Mexicana (en Dodge City y Garden City)
Union Cultural Mexicana (en Kansas City)

TEXAS
SAN ANTONIO

Alianza de Sociedad Mutualista de San Antonio, Texas
Benevolencia Mexicana
Benevolencia Femenil Mexicana
Unión Mutualista "Ignacio Allende" (de ambos sexos)
General Mariano Escobedo (de ambos sexos)

Hijos de América
Hijos de México
Ignacio Zaragoza (de ambos sexos)
Alianza Recreativa Mexicana (integrada por los clubes recreativos mexicanos "Anahuac," "Gardenia," y "Chapultepec")
Cruz Azul Mexicana (beneficencia)

EL PASO

Sociedad Mutualista Zaragoza (independiente)
El Mutualista
La constructora
Circulo de Amigos

Alianza Hispano-Americana (con un gran húmero de sucursales)
Caballeros de Colon (mutualista con fines religiosos)

APPENDIX IX

SUPPLEMENTARY NOTE ON THE NUMBER AND DISTRIBUTION OF MEXICAN IMMIGRANTS

After the manuscript of this book had been prepared for publication, Dr. Gamio made a supplementary study of the amount of Mexican immigration to the United States, and of the origin and distribution of the immigrants, under the title: *Quantitative Estimate, Sources and Distribution of Mexican Immigration into the United States*, Talleres Gráficos Editorial y "Diario Oficial," Lic. Verdad Numero 2, Mexico, D.F., 1930. A brief abstract of this supplementary paper follows:

In estimating the number of Mexican immigrants in the United States it is not possible to adopt the United States statistics. The decennial census is taken at a time of year when the greatest number of temporary immigrants are in the country; many of these return during the winter. Furthermore, the United States immigration laws do not require Mexicans returning to Mexico to register with the authorities. Because the Mexican law requires returning immigrants to register, the Mexican statistics are preferable. Such records enumerate 927,167 Mexicans as having left Mexico for the United States from 1910 to 1928, and 1,085,222 as having returned. Although some Mexicans have probably entered without registering at all, part of this discrepancy is probably due to the birth of children to Mexicans temporarily in the United States. On the whole, the indication is that the movement in one direction has been about as great as the movement in the other direction. The general impression that there are a million or more Mexicans in the United States is probably due to the fact that observers assume that the great number of Mexicans noticed in the United States in the summer and fall are all permanent residents, whereas most of them return the same season to Mexico.

Yearly fluctuations in the number of persons leaving Mexico for the United States are closely correlated with and are attributable to alternating periods (in Mexico) of peace and prosperity, and of revolution and economic disturbance.

Temporary immigration to the United States constitutes a benefit to both countries: to the United States because it supplies cheap labor at a time when it is needed; to Mexico because it prevents difficulties that might arise in periods of great unemployment, and because it gives the temporary immigrants some experience and training in agricultural and industrial technique.

In this supplementary study the consideration of the records of money orders sent from Mexico to the United States was extended to embrace winter- and springtime samples of the nine years from 1920 to 1928. From this it is concluded that there are more Mexicans in the United States in summer and fall than there are in winter and spring. The total amount of money remitted to Mexico has tended steadily to increase; from this it is concluded that the Mexicans in the United States continue to be temporary immigrants, who remit money, rather than permanent residents, who do not.

The study of these additional data as to money orders confirms the earlier conclusion that over half of the immigrants come from Guanajuato, Michoacan, and Jalisco. The origin of the immigrants, and their distribution in the United States, as derived from a consideration of these supplementary data, are shown graphically in tables and maps.

[Dr. Gamio's conclusions on this subject are to be compared with those reached by Dr. Paul S. Taylor in his *Mexican Labor in the United States: Migration Statistics*, "University of California Publications in Economics," VI, No. 3 (1929), 237–55. Dr. Taylor's studies of special areas indicate important increases, due to immigration, in the number of Mexicans, and lead to a conclusion that a considerable part of this immigration is "permanent." In the paper just cited, reasons are given as to why the Mexican southbound figures cannot be compared with either the Mexican or the American northbound figures. A conclusion as to seasonal fluctuation in immigration based on variation in the amount of money remitted by postal order is open to the objection that part of the decrease is probably due to the fact that Mexicans who remain in the United States during the winter suffer from unemployment and have less money to send. Other evidence brought forward indicates a large recent increase in Mexican population in the United States even during the season of slack employment.—EDITOR.]

BIBLIOGRAPHY

In footnotes to the preceding chapters we have made reference to the principal sources of information which have been especially consulted in connection with this investigation of Mexican immigration to the United States. Publications included in the following bibliography refer directly or indirectly to Mexican immigration, and although we have had opportunity to consult only some of them, we include others for the convenience of those who may pursue the subject.[1]

A. Mexican Backgrounds

I. PHYSICAL AND CULTURAL ANTHROPOLOGY

BOAS, FRANZ. "Handbook of American Indian Languages," *Bur. Amer. Ethn. Bull. 40*. Washington, 1911

DIGUET, L. "Anciennes sépultures indigènes de la Basse Californie mèridional," *Jour. Soc. Amer.* (N.S.; Paris, 1905), Vol. II.

———. "La sierra du Nayarit et ses indigènes," *Extrait des nouvelles archives des missions scientifiques* (Paris, 1899), Tome IX.

GAMIO, MANUEL. "Las excavaciónes del Pedregal de San Angel y la cultura arcaica del Valle de Mexico," *Amer. Anthr.*, XXII, No. 2 (N.S.; April–June, 1920).

———. "The Sequence of Cultures in Mexico," *ibid.*, XXVI, No. 3 (July–Sept., 1924).

———. Introduction, synthesis, and conclusions of the work: *The Population of the Valley of Teotihuacan*. Published by the Department of Anthropology. México: Talleres Gráficos de la Nación, 1922.

GAMIO, MANUEL, AND OTHERS. *La Población del Valle de Teotihuacan*. México: Talleres Gráficos de la Nación, 1922.

HOLMES, WILLIAM H. "Antiquity of Man on the Site of the City of Mexico," *Trans. Anthr. Soc. of Wash.*, Vol. III (1895).

HRDLICKA, ALES. "Notes on Painting of Human Bones among the Indians," *Ann. Rep. Smiths. Inst.* Washington, 1904

———. *Contribution to the Physical Anthropology of California*, "Univ. of Calif. Pub. Amer. Arch. Ethn." (Berkeley, 1906), Vol. IV.

[1] See Emory S. Bogardus, *The Mexican Immigrant: An Annotated Bibliography*. The Council on International Relations, 715 South Hope St., Los Angeles, 1929. Pp. 21.—EDITOR

HRDLICKA, ALES. "On the Stature of the Indians of the Southwest and Northern Mexico," *Anthropological Essays*. New York, 1909.

———. "Notes of the Indians of Sonora, Mexico," *Amer. Anthr.*, Vol. VI (N.S., 1904).

———. "The Chichimecs and Their Ancient Culture with Notes on the Tepecanos and the Ruin of La Quèmada," *ibid.*, Vol. V (N.S., 1903).

———. "Genesis of the American Indian," *Proc. Sec. Panamerican Scientific Congress* (Washington, 1917), Vol. I, sec. 1.

JENKS, A. *Indian White Amalgamation*, "Univ. of Minn. Studies in the Social Sciences." Minneapolis, 1916.

JOYCE, T. A. *Mexican Archaeology*. New York, 1920.

LUMHOLTZ, KARL. *Unknown Mexico*. New York, 1902.

———. *New Trails in Mexico*. New York, 1912.

———. "The Huichol Indians," *Bull. Amer. Nat. Hist.* (New York, 1898), Vol. X.

MARTINEZ, GRACIDA MANUEL. *Monografías de las trece agrupaciónes indígenas del Estado de Oaxaca* (inéditas).

MCGEE, W J "The Seri Indians," *17th Ann. Rep. Bur. Amer. Ethn.* Washington, 1898.

NORTH, ARTHUR W. "Tribes of Lower California," *Amer. Anthr.* (N.S.; Lancaster, Pa., 1908), Vol. X.

PREUSS, K. T. *Die Religion der Cora Indianer*. Leipzig, 1912.

RIVET, PAUL. Recherches anthropologiques sur la Basse Californie. *Jour. Soc. Amer.* (N.S.; Paris, 1909), Vol. VI.

SCHENK, A. "Notes sur un crâne otomi," *Mexique, Neuchatel. Bull. de la Soc. Neuchateloise de Géographie*, Vol. XX (1909-10).

SILICEO, PAUER PAUL. "Conocimiento antropologico de las agrupaciónes indígenas de México," *Ethnos* (revista dedicada al estudio y mejoría de las poblaciónes indígenas de México) (2a época; México, D.F., 1922-23), Tomo I, No. 1.

———. "Índice craneométrico de los indígenas prehispánicos y actuales de la Mesa Central de México," *Anales del Museo Nacional* (México; 5a época), Tomo I, No. 4.

SPINDEN, HERBERT J. *Ancient Civilizations of Mexico and Central America*. New York, 1917.

STARR, F. *The Physical Characters of the Indians of Southern Mexico*, "Decen. Pub. Univ. of Chicago." Chicago, 1902.

———. *Indians of Southern Mexico* (album). Chicago, 1900.

BIBLIOGRAPHY 251

TEN, KATE H. "Matériaux pour servir à l'anthropologie de la presqu'île de Californie," *Bull. Soc. d'Anthrop.* Paris, 1884.

THOMAS, CYRUS, AND SWANTON, JOHN R. "Indian Languages of Mexico and Central America," *Bur. Ethn. Bull. 44.* Washington, 1911.

TOZZER, ALFRED M. *A Comparative Study of the Mayas and Lacandones.* New York, 1907.

ZABAROWSKY. "Photographies d'indienes Huicholes et Coras," *Bull. et Mem. Soc. d'Anthrop. de Paris.* (5th ser., 1901). Vol. II.

WISSLER, CLARK. *The American Indian.* New York, 1917.

II. GENERAL WORKS ON PRESENT-DAY MEXICO AND ON THE HISTORY OF MEXICO

BANCROFT, H. H. *History of Mexico.* San Francisco, 1883–90.

BEALS, CARLETON. *Mexico, an Interpretation.* New York, 1923.

BELL, P. L. *Mexican West Coast and Lower California.* Washington, D.C.: Government Printing Office, 1923.

BLAKESLEE, G. H. (Ed.). *Mexico and the Caribbean.* New York, 1920.

CALDERÓN DE LA BARCA. *Life in Mexico.* New York, 1843.

CLELAND, ROBERT G. (Ed.). *Mexican Year Book* (1st ed., 1920; 2d ed., 1924).

CREEL, GEORGE. *The People Next Door.* New York, 1927.

ENOCH, C. REGINALD. *Mexico.* New York, 1916.

EVANS, MRS. ROSALIE. *The Rosalie Evans Letters from Mexico.* New York, 1926.

GRUENING, ERNEST. *Mexico and Its Heritage.* New York, 1928.

JONES, CHESTER LLOYD. *Mexico and Its Reconstruction.* New York, 1921.

McBRIDE, G. M. *The Land Systems of Mexico.* New York, 1923.

MIDDLETON, P. H. *Industrial Mexico.* New York, 1919.

PHIPPS, HELEN. *Some Aspects of the Agrarian Question in Mexico* (pamphlet). New York, 1925.

PRIESTLEY, H. I. *The Mexican Nation, a History.* New York, 1923.

ROSS, EDWARD A. *The Social Revolution in Mexico.* New York, 1923.

SAENZ, MOISES, AND PRIESTLEY, H. I. *Some Mexican Problems.* 1926.

THOMPSON, WALLACE. *The People of Mexico.* New York, 1921.

———. *The Mexican Mind.* New York, 1923.

TROWBRIDGE, E. D. *Mexico, Today and Tomorrow.* New York, 1919.

VASCONCELOS, JOSÉ, AND GAMIO, MANUEL. *Aspects of Mexican Civilization.* Chicago, 1926.

B. The Mexican in the United States

I. PUBLICATIONS DEALING WITH THE OLD MEXICAN HERITAGE IN THE SOUTHWEST

Austin, Mary. *The Land of Journey's Ending.* 1924.

Bancroft, H. H. *History of Arizona and New Mexico.* 1889.

————. *History of California.* 1884–90.

————. *History of the North Mexican States and Texas.* 1884–89.

Blackmar, Frank W. *Spanish Institutions of the Southwest.* 1891.

Bolton, H. E. *The Spanish Borderlands.* 1921.

————. *Spanish Explorations in the Southwest.* 1916.

————. (Trans.). *"Noticias" of Palou.* 1927.

Chapman, C. E. *The Founding of Spanish California.* 1916.

————. *History of California: Spanish Period.* 1923.

Lummis, Charles F. *The Land of Poco Tiempo.* 1893.

McLean and Williams. *Old Spain in New America.* 1916.

Park and Miller. *Old World Traits Transplanted.* 1921.

II. THE RECENT MEXICAN IMMIGRATION

Alvarado, E. M. "Mexican Immigration to the United States," *Nat. Conf. Social Work* (1920), pp. 479–80.

American Federation of Labor. *Proc. 47th Ann. Convention* (Washington, D.C., 1927), pp. 95, 321, 336.

Bamford, C. "Industrialization and the Mexican Casual," *Proc. Fifth Ann. Convention of Southwestern Polit. and Social Sci. Assoc.*

Bamford, Edwin T. "The Mexican Casual Problems in the Southwest," *Jour. and Appl. Soc.*, VIII, No. 6 (July–Aug., 1924), 363–71.

Bloch, Louis. "Report on the Mexican Labor Situation in the Imperial Valley," *Bien. Rept., Bur. Labor Statistics.* California State Printer, 1925–26.

Bogardus, Emory S. "The House-Court Problem," *Amer. Jour. Soc.*, XXII, 391–99.

————. "Second Generation Mexicans," *Sociol. and Social Res.*, XIII, No. 3 (Jan.–Feb., 1929), 276–83.

Britton and Constable. "Analysis of Mexican Patients at Chicago Dispensary," *Nation's Health*, VII, No. 7 (July, 1926).

————. *Our Mexican Patients at Central Free Dispensary* (pamphlet). Chicago, 1925.

BROWN, SARAH A. *Children Working in the Sugar Beet Fields of Certain Districts of the South Platte Valley, Colorado.* National Child Labor Committee, 1925.

CALCOTT, F. "The Mexican *Peón* in Texas," *Survey*, VI (June 26, 1920), 437.

CADY, GEORGE L. *Report of the Commission on International and Interracial Factors in the Problem of Mexicans in the United States.*

CAMBLON, RUTH S. "Mexicans in Chicago," *Family*, VII, No. 7 (Nov., 1926), 207–11.

CLARK, VICTOR S. "Mexican Labor in the United States," *Bull. Bur. Labor*, No. 71. Washington, 1908.

DAVIS, R. A. "Report on Illiteracy in Texas," *Univ. of Texas, Bull. 2328.* 1923.

EL PASO CONGRESS. *Report, Dec., 1926, on Education: International and Interracial Factors, Religion and Social and Economic Factors.* New York: Home Missions Council.

ESQUIVEL, S. I. "The Immigrant from Mexico," *Outlook*, May 19, 1920, pp. 125–31.

FOERSTER, ROBERT F. *Racial Problems Involved in Immigration from Latin America and the West Indies.* Washington: Government Printing Office, 1925.

"Getting God Counted among the Mexicans," *Miss. Rev. of the World*, May, 1923.

GIBBONS, CHARLES E. *Children Working on Farms in Certain Sections of the Western Slope of Colorado.* National Child Labor Committee, 1925.

GWINN, J. B. "Social Problems of Our Mexican Population," *Nat. Conf. Social Work* (1926).

HANDMAN, M. S. "Social Problems in Texas" and "The Mexican Immigrant in Texas," *Southwestern Polit. and Social Sci. Quart.*, V, No. 3 (Dec., 1924), and VII, No. 1 (1926).

HEALD, T. H. "The Mexicans in the Southwest," *Mission. Rev. of the World*, XLII (Nov., 1919), 860–65.

HOOVER, GLENN E. "Our Mexican Immigrants," *Foreign Affairs*, VIII, No. 1 (Oct., 1929), 99–107.

HUGHES, ELIZABETH A. *Living Conditions for Small-Wage Earners in Chicago.* Chicago: Department of Public Welfare, 1925.

Immigration and the Southern States. From a Railway Standpoint. Philadelphia Railway World Pub. Co., 1904.

JENKS, J. W. *The Immigration Problem.* Funk & Wagnalls.

McComBS, Vernon M. *From over the Border.* New York: Council of Women for Home Missions, 1925.

———. "Rescuing Mexican Children in the Southwest," *Mission. Rev. of the World,* July, 1923.

McDowell, John. *A Study of Social and Economic Factors Relating to Spanish-speaking People in the United States.* Home Missions Council.

McLean, R. N. "Rubbing Shoulders on the Border," *Survey,* May, 1924.

McLean, R. N., and Thomson, C. A. *Spanish and Mexican in Colorado.* Board of National Missions of the Presbyterian Church in the U.S.A., 1924.

McLean, Robert N. *That Mexican.* New York: Revell, 1928.

McLean, Robert, and Williams, Grace. *Old Spain in New America.* Council of Women for Home Missions, 1916.

"Mexican Invaders Relieving Our Farm Labor Shortage," *Lit. Dig.,* July 17, 1920.

"Mexican Journeys to Bethlehem," *ibid.,* June 2, 1923.

Oxnam, G. B. "Mexicans in Los Angeles from the Standpoint of the Religious Forces of the City," *Ann. Amer. Acad.,* Jan., 1921, pp. 93–130.

Paschal, F. C., and Sullivan, C. R. *Racial Influences in the Mental and Physical Development of Mexican Children* (1925).

"Results of Admission of Mexican Laborers under Departmental Orders for Employers in Agricultural Pursuits," *Monthly Labor Rev.,* XI (Nov., 1920), 1095–97.

Roundy, R. W. "The Mexican in Our Midst. III," *Mission Rev.,* XLIV (May, 1921), 371–77.

Sheldon, William H. "The Intelligence of Mexican Children," *School and Society,* XIX (Feb., 1924), 139–42.

Simpich, Frederick. "The Little Brown Brother Treks North," *Independent,* Feb. 27, 1926, pp. 237–39.

———. "Along Our Side of the Mexican Border," *Nat. Geog. Mag.,* XXXVIII (July, 1920), 61–80.

Slayden, James L. "Some Observations on Mexican Immigration," *Annals Amer. Acad. Polit. and Social Sci.,* XCIII (Jan., 1921), 121–26.

Stowell, Jay S. *The Near Side of the Mexican Question.* New York: Doran, 1921.

Strego, V. L. "Progress of Adjustment in Mexican and United States Life," *Nat. Conf. Social Work,* XX, 481–86.

SULLENGER, T. EARL. "The Mexican Population of Omaha," *Jour. Appl. Soc.*, VIII, No. 5 (May–June, 1924), 288–93.

SULLIVAN, LOUIS R., AND FRANKLIN, CRESSEY PASCHAL. "The Effect of Race and Environment on the Physical and Mental Development of Our Mexican Immigrants," *Proc. Amer. Anthr. Assoc.* (Dec. 27–28, 1923).

TAYLOR, PAUL S. *Mexican Labor in the United States: Imperial Valley*, "University of California Publications in Economics," VI, No. 1, 1–94.

——. *Mexican Labor in the United States: Valley of the South Platte, Colorado, ibid.*, No. 2, 95–235.

——. *Mexican Labor in the United States: Migration Statistics, ibid.*, No. 3, 237–55.

——. *Mexican Labor in the United States: Racial School Statistics, ibid.*, No. 4, 257–92.

THOMPSON, EDYTHE TATE. *Summary of Mexican Cases Where Tuberculosis Is a Factor.* California State Board of Health, May, 1926.

——. *A Statistical Study of Sickness among the Mexicans.* California State Board of Health, 1925.

THOMSON, CHARLES A. "The Man from Next Door," *Century*, Jan., 1926, pp. 275–82.

WALKER, HELEN W. "Mexican Immigrants as Laborers," *Sociol. and Social Res.*, XIII, No. 1 (Sept.–Oct., 1928), 55–62.

WALLIS, WILSON D. "The Mexican Immigrant of California," *Pac. Rev.*, II (Dec., 1921), 444–54.

WARD, KIRKBRIDE, AND HOLMES, "Mexican Immigration," *Trans. Commonwealth Club of California* (March, 1926).

WHITE, OWEN B. "A Glance at the Mexicans," *Amer. Mercury*, Feb., 1925.

"Without Quota," *Survey*, May 15, 1924.

III. GOVERNMENTAL PUBLICATIONS[1]

Censuses of 1900, 1910 and 1920. Washington, D.C.: Bureau of the Census Department of Commerce.

Statistical Abstracts of the United States, 1924. Washington, D.C.: Bureau of Foreign and Domestic Commerce.

Immigration Laws. Washington, D.C.: Bureau of Immigration, Department of Labor, 1925.

[1] Including those not listed above.

Annual Reports of the Commissioner General of Immigration. Department of Labor.

Monthly Labor Review. Bureau of Labor Statistics, Department of Labor.

Annual Reports of the Commissioner of Naturalization. Department of Labor.

Hearing before the Committee on Immigration and Naturalization. House of Representatives, 1926.

Immigration in the United States (showing number, nationality, sex, occupation, destination, etc., from 1820 to 1923). Bureau of Statistics, Department of the Treasury.

"Immigration of Aliens," *Conf. Rept.* (1924).

Immigration Problem in the United States. National Industrial Conference Board, 1923.

Register of Money-Order Post Offices in the United States (including Mexico and other foreign postal regions).

Hearings on Temporary Admission of Illiterate Mexican Laborers. Committee on Immigration and Naturalization, House of Representatives, 1920.[1]

6th and 9th Annual Reports of the California Housing and Immigration Commission.

Annual reports of Immigration Association of California.

Ley de Migración de los Estados Unidos Mexicanos. México: Talleres Gráficos de la Nación, 1926.

Estadística nacional (revista quincenal: órgana del Departamento de Estadística Nacional). México: Correo Mayor 31.

Censo Gral., de habitantes. Es dirección Gral., de Estadística y Departamento de la Estadística Nacional.

Otras publicaciónes y documentos inéditos de las Secretarías de Gobernación, Relaciónes, Agricultura e Industria, y Comercio.

[1] The foregoing were all printed in the Government Printing Office, Washington, D.C.

INDEX

INDEX

DATE DUE

OCT 09 1995	
DEC 11 2006	

GAYLORD   PRINTED IN U.S.A.